SONS:

A Mother's Manual

SONS:
A Mother's Manual

ELYSE ZORN KARLIN
with Muriel Warren, M.S.W.

AVON BOOKS ◆ NEW YORK

SONS: A MOTHER'S MANUAL is an original publication of Avon Books. This work has never before appeared in book form.

Permission to publish excerpts from the following books is gratefully acknowledged: *The Sissy Boy Syndrome* by Richard Green, M.D., J.D., published by Yale University Press, 1987; *Boys Will Be Boys* by Myriam Miedzian, published by Doubleday Books, 1991; *Boys and Sex* by Wardell P. Pomeroy, Ph.D., published by Dell Publishing, 1981; *Finding Our Fathers: The Unfinished Business of Manhood* by Samuel Osherson, Copyright © 1986. Reprinted with the permission of the Free Press, a Division of Macmillan, Inc.

AVON BOOKS
A division of
The Hearst Corporation
1350 Avenue of the Americas
New York, New York 10019

Copyright © 1994 by Elyse Karlin
Published by arrangement with the author
Library of Congress Catalog Card Number: 93-90671
ISBN: 0-380-76997-2

First Avon Books Trade Printing: April 1994

AVON TRADEMARK REG. U.S. PAT. OFF. AND IN OTHER COUNTRIES, MARCA REGISTRADA, HECHO EN U.S.A.

Printed in the U.S.A.

OPM   10   9   8   7   6   5   4   3   2   1

To all the sons who have touched my life—
in memory of my father, Edgar;
for my husband and friend, Andrew;
and for my darling son, Harris.
—E.Z.K.

To Howard, and to all my children:
Joel, Sandy, Jenny, George,
Ashleigh, Kristina, Taylor;
and to the new arrivals,
and to my mother and father,
who made everything possible.
—M.P.W.

Acknowledgments

We would like to thank the following people for their cooperation in writing this book:

Janet Anfuso, who drew all the medical illustrations; Dr. Stephen Boris, who reviewed the medical material in the Appendix; Dr. Rene Bouchard, Dr. Irene Kaminsky, Debbie Jurkowitz, Dr. Andrew Karlin, Suzanne Lipsett, Jenifer McLauglin, Jody Rein, Rabbi Michael Rovinsky, Dr. Brad Sachs, Dr. Charles Schaefer, Daisy Spier, Nancy Yost, and all the mothers who shared their time and their thoughts with us.

SONS:
A Mother's Manual

Table of Contents

Introduction

From the first moment she sees that her little bundle of joy has a penis, a mother enters a mysterious new world—the world of males. Instantly she faces a difficult and controversial decision: whether or not to have her baby circumcised. And as her child grows, she finds herself becoming uncertain again and again: "Should I let him act so rough?" "Should I cuddle him so much?" "Is a boy really so different from a girl?" Were she raising a daughter, she would be able to rely on her own background, but when she searches for ways to proceed with her son, she is likely to find more questions than answers.

Throughout the toddler and preschool years, when her son is pulled like a magnet to trucks and guns, and during the school-age years, when he begins to draw away from her and identify with his father, her son continues to reveal more enigmatic aspects of his body and personality. Certain medical problems that occur only or more frequently in boys can catch her completely unprepared, as can some of the psychological issues. To his mother, even the most cherished son begins as, and remains in part, the "other."

One of the authors of this book is the mother of a little boy who continues to mystify her; the other is the mother of a grown son. In discussing our feelings with other women about having entered these uncharted waters, we found that many mothers shared our concerns. Mothers see striking differences between both the way their sons and daughters behave and the way they themselves interact with their sons and daughters. But as to precisely what these differences are, why they exist, what they mean, and how it is best to handle them, mothers are

1

likely to respond, "I'll let you know when I figure it out. Call me
again in eighteen years."

We were intrigued by the degree to which many mothers felt
different from their sons. As we compared notes—one of us
drawing from the active world of playground and play group,
the other from her busy psychotherapy practice—we both
agreed that most mothers admitted to having at best a cloudy
understanding of their sons' emotional needs and motivations.
A book providing factual information on the physical and psychological issues exclusive to growing boys would, we concluded, meet a clear and present need.

We developed a questionnaire designed to elicit the major
issues, fears, and problems with which mothers of boys have
had to contend—as well as their major pleasures—in raising
their sons. Through this questionnaire, we invited mothers to
share their ideas as well as their experiences, and to give us a
sense of the quality of their relationships with their sons. We
mailed these questionnaires to mothers nationwide; while not
devised to be a statistically relevant sample, our group of mothers reflects a diversity of backgrounds, ages, ethnicities, and
lifestyles. Some of our respondents work full-time outside the
home, some part-time, some not at all, and many had daughters as well as sons. In writing this book, we drew heavily from
these written questionnaire responses as well as from many
discussion groups we held with mothers of boys. These groups
gave women an opportunity to discuss their mothering experiences in more depth and ran well into overtime because the
women enjoyed sharing their stories so much that they didn't
want to leave. In this book, they will be sharing their experiences with you.

Our mothers varied a great deal about how they felt when
thrust into the role of becoming the mother of a little boy. We
heard comments from those who approached this role with
some trepidation:

> "I was raised in an all-female family, so every day with my
> son brings surprises. Sometimes I have no idea what's
> expected of me or what I should do!"
>
> —*Marie, mother of a five-year-old boy.*

> "For one who was raised an only child and as something of
> a princess, relating to boys can be very hard sometimes."
>
> —*Linda, mother of a one-and-a-half-year-old boy.*

"I was afraid of the challenge of raising a son. In fact, I was totally terrified."

—Maria, widowed mother of a sixteen-year-old son.

Overall, the results of our survey, the discussion groups, and, of course, our own experiences made it clear that many women perceive mothering a boy as quite different from raising a daughter. For some like Maria, Linda, and Marla, parenting a son was downright daunting. Others saw it simply as an opportunity to experience something new:

"Having a son has been a wonderful experience for me. I have four sisters and no brothers, so it's been a learning experience by trial and error."

—Nancy, mother of an eight-year-old boy.

"Since I never had a brother, having a son is a most exciting adventure into the world of men."

—Leslie, mother of a ten-year-old boy.

Even those mothers who responded with enthusiasm or excitement about this novel experience reported that there were times when they felt uncomfortable or even at a complete loss as to what to do. For example, they were always aware of the ways in which their sons differed from themselves, even if boys had personalities similar to their own. And they were constantly facing questions to which they had no answers, questions to which they had never given much thought before. Are boys by nature more aggressive? Do they really play more roughly? Should I worry because my son learned to talk a full year later than my daughter? Is it okay for my son to hold his penis in public so much? Such questions peppered the responses to our mothers' questionnaire.

The goal of our book is to provide answers to these questions as well as to ones we ourselves had about mothering our sons. We've addressed the issues we felt specifically applied to the raising of sons, rather than discussing general parenting issues. For example, we did not cover issues that arise between siblings. No doubt family dynamics may work differently in a family with all boys versus one with girls and boys. Yet so many variables come into play—birth order, age of the children and the spacing between them, and personalities. We would have to write another whole book to cover these issues too!

Sons: A Mother's Manual focuses primarily on boys up to the age of twelve. Where we felt it appropriate, we discuss some issues which go beyond this age. Our reason for making this cutoff is that we feel living through puberty and the teenage years is so different from boyhood that it is almost like going to live in a country where you don't speak the language. There are a number of good books available to help parents survive this often difficult time, and we've listed them in our Selected Bibliography at the back of this book. The purpose of our book is to help mothers feel as comfortable as possible with their sons before they hit the teens years. We invite you, our readers, to consider the energetic, and sometimes exhausting, world of little boys with two mothers who have been there—and who wouldn't trade it for the world!

1

Sex Differences: Fiction and Fact

Before we can begin to talk about how to mother a son, we need to define how or why this experience differs from being the mother of a daughter. We find the best place to start this discussion is by addressing sex differences in children.

There are many misconceptions about how boys and girls differ—some rooted in half-truths and some having no sound basis at all. We will address these truths and misconceptions by answering the questions we most often heard from the mothers we surveyed. Our purpose is to clear up mysteries and myths at the outset, to explain which are rooted in biology and which in culture, and to allay the anxieties felt by mothers of sons.

In a public television program on gender and identity produced by the Smithsonian Institute, the narrator began by saying that becoming a boy or a girl was "merely a toss of genetic dice," so let's start our exploration of sex differences from when the toss lands on "male." We must explain before we begin that for some of these questions, there are no conclusive answers. Although scientists have been conducting numerous studies about sex differences, in many aspects the jury is still out as to whether some of these differences really exist or not.

COMMON QUESTIONS RELATING TO THE PHYSICAL MAKEUP OF GIRLS AND BOYS

DO BOYS HAVE MORE CHROMOSOMES THAN GIRLS?

The answer to this question is no; they have different kinds of chromosomes, not more. Chromosomes are tiny threads of DNA and molecules of other chemical compounds which are in the nucleus of every cell in our bodies. Chromosomes in turn are made up of genes which carry the traits that determine such things as hair color, color blindness, propensity to baldness, etc. All human beings have forty-six chromosomes in every cell, except for sperm cells and ova (eggs) cells, which have only twenty-three apiece. Other than the sperm and ova, each cell has twenty-two pairs of chromosomes—one half of each of these pairs has been inherited from the mother and one half from the father. In addition, each cell has two sex chromosomes, again one deriving from each parent. Mothers can pass on only an X chromosome to their children; fathers can provide either an X or a Y. If both provide an X, the embryo that results will develop into a girl fetus (XX). If the father provides a Y chromosome, the embryo will develop into a male fetus (XY). The sperm and the egg chromosomes fuse together when the egg is fertilized, and this is how the resulting embryo comes to have forty-six chromosomes in each cell. (There are mistakes that can occur during the development of the embryo which result in too many chromosomes, too little chromosomes, or chromosomes that stick together, but statistically this doesn't happen very often.)

IS TESTOSTERONE (A MALE HORMONE) WHAT DETERMINES IF THE BABY WILL BE MALE?

No. As we described above, it is the chromosomes that determine if a baby will be a male, but male hormones play an important role in the male's development. The embryo does not physically begin to become either male or female until it reaches the age of six weeks. At this point, the male fetus begins to develop cells that make androgens (male hormones), of which testosterone is the most significant. The androgens help to start the growth of male genitals. Boys have ten times more testosterone in their bodies than girls, which sustains the growth of male tissue. When a boy reaches puberty, testosterone begins to be released into the bloodstream, and this gives his body the ability to ejaculate semen.

DO BOYS HAVE BIGGER BRAINS THAN GIRLS? DOES THIS MEAN THEY ARE MORE INTELLIGENT?

There is probably not much difference in brain size between a little boy and girl. The **average** adult-white-male brain weighs about 3.07 pounds and the **average** adult-white-female brain is about 2.76 pounds, not a terribly significant difference. (Weights vary slightly by ethnic group.) The fact is that the brain is about 2 percent of the weight of a human being's body. Because the **average** male is taller and heavier than the **average** female, it follows that his brain would be a little bigger proportionate to his body size. While some researchers have tried to claim this indicates males have higher intelligence, there is absolutely no proof to this theory. The concept of a larger brain indicating greater intellect is addressed by biologist Anne Fausto-Sterling in her book *Myths of Gender:* "This logic, however, ran afoul of the 'elephant problem.' If size were the determinant of intelligence, then elephants and whales ought to be in command."

DO BOYS HAVE HIGHER METABOLISM RATES THAN GIRLS?

Yes. This is one of the areas of differences where boys are in luck. Males do have higher basal metabolism rates than girls, which means that they can consume more calories. However, this aspect does not really come into play until puberty.

DO BOYS HAVE ANY DIFFERENCES IN THEIR PHYSICAL STRUCTURE BESIDES THE OBVIOUS DIFFERENCES OF INTERNAL AND EXTERNAL SEXUAL ORGANS?

The answer to this question is yes and no. Some of the differences that will exist in adulthood will not have occurred yet during childhood. Although males and females basically have the same skeletons, organs, muscles, etc., there are some differences. For example, the average male heart (adult) weighs about two ounces more than a female heart; adult men will have a greater quantity of blood than adult women and more red blood cells as well. Other examples which are less obvious are that the muscular markings tend to be more delineated in the bones of males—these are grooves and ridges where the muscle attaches to the bone—males are **on average** larger than females and so have larger muscles. Girls' bones tend to ossify (mature) a few years earlier than boys' and are generally lighter and smaller. The development of a girl's thorax (the bony case of the chest) is also complete a few years earlier than a boy's. Boys tend to be heavier than girls of the same age during babyhood and childhood, and then, around the age of puberty, girls get heavier. After the first year or two of puberty, the boys become heavier again and stay that way (on average). Also during puberty, a boy's larynx will become about twice the size it was at birth, while a girl's will get only about one-third larger. Boys will continue to grow until age twenty; girls stop growing at about age eighteen. There are other minor differences as well, but none that have any great significance.

DO BOYS HAVE MORE MUSCLE AND LESS FAT THAN GIRLS?

The body of an **average** adult male has only about 15 percent fat, while that of a female has 27 percent fat. With children there is not much difference in body fat, but when kids hit puberty, girls begin to add fat and boys begin to add muscle.

DO BABY GIRLS PHYSICALLY MATURE SOONER THAN BABY BOYS?

Girls do tend to have their bones grow faster and get teeth earlier than boys. In general they sit, crawl, and walk earlier than boys.

COMMON QUESTIONS ABOUT DEVELOPMENT

We heard equally as often from mothers who wondered about developmental issues, some of which arose very early in a little boy's life.

DO BOYS HAVE A DIFFERENT TEMPERAMENT THAN GIRLS?

This question addressed a rather complex issue. Each child has its own unique personality irrespective of its sex. Temperament refers to personality traits—is a child shy, outgoing, gregarious, introspective? These are not sexual differences but individual differences. However, studies show that as a group, boys tend to be more aggressive than girls. Whether or not this stems from a biological basis or is learned by boys is a question of some debate among child behavior experts. We discuss this issue more fully in Chapter Ten.

DO BOYS TAKE SECOND PLACE TO GIRLS IN VERBAL SKILLS?

This subject is rather controversial and one for which there is no unequivocal answer. While very young girls do appear to score higher in verbal ability in some studies, this result is not consistently true: in many studies they don't test any better than boys. Researchers Eleanor Emmons Maccoby and Carol Nagy Jacklin report that girls mature faster in verbal abilities but boys catch up until age eleven, when girls do surpass boys. What this means is not clear, exactly, because there are so many variables in looking at this kind of research. For example, it may be that girls receive more attention from teachers when it comes to verbal skills; it is believed that teachers favor boys in math and science instruction, so the opposite may be true as well. Also, as social scientist Carol Tavris explains in *The Mismeasure of a Woman*, "The meanings of verbal abilities keep changing depending on who is using them and to what purpose." Tavris points out that although most surveys show that boys are more likely to have reading problems, like dyslexia, some scientists say that there are no differences and that the confusion lies in the fact that boys get referred more often than girls for these problems.

DO BOYS HAVE BETTER VISUAL-SPATIAL ABILITY THAN GIRLS?

Visual-spatial ability, which means a person's ability to visualize objects three-dimensionally in his or her mind, does appear to be greater in boys. This is true not so much in childhood but in adolescence and adulthood. Again, the reasons for this are not clear. While there are scientists who have postulated that this ability may be linked to a recessive X-linked gene, a number of studies have failed to support this belief. Biologist Anne Fausto-Sterling postulates why boys may excel in this area with a number of reasons that have no biological basis. She says that although it is possible that either physical maturity or hormones may affect male and female brains differently, it is also possible that boys are encouraged to play more games, such as model construction and catch, which may develop these skills; she makes this point because it is known that these skills can be learned. Studies show that girls who are taught these skills can catch up to boys rather readily. Fausto-Sterling theorizes that early parent-child relationships may have an effect on boys' and girls' visual-spatial skills in other ways. Studies also show that children who experience more independence and less verbal interaction (which is the way most parents tend to proceed with little boys rather than with little girls) have stronger spatial skills. Also, studies have indicated that mothers are more likely to imitate sounds that baby girls make and to dangle an object in front of a baby boy, reinforcing different skills.

ARE BOYS REALLY INNATELY BETTER AT MATH THAN GIRLS?

There are certainly a lot of researchers who keep trying to prove this is so. Most studies reveal that there is no discernible difference in math skills before adolescence, but when a study does show a difference, it is boys who are slightly ahead. Upon reaching adolescence, boys pull ahead in math (and science) somewhat, and many researchers believe this may be because boys have a greater interest in these subjects. Anne Fausto-Sterling, in *Myths of Gender*, reports that this is another area where scientists have attempted to link male math ability with an X-linked gene, and again, no studies have been able to support this thesis. She also suggests that boys and girls in the same classroom do not receive the same instruction—that boys receive more direct instruction in math than girls. Furthermore, she says that parents tend to encourage boys more by giving them microscopes, science kits, etc. (One of the authors of this book still remembers with anger watching her grandmother give a chemistry set and a microscope with slides to her male cousin. The same cousin started a fire with his chemistry set in her grandmother's store—giving this author some measure of guilty satisfaction!) Carol Tavris, in *Mismeasure of A Woman*, also focuses on this subject. She points out that although most math geniuses are male, overall there isn't much difference in math scores between males and females; it is the gifted males who throw off the curve.

WHAT IS ALL THIS TALK ABOUT RIGHT-BRAIN AND LEFT-BRAIN DOMINANCE? IS IT TRUE BOYS USE THE RIGHT SIDE OF THEIR BRAIN AND GIRLS USE THE LEFT?

It is true that we have two hemispheres in our brain that seem to be used for different tasks. In *Myths of Gender*, Anne Fausto-

Sterling explains that we know fairly well how the two hemispheres work in right-handed people, but in left-handed people research is still required. The right hemisphere governs spatial skills, nonverbal skills, and artistic ability. The left hemisphere controls all verbal activities and analytical skills. But even knowing this to be true, we must still bear in mind that the brain is a single unit and there may be other divisions beside the two hemispheres that we have yet to discover. A number of years ago some scientists set out to prove that the male brain is lateralized—that is, that males tend to use the right side of their brain more. They felt, based on a study of a relatively small number of brains, that the female brain stem contained more fibers which connect the two hemispheres and therefore allows females to use both sides of their brains more easily. The support for this theory is the belief that since boys are flooded with testosterone as fetuses, the brain must be affected by this flood of male hormone, and the development of the left side of the brain is slowed down.

Carol Tavris, in *Mismeasure of A Woman*, argues rather convincingly that this theory doesn't make too much sense. Tavris says that most researchers today feel the two sides of the brain complement each other and that many skills involve using both sides of the brain. More importantly, most research on male brain lateralization was carried out on rats and is not necessarily reliable when applied to humans. It is also significant, she says, that the differences in male-female abilities became less distinguishable as girls are encouraged to pursue mathematics and science. "Theories of sex differences in the brain," says Tavris, "cannot account for the complexities of people's everyday behavior . . . nor can theories explain why abilities and ambitions change when people are given opportunities previously denied to them."

DO BOYS REALLY USE THEIR GROSS MOTOR SKILLS MORE THAN GIRLS?

Boys do seem to move around more than girls even at a very young age, according to a number of studies. They tend to be more adept at using arms and legs (gross motor skills) and are more coordinated, while girls are better at fine motor skills (not manual dexterity {hand}, but in the use of their fingers). Some studies have shown that parents are more likely to encourage gross motor skills in baby boys—pulling on their arms and legs more than on girls', which may be one contributing factor to this difference as well as the fact that boys tend to have more physical strength.

DO BOYS AND GIRLS REALLY PLAY DIFFERENTLY?

As we said before, all children are individuals with their own preferences, but overall, there is a difference in how boys play and the category of toys they gravitate to. In the first few years of life the differences in play between boys and girls is not that pronounced. By the age of three, boys have already assumed sex roles in their play that are identified with males—superheroes (the favorite), policemen, firemen, fathers, etc. Girls overwhelmingly choose domestic play.

By the age of four, boys are primarily interested in playing only with other boys, and their method of making contact with other boys includes vying for power. Boys play in a more aggressive manner than girls and are very interested in dominating each other, while girls are just interested in playing amicably. Little boys tend to be more active, engage in rough-and-tumble play, and are quicker to resort to fighting. They also tend to insult each other more and participate in a lot of name-calling. Around the age of five, they begin making jokes about bodily functions, their posteriors, their penises, and farting.

Mothers, take heart: this stage doesn't last too long!

Peer relations play a very important role in how little boys learn sex roles through play. Boys tend to play in larger groups than girls, which only serves to exacerbate their tendency for aggression. They are more likely to respond to physical assaults from other boys than girls are to respond to a child of either sex. Boys also seem to play in a way that demands attention from their playmates.

Most boys have a preference for superhero toys, guns, cars, blocks, construction sets, and other toys traditionally considered to be masculine. To a certain extent this is a result of their environment; parents, particularly fathers, tend to encourage boys to play with "sex-appropriate toys," and the media reinforce this message.

IS THERE A DIFFERENCE BETWEEN BOYS AND GIRLS IN THE FIVE SENSES?

Some studies suggest that boys have less acute hearing than girls (their mothers certainly think so), and we know that boys are far more likely to be color-blind than girls. Boys also have a higher propensity for stuttering.

THE INFLUENCE OF SOCIETY

What we haven't yet focused on is a most critical part of a little boy's world—the societal and familial influences that shape boys into men. From birth on, boys and girls are treated differently. Unlike the hit recorded by Johnny Cash, "A Boy Named Sue," we give our sons names that are clearly masculine. We decorate our boys' rooms in blue or yellow, red and white, or some neutral color—never pink or purple or filled with white eyelet and lace. We dress them in the same colors we paint their rooms and take care not to put clothes on them that are feminine. But the way we approach the raising of our little boys differs from the way we raise girls in even more significant ways.

Through our research we found that the majority of families express a desire for their firstborn to be male. Although we knew what the research tells us, we were frankly quite surprised at the passion we heard in our discussion groups. We found that prizing a male child, although seemingly an old-fashioned notion, is still widespread. We heard over and over again how giving birth to a son made a woman seem to have more value to her in-laws and even to her own family:

> *"My husband is Chinese and boys are revered in the Chinese culture. His family wasn't very happy when he married me, because I'm not Chinese, but having a boy put me in great standing with them."*

> *"Because I wasn't Jewish, having a boy made it better with my husband's grandmother that he had married a Gentile."*

> *"We finally got the Italian aunts to stop bothering us!"*

> *"I gave him my maiden name as his first name to please my father!"*

> *"The best part about having a boy is giving your husband a son!"*

We also know that this strong desire for boys in the family translates into a difference in fathering. Studies show that men play with boy babies more than girl babies and in general are more involved with their families if they have at least one son. Marriages, on average, last longer if there is a son. Even divorced fathers tend to see their sons more than their daughters (at least until adolescence).

Boys bring out a somewhat different style of mothering as well. Studies show that mothers spend less time fondling infant sons than daughters and punish their sons more often than their daughters. They tend to engage their little girls in more verbal exchange than their sons, and allow their daughters less physical freedom. Mothers worry less if their sons have dirty clothes or their hair isn't combed, and both fathers and mothers involve their sons more than their daughters in rough-and-tumble play. Clearly the attitudes of parents and extended families help to shape the differences between boys and girls.

In the following chapters we will focus on many of the ways in which the family and society tell a boy what kind of man he is supposed to grow up to be. We will address the roles of both of his parents in all of his developmental stages, the greater propensity for aggression that boys have and how it affects their lives, how they learn about their gender identity and sexuality, as well as other critical influences, pitfalls, and advantages boys face as they are growing up.

2

A Boy's Body:
Anatomy and Growth

"My son pulls on his penis like it's a rubber band. I wonder if it hurts."

"It can be shocking to a mother to see the enlarged testicles a newborn baby sometimes has . . . my son's looked *huge!*"

"I realized when my son hit puberty that I didn't know very much about the male reproductive system!"

Many mothers are surprised at and anxious over how constantly sons handle their penises during the early years. They wonder, can their sons actually harm themselves physically? And what about the psychological aspects of all that touching, playing, pulling, and tugging?

Although mothers thought they understood "how little boys were made," when we asked them specific questions about the male anatomy, they discovered they knew less than they thought. For this reason, we feel it's important to discuss the obvious difference between our bodies and our sons' early in the book; we'll talk about the structure and function of their genital organs and other related issues.

As we mentioned earlier, this book is focusing on boys up to the age of adolescence. In this chapter, however, we make an exception and discuss the physical changes that take place during puberty as well because we believe strongly that mothers should be entirely familiar with their sons' normal sexual

15

development. We hope to make you feel completely at ease with your boys physically and to anticipate and allay your fears as we go along.

The Male Reproductive System

We start with the most familiar part of a boy's anatomy—the penis. The penis is a sexual organ made up of spongy tissue (no bones) with muscles at the base that aid in erection. It is actually composed of several parts: the tip or head is known as the **glans,** the long part of the penis is called the **shaft,** and the area where the shaft and the glans meet is known as the **corona.** At the tip of the glans is the **meatus,** the opening through which a boy urinates and, after puberty, ejaculates.

If a boy is not circumcised (circumcision will be discussed in more detail later), his penis will be covered with a **foreskin,** which is like a sheath that protects the penis. In about 4 percent of newborns this foreskin will already be retracted, which means that it can be pushed back toward the abdomen. This usually doesn't happen until a few months to several years after birth and can occur even as late as puberty or beyond. Until it does retract, it is still attached to the glans. Parents often try to force the foreskin back, but this may cause damage. The foreskin will eventually retract by itself.

While it is still attached to the glans, the foreskin does not get in the way of a boy urinating. As a male gets older, retraction is a necessity for cleaning the penis and will occur automatically for urination and during an erection. Penile cleanliness is of **extreme importance,** particularly after puberty, because at that time boys' bodies secrete an oily substance known as smegma which collects on the penis and under the foreskin. If the penis is not cleaned regularly, this secretion can cause infections, sexually transmitted diseases, and a higher incidence of penile cancer. It has also been linked to a higher rate of cervical cancer in a male's sexual partner.

The **frenulum** is a band of tissue under the glans which stops the foreskin from retracting too far during an erection. The corona and the frenulum are the most sensitive parts of the penis.

The **urethra** is the passageway that runs from the bladder to the penis and carries both urine and sperm. After puberty it also carries semen from the **vesicle** (two pouches that produce some of the seminal fluid) to the penis. It ends at the meatus, the opening through which a boy urinates or releases sperm when he is old enough for his body to produce it.

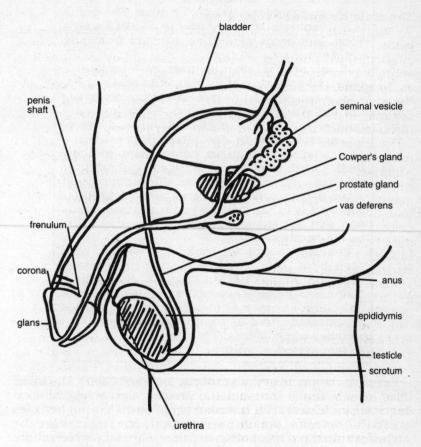

Illustration I: The Male Reproductive System

THERE are a number of old wives' tales about penises, none of which is true. Penis size does not affect sexiness, and there is no relationship between penis size and other parts of the body, such as feet, hands, or nose. The penis is also not related to the overall size of a man's body, and penis size does not vary from one ethnic group to another.

In an adult male, the average length of a penis, when not erect, is four and a half inches, with a range of from two to six inches being normal. An erect penis averages six and one-quarter inches in length and one and three-quarters inches in diameter. Boys' penises stay relatively small in comparison to their bodies until they reach the age of puberty; for this reason, little boys are often concerned when they compare their genitals with their fathers'. It is important for you to reassure your son that his sexual organ will someday to be as big as his father's.

Penises do not all look alike—some may even be a little "lopsided"—but their visual presentation has nothing to do with how they function. The only exception to this rule is the condition known as "chordee," which causes an extreme curve in a penis and can lead to a number of problems. This condition is likely to be noticed by your pediatrician.

Beneath the penis is the **scrotum** (or scrotal sac), the loose "bag" of skin which contains and protects the two egg-shaped **testicles** (or testes). The common slang terms for the testicles are "balls" or "nuts" (for obvious reasons). The testicles are the organs within the scrotum that are necessary for reproduction; they are the male form of gonads or sexual glands. The scrotum hangs as it does because in order to manufacture sperm—its function after a boy reaches puberty—it must be cooler than the rest of the body. Your son may worry if he notices that his left testicle appears bigger or heavier than his right one, but you can assure him that this is true for about 85 percent of males and is entirely normal.

Inside the scrotum, in addition to the testicles, there are sections with tiny coiled tubes **(tubules)** within which sperm are made after a boy reaches puberty. There are also tiny tubes inside the testicle through which the sperm travel for a period of four to six weeks for maturation before being released from the body when a male ejaculates. The testicles are "fed" by the **spermatic cord,** which is made up of arteries, veins, and nerves and hangs from the abdomen through an opening called the **inguinal ring.**

The **vas deferens** (sperm duct) is the location to which sperm go for storage after they have matured; it is here they wait to be ejaculated when a male masturbates or has sexual intercourse. The vas deferens runs from the tip of the penis to the bladder at the other end, where it gets wider. This wider part, where the actual storage of sperm takes place, is known as the **ampulla.**

Another link in the male reproductive system is the **seminal vesicle,** which produces **semen** (the fluid that is released when a boy ejaculates) after puberty. Semen is actually only one-tenth sperm; the rest of what spurts out is a fluid produced by the vesicle and the prostate gland, and it contains a number of chemicals including protein, citric acid, and fructose.

The ring-shaped **prostate gland** is located below the ampulla and the seminal vesicle. In addition to contributing fluid semen, its function is to contract during ejaculation, helping to push the semen into the urethra, the tube through which both urine and semen are released. (In case you're wondering, both cannot happen at the same time—a male can never urinate while he is ejaculating.) Lower down in the urethra is the **Cowper's gland,** which produces a fluid that is secreted when a male is sexually aroused.

The **anus,** located behind the scrotum, is the opening through which excrement is expelled from the body.

Like a complicated machine with many parts, the male reproductive system from time to time may have a problem with one part. In the Appendix you will find a discussion of these potential problems and their treatments. But now we will return to a decision that must be faced early on: circumcision.

To Do or Not to Do—The Circumcision Question

This is my covenant, which ye shall keep between me and you and the seed after thee; every man-child among you shall be circumcised.

And ye shall circumcise the flesh of your foreskins; and it shall be a token of the covenant betwixt me and you.

—the Old Testament, Genesis 17:10

Circumcision is surgery. With any surgery there are inherent risks. Parents should carefully weigh the benefits and risks of circumcision.

—International Childbirth Education Association

The decision whether or not to circumcise your newborn son by surgically removing the foreskin that covers the end of the penis has to be made rather quickly. If you are of the Jewish or Moslem faith, this may not be an option but rather a requirement of your religion. In the Jewish religion a circumcision (bris) is performed eight days after a son is born; in the Moslem religion it may be performed at as late an age as the early teens. Most nonreligious circumcisions take place within a week of birth—often while the mother is still in the hospital.

In many countries circumcision is not nearly as popular as it is in the United States, where there is a 60 percent circumcision rate. Ironically, while we are busy removing "sheaths" from penises, in other cultures men add artificial sheaths as a form of ornament. In the book *Facts & Phalluses,* Alexandra Parsons reports that in New Guinea and South Africa "toothpaste tubes, discarded film containers, open sardine cans and even the leg of a plastic doll have been spotted fulfilling this remarkable role."

"We almost got divorced deciding whether or not to circumcise my son," Anne Marie told us. This statement reminded us of a scene in the British television comedy series *Dear Jane.* In the show, Jane is Jewish and her husband is not, and they strongly disagree on whether or not to circumcise their son. She finally convinces him it's the right thing to do, but he's very nervous about the decision. The doorbell rings at the appointed hour for the bris, and when the husband answers it, there stands the mohel (the religious figure who performs the circumcision) with an enormous pair of hedge clippers, and the husband faints dead away. The mohel apologizes for the scare but says he's just come from a "great garden sale" on his way over to perform his duties.

While sometimes the topic of humor, circumcision can really be quite an emotional issue for many parents. For those who don't have religious rules governing circumcision, it is entirely a personal choice; you're not likely to get advice from your doctor on which route to take. Some parents make their choice solely on a medical basis and others consider the social aspect—or the desire for a boy to look like other males in his family or his peers.

Uncircumcised
Penis

Circumcised
Penis

Illustration II: Circumcised/Uncircumcised Penis

One mother who joined our focus groups told us that in her husband's family there was a tradition of circumcising male babies. The tradition was continued when her in-laws had her husband, the firstborn son, circumcised after he was born. Her mother-in-law got a bit confused when it came to caring for the baby's penis and the stub of the umbilical cord. She put vaseline on the cord and alcohol on the recently cut penis, the opposite of what she should have done, and she had a very unhappy baby. She was so traumatized by the experience that when her second son was born she refused to have him circumcised.

We can't tell you whether or not to circumcise your son, but we will try to provide the most current medical information regarding circumcision to help you make your choice.

To reiterate, the penis is a shaft with a rounded end called the glans and a groove known as the corona or sulcus that separates the shaft from the glans. Both parts—the shaft and the glans—are covered by a layer of skin known as the foreskin (or prepuce) at birth. If left to its own natural course, at some point in a young boy's life the foreskin will eventually detach from the tip of the penis, allowing a boy to push it back toward his abdomen and wash his penis.

This detachment takes place because the inner surface of the foreskin begins to separate from the glans through the normal shedding of cells. The discarded cells may appear as little white balls under the skin and are called **infant smegma.** Before the foreskin separates, it protects the glans from infection.

There are various claims for and against circumcision being better for penile health, but until recently there was little definitive proof either way. A number of recent studies seem to indicate good reasons for circumcision, in our opinion. Before we discuss these studies a little further, we'd like to describe the circumcision process.

Doctors recommend that if a nonreligious circumcision is to take place, it should happen no sooner than twelve to twenty-four hours after birth and no later than a week afterward. The exceptions to this guideline are babies who are born premature, babies who are ill, and babies who have genital defects. In these cases, circumcision should be delayed. For these and various other reasons, such as adoption, circumcision is sometimes not addressed until a boy is several months or several years old. Although at times a delay is unavoidable, it is not preferable, as it may be more traumatic for the little boy as it becomes a more complicated procedure. One study suggests that in 5 to 10 percent of males, infections occur which eventually make it necessary to circumcise later in life, sometimes in adulthood. This may be yet another reason to opt for circumcision early on.

A circumcision, unless done for religious reasons, is usually performed in the hospital. One of several people can perform the procedure—your obstetrician, your family doctor, your pediatrician, or a pediatric surgeon. As we mentioned, in the Jewish religion a person know as the mohel will do the circumcision, and in the Moslem religion it is the mullah who performs the rite. Although these religious figures are not usually medical doctors, they have been trained to circumcise and generally do a good job. In fact, many mohels claim they complete a circumcision in less than a minute, while a doctor may take up to ten minutes. It is always advisable to use someone who has been recommended by others.

There are several methods of circumcision, including the "clamp" technique and the Plastibell technique. In the former, the foreskin is clamped and an instrument is used to free the tissue connections between the foreskin and the penis. The Plastibell method utilizes a plastic ring which is placed over the head of the penis; the foreskin is then stretched over it and cut. The ring falls off by itself in about a week.

The American Academy of Pediatrics suggests that certain procedures will help limit some of the potential "postoperative complications" of circumcision. The doctor performing the circumcision should use a surgical marking pen to indicate the location of the coronal sulcus on the shaft skin before proceeding, and the urethral meatus should be clearly identified to avoid interfering with it. You can discuss the merits of both with your doctor.

Another issue for circumcision is the use of anesthesia. In the Jewish religion it is common for the mohel to put a finger dipped in wine into the baby's mouth to calm him. This seems to work quite well, perhaps because wine contains natural sugar. A study at Johns Hopkins and Cornell medical schools showed that babies undergoing circumcision who were not given a pacifier cried during two-thirds of the procedure. Babies who were given pacifiers that released water cried during half of the procedure, and those who received pacifiers that released a sucrose solution cried during about one-third of the procedure. It is presumed that sugar releases brain endorphins which cause pain reduction.

Because the pain related to circumcision has been shown to be so brief, with no long-term effects, doctors believe that any anesthesia used during a circumcision should be almost risk-free. General anesthesia, in which a baby is put to sleep, has risks that are too high to warrant its use for this procedure.

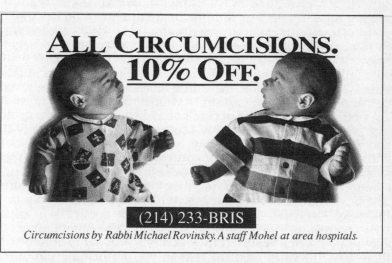

Circumcisions by Rabbi Michael Rovinsky. A staff Mohel at area hospitals.

Illustration III: In the Jewish religion, a circumcision is performed eight days after a boy is born. Rabbi Michael Rovinsky of St. Louis, Missouri, injects mild humor into his advertising in an attempt to alleviate some of the anxiety parents may feel about this procedure.

Advertisement courtesy of Rabbi Michael Rovinsky.

There are two options for anesthesia which remain—both
are considered "local" forms of anesthesia. The first is a penile
block, which consists of injecting lidocaine, similar to the novo-
caine you get at the dentist's, at the base of the penis to numb
it entirely. This type of anesthesia is not used widely, with only
a few hundred cases being reported. It also has some risks
associated with it. For example, even a very low dose of lidocaine when injected into the bloodstream can cause toxicity,
and it is very easy to reach a toxic dose in a newborn. The
second option is to administer lidocaine only at the site of the
circumcision. A baby can also be given acetaminophen (Ty-
lenol) for the pain.

If you circumcise your baby in the hospital, you will be required—as for any other type of surgery—to sign a consent
form, and your insurance may or may not pay for it. Some hospitals will allow you to watch, but that's not necessarily a good
idea. Decide ahead of time if you can handle it. If you can, it
gives you an opportunity to cuddle your baby when he really
needs it. Be certain that your own doctor performs the procedure. If you give birth in a teaching hospital, insist that you
will not allow a resident or a medical student to do the job.

After the circumcision the penis should be kept covered with
petroleum jelly until it heals and should be wrapped loosely in
gauze. It should be not be washed until it is healed, which will
take only about three or four days. However, mothers should
watch for complications, including bleeding, redness, or swelling, and should make certain that urination appears normal.

A note for parents who decide not to circumcise. If you detect
any swelling under your baby's foreskin, clean it with a Q-tip
and water. If it doesn't go away, see your doctor.

There is still a great deal of controversy regarding circumcision. Many parents and doctors believe in "leaving well enough
alone." They are concerned about possible complications,
which include infection, excessive bleeding, scar tissue, or a
"mistake." In truth, few complications ever occur.

As recently as 1983, the official policy of the American Academy of Pediatrics reported in *Pediatrics Magazine* stated that
there was no valid medical reason for performing circumcisions. This might partly have been due to the fact that the policy
statement was formed by neonatologists, who are familiar only
with the pain and potential complications of the procedure.
Urologists, for example, who are more likely to see the later
problems caused by not having a circumcision, tend to favor
it.

The Academy's 1988 task force had a more balanced composition and took the position that "recent studies suggest benefits outweigh the risks." These studies indicate the incidence of urinary tract infection in infants is reduced by circumcision, that circumcision prevents a number of infections related to the penis (see the Appendix), that there is virtually no cancer of the penis in circumcised males, circumcised males have fewer sexually transmitted diseases, and the partners of circumcised males have fewer sexually transmitted diseases, and the partners of circumcised males have less incidence of cervical cancer.

One of the most recent pieces of research that seems to support circumcision was done in Africa. It appears to show that circumcised males are less susceptible to being infected with the HIV virus (AIDS) during sexual intercourse. This is believed to be because uncircumcised males are more likely to have open sores, which offer an entry point for the virus. This research is by no means conclusive and this theory will probably be studied a great deal more.

Please see the box on page 26 for a more detailed listing of the pros and cons of circumcision to help you make an informed decision.

Checking a Newborn's Genitals

When a boy is born, the doctor who examines him should be looking for the position of the urethral meatus, the opening in the penis through which a boy urinates. An abnormal urinary stream could indicate "urethral stricture."

He should palpitate the testes to make certain there is not an atrophied or undescended testicle or hydrocele. (Please see the Appendix for descriptions of all of these conditions.)

Boys and Height

"We adopted two children, so we had no idea what height to expect them to reach. My husband is very short, and I'm happy it appears my daughter won't be very tall so she won't tower over her father. Luckily it looks as if my son will be tall. It's hard for a boy to be short," Marlee told us.

This anecdote very much epitomizes the concerns most families have about their sons' future height—a concern which they express about their sons far more than about their daughters.

So first, let us assure you that all children grow at their own pace, and unless a boy is unusually small for his age, there is

Pros and Cons of Circumcision

Benefits

(1) Urinary tract infections are more common in uncircumcised males, and they can be serious in an infant; a number of studies have shown the risk for infection in infancy is as much as ten times higher for uncircumcised males.

(2) Circumcision prevents phimosis and balanitis, two potentially serious infections of the penis. (See Appendix for more detailed descriptions.)

(3) Sexually transmitted diseases are more common in uncircumcised males, in particular genital herpes, candidiasis, gonorrhea, and syphilis.

(4) Bacterial viruses don't get trapped under the foreskin.

(5) No smegma (the shed skin cells mixed with an oily substance produced by the sebaceous glands) collects as it would under foreskin, which can cause infection.

(6) Studies show female partners have less cervical cancer.

(7) Penile cancer is not common but has a 25 percent mortality rate; it almost never occurs in circumcised males.

(8) Avoids trauma at an older age if a circumcision is required for medical reasons.

(9) Possibly decreases the susceptibility of a male for transmission of the HIV virus during intercourse.

Risks

(1) Pain associated with the procedure.

(2) Potential for excessive bleeding.

(3) Potential infection from procedure.

(4) Potential for surgical error—removing too much.

(5) Scar tissue on the meatus could potentially cause a blocked urethra.

no need for concern. About half of "small for due date" babies are small in childhood but catch up later. And no, big feet or hands do not mean a baby boy will grow up tall; that works for puppies, not for children.

Margo, who is five feet tall, married a man only a few inches taller than she. She told us this story: "When my husband was young his parents were quite upset that he was so short. They took him to a doctor who administered shots to help him grow. Needless to say, the shots didn't work, but what did they expect? They're both *very* short!"

When you take you son for regular checkups, your pediatrician will probably plot on a graph your son's height in relation to his weight and will tell you what percentile he falls into compared with other children. Whether your son is in the "top 75th percentile" or "below the 50th percentile," these are all within the normal range. There has to be some variation in order to create a relative measurement, but not being in the top of the percentile chart doesn't mean there is anything wrong or that your son might not be a normal height in adulthood. The greatest determinant of a boy's height is heredity. If you and your husband (as well as other siblings) are short, don't expect to have your son grow up to be a professional basketball player.

Generally, boys do not hit their stride in height until adolescence, between ages twelve and fifteen, at which point they have probably reached about 82 percent of their adult height. As they enter puberty they begin to have growth spurts, often growing as much as five or six inches in one year, and they continue to grow in height until about age nineteen or twenty. Boys grow first in their arms and legs and later in the bones of the spine.

You should be aware, though, that there are medical conditions which can cause growth problems. Some causes for growth failure are the use of steroids, pituitary or hypothalamic problems, thyroid disease (symptoms include changes in activity level, sleeping patterns, or bowel movements) or the deficiency of growth hormones characterized by the failure to change shoe size and by excess abdominal obesity. The rate of bone maturation actually corresponds better with physical development than chronological age, and this can only be determined by tests and X-rays. If you are concerned about your son's growth, you can discuss it with your pediatrician.

A word about hormones used to stimulate growth in very short boys. Growth hormones are currently used for children who have a medical condition in which their bodies don't make enough of their own growth hormone (h.g.h.—human growth hormone). This treatment has been used for thirty years and is safe and often quite effective.

There is now on the market a synthetic growth hormone which is more readily available than the natural hormone. Some doctors are treating short boys with it who **do** make enough of their own growth hormone for purely aesthetic reasons—simply because their parents want them to be taller. This treatment is still quite controversial, as there is no conclusive evidence that it works, and it is quite expensive.

Body and Weight

Children tend to eat as much as their bodies need to maintain a normal weight level. This equilibrium can be upset by anxious parents who can create an overweight child by putting too much emphasis on food. Some experts suggest that overfeeding may be perceived by a mother as a way to further develop the mother/child bond.

Breast-feeding a baby can help reduce the risk for too much weight gain in infancy (an issue you can discuss with your pediatrician). Mothers should use food as a response to hunger, not as a way to keep a baby quiet. In general, infants gain one to two pounds per month and will double their birth weight in the first six months of life. By age two, they will gain only about one-half pound per month, and even less between the ages of two and three. After age six, weight gain picks up again, with an average gain of seven pounds per year until about ages ten to twelve. A new study suggests that infants actually grow in spurts, and so they may appear not to make any gains for a period of time and then suddenly—even overnight—grow an inch or more.

Once he begins to eat whole food, try to provide your son with a healthy, balanced diet low in fat (but not until after age two; until then, children need the fat), salt, and sugar and then trust him to eat what his body needs. American Heart Association guidelines suggest no more than 30 percent fat in the diet, no more than 300 milligrams of cholesterol per day, and no more than 3,000 milligrams of salt per day after the age of two. Avoid giving him sugared cereals, processed foods, and "fast foods," which are high in fat content. Don't force your son to eat more than he wants to unless he fails to gain weight and grow over a significant period of time; then seek medical attention.

Obesity is increasing among children ages six to seventeen. One study shows that between 1963 and 1980, there was a 54 percent rise in obesity in children ages six to eleven. Mild-tomoderate obesity in children is defined as being in the 85th to 90th percentile, and severe obesity as being in the 95th percentile.

Helping your son to avoid becoming overweight is a lifetime gift from a mother. A recent study indicates that overweight teenagers are more likely as men to suffer from heart disease, colon cancer, arthritis, and gout by age seventy—a risk twice as great as for those who were thin. Men who were fat teenage boys also tend to die earlier, with an average life span of forty-five.

If your son is overweight, he may appear tall for his age. Overweight boys may also seem to have a small penis, but this is more an illusion than a reality, caused by the fact that the penis is hidden by fat. **Gynecomastia,** swelling of the breasts, and **striae,** stretch marks, are often found in older boys who are heavy, frequently before puberty, which tends to arrive early in a heavy child. If a boy is short *and* overweight, this may be caused by a medical condition and should be investigated by your pediatrician.

To a large extent, weight is determined by hereditary factors. If a boy has one heavy parent, he has a 50 percent chance of being heavy himself. If both parents are heavy, the chance goes up to 75 percent, as metabolic rate is inherited. Boys of thin parents have only a 10 percent chance of being obese.

Obese children—those who are persistently 20 percent over normal weight for their height—are born with extra fat cells and the increased ability to store fats. But **overeating does** contribute to the problem, since the fat cells acquired in early life will always stay with a child. While the tendency for weight gain may be inherited, eating habits are **learned.**

Still, diets are not generally recommended for children and should be discussed with a doctor. Most boys don't need to diet but rather to "grow" into their weight. A preferable method of helping a child to lose weight is to slowly reduce his daily caloric intake and encourage more physical activity.

In severe cases of obesity, a medically supervised weight-control program for children might be indicated. Many hospitals and clinics offer them, and your pediatrician can help you locate a program.

Setting the Right Example
Another way you can help to promote weight loss in your son is to set a good example in terms of diet and exercise. Give rewards other than food, make mealtimes pleasant, and have them be a family affair as often as possible. Don't make your

son eat more than he wants to, and teach him to eat a variety of foods. Don't keep foods in the house you don't want your son to eat. Do your best to teach him about nutrition so that he'll grow up armed with the knowledge of how to eat a balanced, low-fat diet. It's easier to develop healthy eating habits as a youngster than to change them when you're older.

Television and video viewing are often blamed for producing overweight children because they take away from the time that might be spent in physical activity and promote snacking, in part by carrying advertisements for a lot of "junk food." In a study authored in 1985 by Dr. William Dietz, associate professor of pediatrics at Tufts University Medical School, Boston, it was shown that for every hour of TV an adolescent watches, his risk of obesity grows by 2 percent. Boys tend to watch more TV than girls.

Video games and computers are also relatively passive activities that should not be overdone. However, an interesting study at the Mount Sinai School of Medicine in New York determined that kids who play video games *instead* of watching TV are less likely to get fat. The reason is that playing video games raises the heart rate and involves some movement that burns calories. (Too much playing can cause carpal tunnel syndrome, a painful wrist-and-hand condition.)

Being overweight is not the only danger for your son if he is not active. A study by Kurt Guld of the University of California suggests that children who watch at least two hours of TV a day are twice as likely to have cholesterol levels over 200 (above normal).

Adolescence poses its own weight problems. When boys who are thin or even those who have an average build reach adolescence, they often become concerned about how their bodies look, and they try to gain weight to develop a body shape that looks more like an adult's. We all realize how little girls are pressured into having the perfect body, but we don't usually think about the standard we set for men—to be large with broad shoulders, sculpted muscles, and "macho" physiques. Movies, TV, advertisements, etc., all contribute to this image, but a mother can be helpful by reinforcing positive body image from the time a boy is small. The opposite behavior is seen in girls, who frequently feel they are not thin enough, which explains why only 5 to 10 percent of children with eating disorders such as anorexia and bulimia are boys.

Boys can **acquire** a weight problem if they eat too much in an effort to "bulk up." They need to know that they should increase **exercise** along with some calories to solidify their lean body mass, rather than just add fat. Keep in mind that it is also normal for many children to get a little "plump" between the ages of seven to twelve and then slim down by the time they are fifteen. In general, a boy's weight will come close to doubling between ages eleven and eighteen.

As boys get older they can usually eat more than girls, although they have the same nutritional requirements. Luckily for them, they have higher metabolic rates—we all know how angry we get when our husbands eat more than we do on a diet and still lose weight faster! Also, the calorie needs of boys and men are stable, while girls' needs from puberty on into womanhood vary with their menstrual cycles.

Recommended Number of Daily Servings From Each Food Group for a Healthy Diet for *Boys*, Beginning From Age Two

	Ages 2–5	Ages 6–10	Ages 11+
Vegetables (½ cup cooked or raw, 1 cup leafy)	2	3–4	4–5
Fruits (1 medium fresh, ¾ cup juice, ½ cup canned)	2	2–3	3–4
Grains (1 slice bread, 1 oz. cold cereal, ½ cup rice or pasta)	3	6–9	9–11
Dairy products (1 cup milk, 1 oz. cheese, 2 oz. processed cheese)	2	2–2½	3 or more
Meats (1 egg, 2 oz. meat, 4 tbsp. peanut butter)	2	2–2½	2–3

There are some other potential dietary-related problems for teenage boys. If a boy is training strenuously for sports and doesn't take in enough nutrients, this can be dangerous and can stunt growth. For example, boys often don't get enough calcium or iron, and between the ages of eleven to eighteen, all kids need more iron. An iron-deficiency anemia is not uncommon in boys who are undergoing a growth spurt.

Some kids also have zinc deficiencies, vegetarian teens may have several nutrient deficiencies, and, of course, too much sugar means cavities. If you feel your son isn't getting the proper nutrients, you might want to discuss how to balance this with your doctor or a nutritionist.

Average Height and Weight and Suggested Calorie Intake for Boys

Age	Weight/lbs.	Height/inches	Calories (average and range)
1–3	29	35	1300 (900–1800)
4–6	44	44	1700 (1300–2300)
7–10	62	52	2400 (1650–3300)
11–14	99	62	2700 (2000–3700)
15–18	145	69	2800 (2100–3900)

Puberty
Puberty refers to the period of a boy's life when his body begins to become more like an adult male body. When the **hypothalamus** reaches a specific point in maturity, it tells the brain to start puberty, and the **pituitary glands** begin secreting the necessary hormones. This usually happens between the ages of twelve and fifteen and a half, but can also begin as early as eight. For this reason, it would be wise to tell your son about the changes that will occur in his body *before* they happen—nothing can be more frightening to a boy than to see his body changing without understanding why it is happening.

Puberty that begins very early may be a medical problem and should be reported to a doctor. Similarly, if by the age of fifteen there is no evidence of the onset of puberty, it would be prudent to consult a doctor, since there may be problems with the hypothalamus or the pituitary gland that could be preventing puberty from taking place.

The hormone which is secreted by the pituitary gland is **testosterone,** a male hormone that causes the sex drive in males *and* females. Male hormones are called **androgens** because they support and sustain the growth of male tissues. Males have ten times more testosterone than females, which maintains their virility for their entire lives. The male body also manufactures the female hormone **estrogen,** but ten times less than females do.

The first sign of puberty is usually a rapid change in height and weight, followed by changes in the genitals and pubic area. Another early sign is when a boy begins to get body odor, particularly under the arms and in the feet.

When a boy is prepubertal, he has no pubic hair and his genitals are still relatively small. In the first stage of puberty he will begin to have enough pubic hair to be counted, and the hair will be straight. The penis will begin to lengthen and darken in color, the testicles will enlarge slightly, and a slight folding and darkening of the scrotum will be noticed.

In the next stage the pubic hair will get darker and begin to curl; there will also be more of it. The penis continues to lengthen and the testicles continue to enlarge.

Following this phase even more pubic hair appears, and it is of a coarser texture covering most of the pubic area. The testicles enlarge even further, the penis gets bigger, and the folding of the scrotum continues to develop.

In the final stage pubic hair will become like an adult's and will also spread to the thighs and lower abdomen. The genitals will have reached full adult size.

Other changes that occur during puberty include those in the larynx and voice—the Adam's apple becomes more pronounced and the voice deepens. A boy may get acne eruptions, which are caused by oil secretions of the sebaceous glands, and hair may grow on his chest and face. Facial hair usually appears about two years after pubic hair is first noticed. It starts growing on the upper lip, then on the chin, and finally along the sides of the face. There may also be a temporary swelling of a boy's breasts.

Boys going through puberty will gain muscular sinew and their strength may double. To support these changes it is important for them to eat enough protein, get sufficient sleep, and avoid alcohol, which can reduce growth.

One of the most significant changes that puberty brings is that a boy begins to ejaculate, which means he is now **physically** capable of fathering a child. Ejaculation (release of semen) usually first occurs around age thirteen or fourteen and

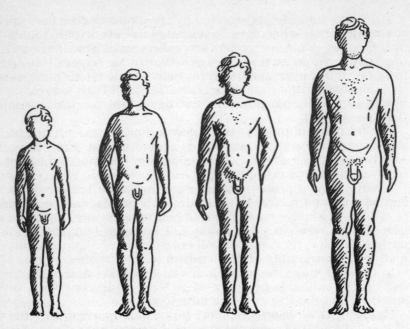

Illustration IV: Changes in Male Body During Puberty

may happen during masturbation or during a boy's sleep. This later phenomenon is known as a wet dream. Wet dreams cannot be prevented, but many boys are ashamed of them and try to hide the evidence—sticky sheets—from their parents. This is another reason to explain puberty early to your son and to let him know this too is normal.

The typical amount of semen in an ejaculation ranges from one-half to one teaspoon and holds somewhere between 100,000,000 and 550,000,000 sperm. Ejaculation happens as three separate spurts with the Cowper's gland, the prostate, and the testicles all contributing to the output. Semen is released as a liquid, but it immediately gels and then within a few minutes returns to its liquid state.

Boys who masturbate sometimes try to prevent their semen from spurting out when they ejaculate. This can force the semen into the tube leading to the bladder, which will cause cloudy urine, and can even wind up in the prostate gland, causing an irritation or an infection. You should tell your son that if he has pain in his genital area or a "milky" discharge, a doctor should be consulted. Boys are often too embarrassed to let their parents know when they have problems of this type.

Another problem boys may experience during puberty or after occurs when they have an erection for a while but don't ejaculate. When blood stays in the penis for a long time, pain may be felt in the testicles or genital area, and this is commonly known as "aching balls" or "blue balls." The pain will usually go away in a few hours.

We'd like to add one more point here which is unfortunately not discussed often enough. Although testicular cancer is rare, it is best detected early. Boys should be taught from puberty to check their testicles regularly for lumps, tenderness, or soreness, just as girls are taught to examine their breasts. This is best done after a hot shower. Any abnormal discharges should be reported to a doctor. Boys should also be taught to check their nipples once a month for lumps, although again, breast cancer in men is rare.

If you're the mother of a very young son, puberty probably seems like a long way off. So in our next chapter we'll turn to issues that mothers must deal with much earlier.

We began this chapter by talking about a mother's concern about her son pulling on his penis and wondering whether it hurt. We'd like to answer that question now as we conclude this section. No, it doesn't hurt. In fact, it probably feels good or he wouldn't be doing it. Don't worry!

3

Zippers? Practical Answers to Embarrassing Questions

There are times when a son's unfamiliar anatomy leaves a mother wondering how to proceed. We've pulled together a listing of the problems we and other mothers we interviewed have faced, and we offer some practical solutions. For example, what do you do if your son's penis get caught in his fly? (We'll answer that a little later in this chapter.)

Handling Your Infant Son

Penises give many mothers a few anxious moments. They fear they must treat them with great delicacy, especially in infants.

For example, many mothers are unnecessarily fearful they will hurt their sons' penises when they wash them. Not to worry. The penis of a baby or a young boy should be washed with soap and water (for babies, a very mild soap like Ivory or Johnson and Johnson), using the same amount of pressure as for any other part of the body. When your son gets old enough, you can teach him to do this himself.

The only difference in diapering a baby boy, which all parents soon discover, is that if you don't get the soiled diaper replaced quickly, you run the risk of getting squirted with urine. After this happens once or twice, you're likely to remember in the future. Some mothers immediately place a cloth or wipe on the penis while they are changing the diaper. You will also be interested to know that there are sex-specific disposable diapers on the market; the boy's version has more padding for absorbency in the front, where it's needed, and they seem to work pretty well.

Diaper rash can occur on the penis, scrotum, and surrounding areas and is treated the same way as it is for girl babies. It's fine to lift the penis and gently clean and then apply a diaper-rash cream (but not on the head). Leaving the affected area exposed to air promotes healing but again may result in Mom or Dad getting squirted.

Mothers are usually terribly embarrassed to ask, but wonder if there is some particular way a penis should be positioned within the diaper or their sons' underpants. Actually, when a baby is little, his penis is so small you'll find that you can simply put his diaper on and not worry about hurting the penis. As your son grows older and his penis grows larger, this issue may seem more important. Again, all you have to do is pull his pants up. If your son is uncomfortable he'll rectify the situation himself. After you see how your little boy pulls on his penis with no thought for gentleness, you'll relax and realize that the organ is not quite as sensitive as you might have imagined.

Zippers
A suggestion for preschool and even beginning-school-age children is to avoid pants with zippers altogether. Young boys often don't have the dexterity to manage a zipper themselves. They also have a tendency to wait until the last minute to run to the bathroom, so all-elastic-waist pants really facilitate matters.

If a boy's penis should get caught in his zipper, don't try to unzip it. Cut the teeth of the zipper below where it is stuck with a scissors, and the zipper will fall apart.

Toilet Training
It's a fact: boys have a tendency to mature a little slower than girls and for this reason may take longer to be toilet trained. Their bladders may also take longer to be ready. Girls are more willing to be bribed with "pretty panties," while many boys seem less interested in "big boy" pants and so are in no hurry.

We are not going to go through toilet-training procedures here. There are whole books on the subject and we've listed some in the Selected Bibliography in the back of this book. We will point out a few differences between training girls and boys often overlooked in these books and will offer some suggestions for handling these differences.

Child psychologist Dr. Charles Schaefer, author of *Toilet Training Without Tears,* says "consistency of the model of a father is important in toilet training boys." Fathers or older brothers help by teaching their sons or younger brothers to urinate standing up. Little boys who don't see their fathers urinate tend to want to sit when urinating, especially if they have older sisters, but if boys have the opportunity to imitate Daddy or a big brother, they're likely to take it. It doesn't really matter if a boy prefers to sit when he's learning to use the toilet, but toilet training may be accomplished more quickly if he wants to stand like Daddy does.

If you are toilet training your son in the warm weather, allowing him to pee on the ground (so much easier for boys than girls) is another good way to get him used to being without diapers. An advantage to this training is that in a real emergency, where no public toilets are available, you can take a little boy behind a car or a tree and let him urinate without him feeling uncomfortable.

One aside regarding this method was heard in our discussion groups. A mother who lives in a tropical climate had told a Northeastern friend she was visiting how easy it had been to toilet train her son when he could run around outside without pants. When the mother who resided in the Northeast found her friend's son peeing into her own son's wagon, it became obvious that something had been left out of this "back to nature" training.

There are some toilet-training aids you can purchase which may also help. "Tinkle targets" are paper targets with animals on them which you son can aim at as they float in the toilet bowl. They make using the potty fun and help to teach a boy to aim, an important aspect of toilet training. At least one company manufactures a urinal meant for use in the home which is scaled down to child size and may help prepare a boy for using public men's rooms and make him feel "grown up" at the same time (see listing under Useful Products in the back of this book). There is also a boy version of a video for children that addresses toilet training.

Also, we'd like to make one suggestion if you use a training potty that comes with a detachable shield or guard. We recommend that you remove the shield, as a boy may hurt his penis on it.

Unlike girls, boys don't usually wipe themselves after they urinate, so the last few drops of urine go into their underpants. A boy can be taught to apply pressure at the base of his penis to squeeze the last drops out, which will minimize this problem.

Boys should be taught to change their underwear every day, and it is best to buy them cotton or cotton-blend underpants, which are absorbent. They should be taught to wipe from front to back after having a bowel movement.

One hint about toilet training boys. If they are in a hurry to finish urinating, or if they stare at a spot on the wall while they relieve themselves, you'll wind up with yellow stains on your floor around the toilet, especially if your son gets up to use the bathroom during the night. If you have bathroom carpeting, it might be wise to protect it with a covering or a mat until your son gets the hang of aiming properly.

We've focused mainly on urination in this section because this is the main difference in toilet training boys and girls. Boys may also be resistant to making bowel movements in the toilet for a number of reasons. Children sometimes use noncompliance as a control mechanism, and little boys often tend to be more willful than little girls. Also, boys are often so busy physically, they are reluctant to stop their play to sit on the toilet for a period of time. If you are experiencing these problems, we again refer you to the books specifically on this subject.

A last bit of advice from Dr. Schaefer. "Be patient with your son." It may seem like he'll never be toilet trained, but he will.

Bed-wetting

Feeding boys ground-up hedgehog testicles and tying a string around the penis are actual methods once used by parents to stop bed-wetting. Needless to say, none of them worked, and while bed-wetting after the age of five (known as nocturnal enuresis) may be disturbing, it is not abnormal. The fact is that 20 to 25 percent of all five-year-olds wet their beds, with twice as many boys falling into this category as girls. In many cases there tends to be a family history of delayed control, and in others there may be psychological factors (such as the trauma of a divorce) or a congenital abnormality of the bladder "neck" that causes a constant dripping of urine. This problem usually resolves itself, but you can discuss treatment with your pediatrician if your son has nighttime bed-wetting and you are concerned. Behavior modification and in extreme cases drugs are used, but there are side effects to some of the medications, so they should be used cautiously.

Using the Men's Room or the Ladies' Room

Another issue that stymies mothers is whether to take their sons into the ladies' room with them or send them alone to the men's room. The answer has a lot to do with your personal comfort level. Obviously, if your son is too young to negotiate the bathroom by himself and Dad is not around, the ladies' room is the answer. But even when a boy is old enough to go by himself to the men's room, we suggest you be cautious. If you are in a restaurant or some other location where you can watch where he is going and only one person at a time can use the men's room, letting him go alone is probably fine. A large public bathroom such as in a bus station or an amusement park might not be a good idea, as your young son might be bothered by strangers.

Cleanliness for Boys

After boys go through puberty they will begin to develop a waxy substance on their penis called smegma, which is formed by the normal shedding of the body skin mixed with oil from the sebaceous glands. It appears white when it is fresh and after a while becomes greenish gray. Boys may not wash this carefully, which can lead to infections, so teenage boys should be taught to use soap and fairly hot water (smegma is oily) to remove it regularly. This is particularly important for uncircumcised boys because the smegma collects under the foreskin. Lack of penile cleanliness can cause serious problems, including infections and a higher risk of penile cancer.

Teenage boys also have a tendency to get "jock itch," a bacterial infection (see Appendix) which is not serious and is easily treatable but uncomfortable. This can sometimes be caused by wearing clothes that are too tight or are not clean and by not keeping the penis clean.

Why Are Boys' Bikes Different From Girls'?

We're not certain we have the definitive answer to this one, but we were told by a bike-shop owner that the bar across the top of a boy's bike adds stability. Women's bikes are probably modified, because at the turn of the century, women still wore skirts to bicycle.

Why Do Boys' Shirts Button The Opposite Way Than Girls'?

According to one explanation we've heard, originally both buttoned the same way—from the left side. In the nineteenth century, when women began to have personal maids, it was easier for their maids to reach them from the right side.

4

The Stages of a Boy's — and Mother's — Life

The well-known psychologist/pediatrician D. W. Winnicott described a mother and her baby as a single unit. In essence, the two are one for the first few months of the baby's life—the baby is attached to the mother by sucking at her breast or by being held close when bottle fed. She holds him most of his waking hours and has the intuitive ability to understand and meet his needs. So crucial is the mother to her baby that if she cannot take care of the child, the baby may fail to thrive or even die of a broken heart.

Yet a mother is confronted from the start with the obvious differences in her son's physical anatomy, activity level, and emotional development.

To begin with, a baby girl's body is familiar to her mother, but a son's is not. From birth, boys are often fussier and sleep less. As we have mentioned, once they begin to move around, boys tend to be more active than girls, rather adventurous climbers, and are more likely to dash away from their mothers. They often display a tendency to get "into things," which vexes and frequently exhausts their unsuspecting mothers. (We'll discuss at some length the biological and environmental origins of this behavior in Chapter Ten.)

Although baby boys and girls start life with essentially the same relationship with their mothers, by the time they reach toddlerhood they begin to travel down different roads. The way their mothers interact with them and the manner in which they relate to their mothers are unique to little boys. A mother may be able to sustain that feeling of unity with a daughter longer than with a son because in her daughter she sees herself; in her son she sees "the other."

All children need to learn to separate from their mothers, and in a sense they begin doing this almost from the day they are born. Boys have an added burden, for they must separate more definitively from their mothers than girls; not only must they learn to be independent, they must also learn eventually that they cannot grow up to be like their mothers. So the boy must separate both from the security of his mother and from identifying with her as a female.

Mom—a Boy's First Love
In the earliest stage of their lives, boys are totally dependent on their mothers—it is through mothers that they experience and learn trust and first love. Because in most families mothers spend more time with their sons than fathers do during infanthood, they generally take care of all of their sons' needs and provide most of their early education. Margaret Mahler, a noted child-behavior researcher and psychoanalyst, described the early stages of a baby-and-mother relationship in this way: "The mother's ego functions for the infant, and it is the mother who mediates between the infant and the external world. The sensations the child experiences from the mother form the core of his sense of self, and this period marks the beginning of the capacity to invest in another person." So you see, a boy's mother means everything to his early development and his view of his environment; without her he would never learn to feel safe in the world.

To explain the subsequent and natural development in a little boy's life as well as the mother's role in that development, we'll jump ahead now from babyhood to the age of three and then work backward. The reason we are doing this will become apparent a little later on.

Understanding the Oedipal Stage (Ages Three to Six)
On one episode of *Mr. Rogers' Neighborhood,* the popular children's television show, Mr. Rogers had a little chat with his young viewers. He showed them a picture of his parents and then his own wedding pictures with both his parents and his wife's in the wedding party. He then went on to explain that when he was a little boy he decided he was going to marry his mother and told her so. His mother gently explained that this

would not be possible because she was already married to his father. Mr. Rogers had just described the Oedipus complex.

The Oedipus complex was labeled and defined by Sigmund Freud about eighty years ago, based upon the Greek legend of Oedipus, who unwittingly killed his father and married his mother. Although many of Freud's theories have been expanded upon or displaced by more modern psychoanalytic theory, this concept has basically held up throughout the years and is acknowledged by experts in the field of psychology. Freud determined that between the ages of three and five, a boy who has had his mother as the first love of his life becomes aware that his father is a rival for that love. Although he loves his father, he fantasizes about his father's removal from the family circle and *his* replacement of his father in his mother's affections, even in his parents' bed. Freud did not mean this literally; we should understand that this desire is unconscious on the part of the little boy—that is, it is only a fantasy. The average little boy would no more try to make this fantasy a reality than he would jump off a roof to try to really fly while fantasizing that he is Superman.

No observer would dispute the bond between mother and son at this young age. In fact, we note at this stage of life that little boys are often far more affectionate with their mothers than are little girls, and they show a definite preference for their mothers over their fathers a good deal of the time. Our questionnaire respondents provided us with some interesting stories of how they observed this to be true in their own sons:

Carole told us that her son insists that his father lives in a separate house, although he knows in reality this is not true.

Megan told us that one day her husband and her three-year-old son, Jessie, were getting ready to go on an outing in the car. Jessie implored her to sit with him in the back and she finally agreed. He then turned to his father and said with spiteful glee, "Mommy is sitting with me in the back and you have to sit in the front alone. Ha-ha!"

Anna told of the day she and her husband were at the beach with their four-year-old son. Her son asked her to take him down to the water and told his father not to come. On the way he turned to his mother and said (referring to his father), "I wish he didn't have any legs!"

These anecdotes demonstrate rather dramatically both the need to have Mommy and the desire to shut Daddy out of the relationship.

Boys often express themselves quite openly about their fantasy by saying, "When I grow up I'm going to marry Mommy," as Fred Rogers did. The majority of women who filled out our questionnaire told us their sons did indeed declare their intentions to marry them. One mother's son described a slightly different scenario to her—he told her he was never getting married and would never leave her. Another mother told us, "When my son was three, he kissed me like he was my lover and said, 'That's the way Daddy kisses you. I'm going to marry you—I'll talk to Daddy about it.'" One little boy even announced to his mother that not only was he going to marry her, but they would also have a baby together!

Verbalizing the wish to marry Mommy is not the only outward sign that makes it apparent the Oedipal stage has arrived. Your son may begin acting unusually attached to you. He'll want to hold on to you, sit next to you, touch you, and may seem to be practically joined at the hip with you. We suggest you enjoy the closeness and the cuddling your son seeks, knowing as he grows he will eventually draw away from you physically.

Hugs and kisses are fine between a mother and a young son, but a mother who encourages behavior that is overtly sexual and that goes beyond the "normal" boundaries of a mother-son relationship can cause problems for herself and her son (see Chapter Eight). It is during this Oedipal stage, when our sons may be the most seductive, that we must be aware not to feed this attachment either physically or emotionally. A boy must be free to separate from his mother so that he will look outside his relationship with her for other relationships. This task will be made difficult if his mother encourages him to be "in love with her." This exaggerated love is also certain to interfere with the relationship they both have with the boy's father.

There is another pitfall to the Oedipal stage that is the reverse of what we have just described. Some mothers are frightened by the show of affection and the sometimes overt sexuality their little boys display at this age. Unable to cope with their feelings, they push their sons away both physically and emotionally. Boys who encounter this rejecting treatment may also have trouble with love relationships as an adult; they may be unable to get close to a woman for fear of being pushed away, just as they were by their mothers. This could mean that a boy may grow into a man who is unable to have a satisfactory physical relationship with a woman or one who can't allow himself to get involved emotionally.

This isn't an easy time for boys. Behavior problems that occur at this age may be due to the internal conflict with which a boy is trying to cope. For example, a boy may unconsciously be trying to get himself punished as a way of ridding himself of the bad feelings he has toward his father. He is torn with guilt because even though he loves him, he wishes his father would go away. The ambivalent feeling is quite difficult for a small child to resolve by himself.

The mother who understands the Oedipal stage can help her son handle these conflicts by letting him express his wishes and feelings, accepting them, but not feeding or encouraging them. Understanding this phase may help her not to be frightened of her son's attachment to her or may give her the wisdom to set comfortable limits on the attachment if it is excessive. She can also help in another way. Little boys still need their fathers at this age, but sometimes fathers are jealous of the sons' preference for their mothers, and the relationship can end up looking more like an unhappy love triangle than a family. A mother can diminish this tension if she explains to her husband that his son does not really love her more than he does his father; he is simply passing through a developmental stage. She can point out that his turn will be next.

The Oedipal phase is just that—a phase—and it will begin to fade as a boy grows a little older. At some point he begins to realize that wooing his mother is pointless because Dad has gotten there first. He begins to see that he has an alternative: he can identify with his father, and so he begins to do so.

As he gets older, it is unlikely your son will consciously remember having had these feelings of being in love with you. Yet they do not go away completely. In part they remain suppressed, and a sort of "mini" Oedipal stage may take place during the confusing time of adolescence, when hormones begin surging in your son's body.

It may sound as if a tremendous responsibility has been placed on you as a mother to get your son through the Oedipal stage safely. We'd like to reassure you that mothers in our discussion groups made it clear to us that for most women, this is simply intuitive and works out exactly as it should. "My son kept saying, 'I want to marry Mommy,'" said Jane. "I thought it was kind of sweet, so it didn't bother me. I knew he would grow out of it, but still, I didn't encourage it."

Adele gave her account of her son's resolution of the Oedipal stage with a wry smile. "It all blew over when he fell in love with an eight-year-old girl in his class!"

The First Separation
The Oedipal stage is the developmental stage which usually gets everyone's attention, perhaps because it so clearly can cause problems if a boy fails to negotiate this passage by de-

taching from his mother. It is also so fraught with sexual over-tones that we can't help but take notice that something is happening in our sons' emotional lives. Yet the Oedipal stage—although more dramatic to view—is actually the second stage of an evolving separation between mother and son.

We now return to infancy with a better understanding of the emotional upheaval that lies ahead for a little boy in only a few short years. We quoted psychoanalyst Margaret Mahler in the beginning of this chapter. Mahler believed Freud's theories about separation to be correct, but with the perspective of several decades of additional psychoanalytical thinking, she theorized that the Oedipal stage might actually not be the first stage of mother/child separation. In the 1930s, she began to research her idea by observing infants and toddlers to see how this individuation/separation process might work. Her conclusions are the following:

After the first three weeks and up to the first five months of a baby's life, he begins to have some awareness of his mother as an external object and he begins to distinguish between good (pleasurable) and bad (unpleasurable). He is learning that the world is not an entirely benign place—it is good when he is given food and bad when he is hungry and not fed. It is good when he cries and gets picked up, but is bad when he is left to wail alone in his crib.

Next he moves into a stage where he begins to explore his mother physically—he pulls her hair, sucks on her skin, may even bite her. At the same time, he begins to explore the world around him and will eventually venture beyond her lap, although still staying very close to her.

At about ten months old, the baby boy moves into the next developmental stage, in which he begins climbing and crawling farther away from his mother. His adventures still end with him returning to her side for security. It is at this stage that a mother may first begin to notice an appreciable difference between boys and girls, as boys may climb and move around more than baby girls.

The Psychological Birth

A few more months pass and the baby boy begins to walk, and he experiences what Mahler dubbed "the psychological birth of the child." He finds pleasure in his own body now that he is mobile and falls in love with the world around him. This is a critical stage for the little boy because it requires specific responses by his mother if his development is to continue smoothly. The mother must be willing to allow, and even enjoy, his increasing capacity to operate at a distance from her and enter into an expanding, exciting world. For example, she should let him run a little ahead of her and not force him to stay by her side. She must be attuned to her son's maturational and developmental paces and respond to him as his own person, placing aside preconceived notions of how she might want him to be. In fact, mothers may actually have an easier time doing this with their sons than with their daughters because they have less rigid ideas of how a son should behave.

Rapprochement
According to Mahler, children enter a stage she called "rapprochement," beginning around the age of fifteen months. Up until this point a child feels that nothing can happen to him because his mother is always there to protect him, but suddenly he begins to understand that he is a small person in a very big world. He also recognizes that his mother may not always be there to help him. This frightening realization may be reflected by behavior which we have come to know as separation anxiety. Separation anxiety may manifest itself by the child's fear that his mother will not return when she leaves, his resistance to going to a baby-sitter's house or to preschool, or his refusal to go to sleep without his mother, and other similar behaviors.

By the time he reaches the ages of eighteen to twenty-four months, your son will begin to go through a sort of crisis—the result will be that he may alternate between clinging to you and battling with you for his independence. He is simultaneously fighting conflicting emotions—the fear of losing your love by being separated from you and the fear of being engulfed by you because he needs you. To add to his increasingly complicated view of the world, around this time your son may become aware that boys have penises and girls don't have them, and that he is a boy.

He then begins to form a "core-gender identity," or a sense that he is a boy, which is different from his mother's gender identity, and he will be a boy and different from her for all of his life. The ability to go through this separation, or to "disidentify" from his mother, is far more critical for a boy than for a girl. Girls can continue to identify with their mothers throughout their lives, but for boys to grow up to be men who are comfortable with their own sexual identity, they must separate from the female identity. (Some psychologists suggest that even though boys face this difference in dealing with sexual identity, in some ways it is easier for them because they can transfer their need for identity to a father or an older brother. Girls will have a harder time separating from their mothers because it's harder for a girl to see herself as an individual when she is so much like her mother.)

A boy's behavior during the rapprochement phase places a whole new set of demands on the mother. The onset of rapprochement looks very much to her like regressive behavior—her independent child is suddenly needy, anxious, and demanding. He insists on help, then rejects it. Some mothers welcome the opportunity to reimmerse the child in their caretaking, stifling the drive toward separateness by encouraging passivity and regressions. Some overlook the legitimate needs of this phase and reject the child's new dependency. These types of actions by a mother make the rapprochement stage an even bigger struggle. The correct response will come from the mother if she is able to recognize that her son has reached this stage and if she accepts and responds to her son's needs.

An example of this can be found in Margaret Mahler's clinical observations of mothers with their babies. Mahler recalled that the mothers who understood their children's need to move about stood in one place while their toddlers ran around the room. Mothers who put their own need first—the need to know where their children were—kept turning in all directions and following their children around the room.

The way in which a child resolves the rapprochement crisis is critical in his development. Mahler suggests that the mother "move with" her child's stage of development, and not try to hold her son back or force him forward until he is ready. This means she takes her cues from her son when he is ready to venture out on his own and she follows at a safe distance to avoid being overprotective. Neither the mother nor the son should lead the way, but instead, mother and son should walk the path of development together.

Mahler noted both appropriate and inappropriate behavior in mothers. She once observed a mother and son interacting in a train station. The mother shadowed the child every time he took a step and said, "Come back"; the child didn't have a right to choose his own way.

Gertrude Blanck, a psychologist, provided another Mahler anecdote at a 1990 conference for psychologists at which she was a speaker. She described how Mahler noticed a mother and child at the beach one day. The mother walked behind the boy but allowed him to choose his own direction in which to walk. This mother's behavior contrasts sharply with that of the mother in the train station.

Consolidation

The final step in this initial stage of separation occurs from ages twenty-four to thirty-six months, when the child is able to function without his mother and not suffer from extreme anxiety. The child now has a stable concept of himself and his mother, or what Mahler called "consolidation." By letting her son learn that he can go away from her, be on his own, and still return to their relationship, a mother teaches him the basis for all the relationships in his life.

As we described earlier, the boy will then move into the Oedipal stage, where, now that he has become aware of the differences between sexes and sees himself and his mother as very separate entities, he "falls in love" with her. When the Oedipal stage begins to resolve itself, at approximately the age of six or seven, it is time for Dad to get his turn.

Daddy's Boy (Ages Six to Ten)

It is at this point that a boy accepts that he cannot hold on to his mother and he begins to identify with his father. He can see that he is more like his father, and in a sense he is no longer competing with his father but is now trying to become like him. In order for a boy to become masculine, he must reject the side of him that is feminine—the part of him that has identified with his mother. This is a difficult period for boys, since they experience a sense of loss as they relinquish some of the closeness and intimacy they have had with their mothers.

In psychological terms, a boy who is trying to get beyond the Oedipal stage goes through three stages. The first is **imitation,** which is characterized by wanting to do the things his dad does—shave, wear pants with a fly front, perform tasks that require strength, and so on. Through imitation he begins to **identify** with his father, to start to understand what it will mean to grow up to be a man. And in the final stage, which psychologists call **introjection,** a boy beings to incorporate parts of his father into himself.

Though it may sound like it—and sometimes even feel like it—you are not losing your son. He is struggling to somehow hold on to the parts of himself that are like you while trying to be like his father and other men he knows. Boys need different things from their parents . . . Mother will still play an important role. In fact, a mother should be more concerned if her son doesn't pass through these stages.

The ways in which boys become closer to their fathers may not appear as dramatically as the love affair with Mother in the Oedipal stage. It may simply be that they start to find a common ground with their fathers, such as participation in sports, hobbies, or other masculine pursuits they can share with their fathers or of which they think their fathers will approve. They may also decide at this age to grow up to pursue whatever it is that Daddy does for a living. If the father is there for his son and creates an atmosphere in which his son can relate to him not only through shared activities but also through shared emotions, the pain of the separation from Mother can be softened.

Knowing that this transfer of identification to fathers is a healthy turn of events doesn't prevent many mothers from feeling left out of their sons' lives at this point in time, particularly if they do not have daughters. However, this need not be an all-or-nothing proposition. A sensitive mother may be able to help her son through this difficult transition period and yet encourage him to retain things they have shared. This will help her feel she is not losing her son and will allow her son to grow up to be a more emotionally integrated man; he will have a greater chance of not having that sense of loss that many adult men carry around for most of their lives. An astute mother can negotiate this time of change by encouraging her son to stay in touch with the feminine world he has known, while at the same time doing nothing to ridicule or suppress her son's need to join the "boy's club."

A mother can do this by letting her son know that boys often grow up to be somewhat like their mothers *and* fathers, yet are men in their own right. For example, she can point out traits in her husband which he may have received from his mother—a love of music—and from his father—the ability to tell good jokes. She can also identify and point out to her son men who are quite masculine but not macho—who have caring, loving sides to them. These could be prominent men, or someone her son knows, such as a pediatrician or an uncle. This information should be related to her son in casual conversation, not phrased as if a lesson were being taught.

Of course, there are many activities mothers and sons can continue to enjoy together; although a boy may want to participate in more masculine pursuits, this doesn't preclude going ice-skating with Mom or going to a movie together. The goal here is to step back and let your son move ahead, but still be there for him as well.

Preadolescence . . . Next Stop, Puberty
(Ages Eleven to Twelve)

Life has settled down a bit; the Oedipal stage is over. Your little boy has one foot in the world of males but still needs his mom to talk to and take care of him. All should be smooth sailing for a while—right? Not necessarily.

A boy *and* his mother may hit a few rough spots when he is approaching puberty, particularly around the ages of eleven and twelve. Although for most boys full-blown puberty does not occur before age twelve, and often reveals itself several years later, some of the changes begin to occur earlier. Mothers are not always prepared for them.

Patricia told us her son is only seven, but he is very big for his age. It makes her uncomfortable to see how big he's grown in only seven years, and she doesn't recognize her little boy any longer. Another mother reported that she felt awkward around her almost teenage sons when they unexpectedly became "big guys." Both she and her husband are quite tall, but having her sons suddenly shoot up to the same height was startling.

Mothers are not the only ones who are not ready for adolescence. A boy is confused when his body begins to undergo changes he does not fully understand. If boys haven't been told what changes are to come, they may be frightened, and even if they are prepared, they may be embarrassed at the changes in their bodies. Boys can feel quite awkward physically when their bodies take on new dimensions, and some time is needed for them to learn to be comfortable with their new bodies. It is tempting for some mothers at this stage of their sons' development to try to hold them back. They treat their growing sons like little boys, as if behaving this way will make it so. But in fact, all this will do is create more guilt and confusion, make it more difficult for your son to grow up and sustain healthy relationships. He will grow up—but not necessarily in a way that will benefit him.

Our advice for handling this stage of your son's development is much the same as it is for other periods of his life—allow him to move ahead; you can't make time stop emotionally for your son and have him develop as he should. In most cultures, boys go through a rite of passage to clearly mark their entry into adulthood. For example, according to anthropologist David D. Gilmore, author of *Manhood in the Making*, adolescent boys in the East African Samburu tribe undergo a ritual circumcision. Next they must pass by their mothers' huts one last time and swear in front of the entire tribe that they will no longer eat meat from women of their mothers' social status or drink milk that comes from outside their village.

In the United States the rite of passage to manhood is not as defined; perhaps it might be seen as the day a boy gets his driver's license or makes the football team. It seems to us that a rite of passage, in addition to making the boy feel he is embarking on a new phase, also serves the purpose of signaling to the mother that her son must move ahead to a new place in his life. Because the rite of passage for American boys is not prescribed, a mother must rely on her own understanding and love for her son to provide the support he needs. Or she might create a rite of passage of her own—a special birthday party or a celebration when her son attains a specific goal.

There is another issue related to a mother's feelings about the physical changes she sees in her son which is often not discussed. As boys mature, mothers may be aware of their growing sexuality and may even feel somewhat attracted to their sons. Such feelings can be very frightening for a mother, but they are not uncommon and are not harmful to mother or son as long as the attraction is not acted upon. Still, dealing with and managing the fear or shame these feelings provoke is not always a simple matter.

One mother told us that her eleven-year-old boy still likes to hug her and be close to her. She pushes him away, telling him he is "too old," while still being openly physical with her younger son. To the older boy, who is not quite aware of his impending manhood, this must be a terrible rejection.

Another mother, of a twelve-year-old boy, says she can't bring herself to push her son away, but she feels very uncomfortable when he presses his body against her, because she can feel his genitals; she is quite aware of the physical maturity that is beginning to take place in his body.

Danielle's son is twelve and just beginning to exhibit signs of puberty. When he recently began taking serious swimming lessons, she innocently said to her son, who has always been very thin, "Maybe you'll wind up with one of those great swimmer bodies." Her son turned to her and said, "What is it with you, Mom? Do you want to date me?" Danielle turned purple.

Susan, who has always been very open with her son, has suddenly noticed a difference in their relationship. She found herself watching a movie with her son that had some steamy kissing in it and realized that she felt embarrassed to be watching it with him.

This is an issue that must be handled by each mother according to her own comfort level. Many boys who are on the verge of adolescence do not feel awkward having a lot of physical contact with their mothers and are unaware that their mothers do. Mothers who are distressed by physical closeness to growing sons because they are aroused or are afraid they will be aroused should try to explain to their sons that because their bodies are maturing, they feel this type of intimacy is no longer appropriate. At the same time, they must stress their love and support for their sons and discuss with them the fact that changes in relationships between people who love each other are normal and healthy. If we push our sons away without explanation, we may appear to be rejecting them, which, once again, has the potential to affect the way a boy relates to a woman when he becomes an adult.

Some mothers experience adolescence in an entirely different way. While they still want to hug or kiss their sons, *they* are pushed away. Their sons do this in order to establish their feelings of manliness; hugging and kissing Mom may be viewed as "sissy." Although their boys may seem to be growing apart from them, mothers must understand that their sons are not rejecting them or have any less love for them. They are simply finding, and occasionally stumbling, their way toward manhood.

You will remember that we discussed earlier that during the Oedipal stage a boy eventually gets over being in love with his mother. He is able to do this in part by suppressing the feelings he has for her. In adolescence, when a boy is on the verge of entering into opposite-sex relationships, his strong feelings for his mother may be resurrected and cause him anxiety. In order to get them out of his way again, he must behave in a similar manner that he did in the post-Oedipal stage and reject the feminine world that is deep inside of him. He is not distancing himself from his mother because he doesn't love her, but because he loves her too much.

While we can easily conjure up images of grown daughters walking arm-in-arm with their mothers, we think of grown sons having little physical contact with their mothers. We must push our sons away several times in their lives because we love them, but we must remember to use only gentle pushes that treat both our sons and ourselves with dignity.

5

Raising a Son in the Brave New World

The world around us has been rapidly changing with the women's movement and the newer men's movement. We have learned that girls can do just about anything that boys can do—excel at math and science, play sports, go into politics. We know boys can grow up to take care of babies, share household responsibilities with their wives, and be allowed to show emotion without jeopardizing their manhood. Does this mean we should treat our sons exactly the same as our daughters—should we treat them in a manner that addresses no difference in their gender? The answer is, emphatically, no.

We know of a mother who decided to raise her boy and girl in an entirely nonsexist atmosphere. She chose not to acknowledge any difference between her son and daughter. She dressed them alike, meaning that her son at times was put in a dress as a child and her daughter in pants. Her son and daughter both had their rooms painted the same color. You may think, Why not? After all, these are just "traditions" and don't mean anything. The children are grown now, and the son is a psychotic adult, unable to sustain relationships or to function in the normal world. We strongly believe that this suppression of normal sex roles was clearly a contributing factor.

It is not specifically the color of a room or the type of clothing that is at issue. Until around the turn of the century, pink was actually considered the preferred color for little boys, who were

54

often dressed in kilt outfits or even dresses—a practice that would raise eyebrows today.

The story is told that Ernest Hemingway's mother chose to put him in dresses as a little boy. He seemed to have rejected this behavior in a rather dramatic way. He became the epitome of the "man's man"—boozing, hunting, womanizing, and writing about tough, macho men. This is an example on one end of the spectrum. It is more likely that nonexposure to masculine concerns will result in boys who become labeled as sissies because they can relate only to females or female concerns. Either way, emotional damage can result when boys are treated differently from their peers and when they are forced to be different from the accepted masculine standard in society.

We may like to believe there are no differences between boys and girls except their sexual organs. It simply isn't true, and even if it were true from a strictly biological point of view, we don't live in an androgynous culture. You have to prepare your son to live in the world around him.

This is not to say that there aren't ways a mother can help her son to bridge the dichotomy between accepted male and female behavior. Ironically, even mothers who wish they could raise their sons in a nonsexist manner overlook ways in which they could help change their sons' consciousness about what it means to be masculine.

We're not always aware of subliminal messages we send, like "Big boys don't cry" or "Stop whining," which is a reflection of society's credo that men should not show their emotions. Boys and men **are not inherently less emotional than women;** they are taught to be that way, which means that mothers and fathers have an important responsibility in raising sons who are aware of their emotions. While many women complain that their husbands never "open up to them," they may still worry about their sons' masculinity and discourage them from crying and exhibiting emotional outbursts.

A mother's guidance can make an unquestionable difference—she can let her son know that it's normal for people to cry when they are sad or in pain; no one needs to be so strong that he or she never cries. This does not mean giving your son a license to use tears to get his own way and to manipulate situations. If he uses tears in this manner, you can explain to him that as he gets older he must learn to express some of his needs in other ways.

You may be confused by now; how can a mother encourage her son to feel emotions traditionally associated with femininity and yet grow into his natural state of masculinity? As with most of the topics we discuss in a boy's emotional and psychological development, the key to successful mothering is creating a delicate balance. A mother needs to understand that her fear of emasculating her son is unfounded unless she attempts to keep him at bay from all that is masculine. She must realize that she has the opportunity to do what previous generations of mothers did not do out of ignorance: she can help her son to have a more gentle side—to have a part of him that can express and not be ashamed of his feelings, a part of him traditionally associated with women—and yet still be comfortable with being a man.

A boy's father can make a difference in achieving this balance. For example, although we tend to think of nurturing as almost an exclusively female trait, the fact is that women have no special skills for this activity that men don't have as well (outside of the ability to breast-feed). When a mother responds intuitively to her son and reflects that his feelings have been seen and heard, she is nurturing him. Logic would tell us that she will teach him by example and he will know how to be a nurturing father when he grows up. This may or may not be the case. We have seen that at various stages a boy feels the need to repudiate those things he loves best about his mother in order to be unlike her—that is, to be male. If only his mother participates in this activity, the lesson may not be learned. When both parents participate, the boy will see nurturing as a skill that crosses gender lines and he will more likely be able to nurture his own children someday.

Samuel Osherson, a psychologist, says in his book *Finding Our Fathers:* "How much of a wrench for the boy is it to leave the feminine world behind, the wet, soft, timeless world of the body, of the preconscious, of the imagination, all of the sides of life attributed to women by men, and which we all need to be able to be nurtured, nurture, and feel rooted in humanity? When emotional holding and caring is a feminine task and masculinity is activity and conquest, the male child is put in the precarious position of having to identify with that image of masculinity. . . . It is the residue of that struggle that I suspect leaves men feeling that deep down they are basically destructive or 'unlovable' and that leads us to withdraw emotionally and become silent when we are vulnerable."

How wonderful would be the gift from mother and father to their son to help him grow up without feeling the struggle within himself of feminine versus masculine, but simply being allowed to be a whole man.

A son who is taught to talk about his feelings may be able to have a more open relationship with his own family when he grows up. His future wife may not feel the same frustrations many women do today when their husbands can't tell them what is bothering them. If a little boy is not forced into a "be tough" masculine role, he will reap other benefits from what he has learned as a child as well. The man who learns as a boy to express his feelings as an adult will be less prone to medical problems including heart attacks and other conditions caused by unresolved stress, to which men are far more susceptible than women.

How else can a mother have an impact on how her son sees the world? As simple as it seems, by allowing him freedom in his choice of toys. Play is one of the earliest ways children learn about themselves, their gender roles, and the world around them. If your son prefers trucks and action figures—which is likely—you shouldn't *make* him play with dolls. On the other hand, we don't think you should ever tell your son he can't play with a toy because it's a "girl's" toy. Some children will play with a "girl toy" secretly anyway, but the lesson is learned—he accepts the arbitrary boundaries of feminine and masculine.

The best route to take is to provide your son with a range of toys which *includes* dolls, cooking toys, etc., as well as blocks and trains, and let him choose for himself the things he likes best. Some experts recommend making some of your own toys or buying toys which stress skills rather than gender-specific roles. This is another area where a father can make an impact. If he plays games or involves his son in activities that might be considered feminine as well as those associated with the masculine, he will by example make these activities acceptable for his son.

A Word About Working Mothers

In 1960, 2 percent of mothers with children under the age of six were working. In 1991, this statistic had climbed to 58 percent. Most mothers wonder if their decision to work will harm their children in any way. We were interested in learning if boys are affected in any specific way when their mothers work outside the home.

Our search did not produce much useful information—very few gender-specific studies have been attempted regarding working mothers. One study conducted at Arizona State University determined that boys in "two-earner families" spend less time "cooking, doing laundry, car and household repairs" than sons of homemakers. (Three hours versus seven hours.) The authors of the study surmised that working mothers, who had less spare time, felt boys took longer than girls to perform these tasks. With their time at a premium, working moms found it easier to take care of these tasks themselves than to supervise their sons. Another study, which partially helps to support the results of the Arizona State study, found that married working moms spend just as much time on child-care activities as stay-at-home mothers, but spend less time on household chores and their own leisure.

The only other gender-specific study we came across found that young boys with nonmaternal care scored more poorly than girls in cognitive tests, although the gap was small. There might also have been outside factors such as income level that skewed the results of this study.

In a National Institute of Health and Human Development study, an attempt was made to determine if there was a difference in how babies of both sexes behave in a "strange situation" depending on whether they had working or nonworking mothers. Babies with stay-at-home mothers showed a slightly greater sense of security, but again, the differences were very small.

The fact is there really has not yet been very much research on the effect on children who have working mothers, but the federal government has begun a large study of this issue and the results may finally shed some light on the subject.

We believe there are two key issues for mothers to consider if they are going to work when their sons are young. The first is the quality of child care—you owe it to yourself and your son to get the very best child care you can afford. Your son will be happy with the right caregiver and you will have peace of mind. If you worry every day at work if your son is being taken care of properly, the stress will spill over into your relationship with him. Babies and young children are very adept at sensing their parents' feelings; if you are feeling stress, your son will too. You will also have to accept that some of the developmental stages we've described may have your child-care worker as their focus, rather than yourself, if you have full-time child care. You can also educate your child-care worker as to what to expect in your son's development and behavior.

The second issue is whether a mother has a strong desire to work (assuming she has an option). If a mother really wants to work, she will probably be a better mother than if she stays home. Ethel Roskies, a University of Montreal psychoanalyst, recently released the results of a survey sent to 1,123 Canadian female doctors, lawyers, engineers, and accountants. She found that married women with children scored the highest in terms of self-esteem and satisfaction with their lives—a clear indication that careers and children do mix.

While it would seem that a working mother would be a good role model for a son, this is only a half-truth. If working makes a woman feel better about herself, this is a positive aspect of her personality which can be good for her son to see. However, when it comes to the subject of holding a job, a boy is more likely to take his cue from his father because he identifies more strongly with him.

We offer some rules of thumb for working mothers which might make life a little easier:

- Get the best child care you can afford. There's no price for peace of mind.

- Don't try to be supermom—it's okay to have a dusty house and serve spaghetti instead of soufflés; set your priorities so you won't feel overwhelmed.

- Take good care of yourself, which means some alone time too—you're no good to your son if you're tired and grouchy all the time.

- Let your son have some responsibilities around the house appropriate to his age—it will free up a little time for you, and start teaching him how to take care of himself so he doesn't grow up to expect women to take care of all of his needs.

- Set aside time when you do specific activities as a family.

- Get your husband to share responsibilities with you; seeing him do household chores allows your son to view him as a good role model, and having him spend time alone with your son is essential to the development of the father-son relationship.

Being a Good Enough Mother
In the beginning of Chapter Four we spoke of a mother and new baby as one unit, as described by D. W. Winnicott. Winnicott also spent a good deal of time observing and writing about what babies need—a mother who is **good enough.**

"Become a good enough mother" sounds like a rather vague piece of advice to give mothers, and in fact, there isn't any textbook which will tell you how this goal is achieved. As Winnicott explained it, a good enough mother offers what a baby needs when he needs it, not according to her own timing and needs. She provides support and ongoing empathy for her son, and if she is attuned to her baby, she will instinctively know when and how to do so. Even though we have defined in broad terms the stages of development your little boy will pass through, every child is on his own timetable and has his own personality; no book can advise you when your child has reached these stages and what he needs from you at any given time—your natural instinct as a mother will let you know.

Although seemingly a contradiction in terms, it is possible to be a **too good** mother, which is as problematic for a boy as a mother who is not good enough. How can you tell the difference between a good enough and a too good mother?

A good enough mother lets her son learn by her own failures that she is not omnipotent, allowing him to know that it is okay for him to fail too; then she lets him experience his own failures. A good enough mother will let her son fall down and pick himself up again; the too good mother won't even let him try. She is oversolicitous, overinvolved, and overcritical with her son.

The good enough mother knows that frustration teaches tolerance and that instant gratification is not always best; the too good mother meets all of her son's needs instantly. The good enough mother knows that a son needs to have ownership of his actions. She stands on the sidelines and cheers him on but lets him run past her in the race. The too good mother keeps her child from becoming independent; she mothers in a way that benefits herself, not her son.

There is an anecdote passed around in psychoanalytical circles, about a boy who for no apparent reason reached the age of six without ever speaking. One night he suddenly said, "Please pass the mashed potatoes." The boy had never spoken before because his mother had always met every one of his needs without him saying a word. This is the epitome of the too good mother.

In our opinion, there are two primary mistakes the mother of a little boy can make. One is not to get involved with her child because he is a male and she fears his otherness. The other is to get too involved with her son, to put him up on a pedestal. We want to raise happy little boys, not demanding little princes who expect to have their every need attended to all of their lives. The good enough mother will know how to find the middle ground between these two ends of the spectrum and raise a fine son.

How can the mother of a little boy be a good enough mother? If she looks into her heart, she will find a visceral response to her son's needs, and that will be good enough for them both.

6

Single Moms and Their Sons

So far we've addressed the issues that relate to how to help your son through his early developmental stages when his father is around. For single moms, this may be more complicated, so we turn to issues that specifically speak to the problems of women who are raising boys alone.

Women who are single through divorce or separation from their sons' fathers may find they have some rough times ahead with their sons. For a variety of reasons, boys suffer more from the effects of divorce than girls, especially between the ages of three to five and nine to ten, according to Linda Bird Francke, author of the book *Growing Up Divorced*. She says that on average it takes boys three to five years to regain their balance after divorce, which is about twice as long as it takes girls. Although things do start to get better in the second year, boys are more prone to become aggressive and exhibit disruptive behavior, primarily because they tend to externalize their feelings, while girls internalize them. In the long run, boys may be better off having gotten their feelings out in the open, and not having to work through them later in life. It still isn't any easier on the mothers of boys.

Single mothers in general have a harder time with their sons than with their daughters, or than mothers in traditional families. A study by the National Association of Elementary School Principals discovered that boys from single-parent families had lower achievement ratings than boys from intact families or girls in either type of family. Divorce has a more

long-term effect on boys as well; a twenty-year study suggests
that men of divorced families suffer more dating anxiety, enter
into early marriages, and have a 33 percent higher divorce
rate.

Preschool Years (Ages Three to Five)

Although a divorce can be difficult for a boy of any age, there
are some specific ages and stages which are more precarious
than others. For example, if his parents divorce during his preschool years, a boy may have some trouble negotiating the Oedipal phase. "This Oedipal resolution, in Freudian terms,
releases the child and allows him to move on," explains Linda
Bird Francke in *Growing Up Divorced.* "But if divorce has inter-
vened, some children can remain stuck in this no-win love affair."

This is why it is extremely important for a preschool boy to
stay in close touch with his father after a divorce, regardless
of how a woman feels about her ex-husband. (The exception
being, of course, a father who is a real danger to the boy.) If he
stops seeing his father, a little boy may believe that he has
made his father go away by his Oedipal fantasy, and this will
increase the normal guilt boys feel at this stage.

Even when a father does maintain a constant relationship
with his son, there may still be some behavior problems. A boy
of this age may exhibit anger, anxiety, aggressiveness, denial,
or regressive behavior such as bed-wetting and tantrums. One
possible reason boys become aggressive is because they have
lost the one person they were allowed to have controlled aggression with: their fathers, who are no longer there to roughhouse
every night. Boys may become angry at all females and may
rebel against this mothers, rejecting them in order to resolve
the Oedipal stage if fathers are not present.

In two-parent homes, mothers usually give about twice as
many commands as fathers, according to Linda Bird Francke.
When a father is not around every day, "the ratio escalates
and the coercive cycle between demands of single mother and
defiant son begins."

Not all boys become aggressive and antifemale. Some boys
have a completely different reaction. Fearing that males are
"thrown out of the house," according to Linda Bird Francke,
they may be afraid to become malelike, will be docile, and may
have trouble with their sexual identity.

From Six to Eight

If boys are six to eight years old when a divorce occurs, they may suffer in a different way. Some may become uncomfortable being around only their mothers, while others will try to become the man of the house and take care of their mothers.

"My son is acting like a little man," Marika told us. "I'm separated from my husband, and even though I don't want him to feel this way, he thinks it's his responsibility to take care of me."

Lysa related a poignant story about a friend who had recently divorced and whose son had taken his role of father substitute to an extreme. "The poor little boy even sets up her toothbrush for her at night!"

For a young boy, this is a tremendous burden—one that some mothers may unconsciously inflict.

This situation can be rectified by a mother in a very direct way. She needs to sit her son down and make it clear to him that it is not his job to take care of her but rather the other way around. She may have to have another talk with him if she starts dating again—young boys are often protective when their mothers date—and mothers need to gently reassure their sons that they can take care of themselves.

Between the ages of six and eight, boys will sometimes blame their mothers for the loss of their fathers, which they feel keenly. Remember, this is the stage when boys start to become more attached to their fathers. If his biological father does not stay in the picture, a boy may attach himself emotionally to the men his mother dates. The risk in this is that if a relationship with a new man doesn't last, the boy can feel rejected all over again. Be discreet about letting your son know when you have a sexual relationship with a man—a boy may see this as a sign that the relationship is serious and that this man will be coming into his life permanently. We're not suggesting you should avoid having a sex life, but the man shouldn't be there in the morning when your son gets up unless the relationship is beginning to look serious. It's a good idea to take it slow in involving a new man in your son's life; wait until you feel that the relationship has long-term possibilities. If the relationship doesn't last and your son has had expectations, it is important to let him know that the reason it ended had nothing to do with him, but only with what transpired between you and this man. It's also a good idea to explain to your son that dating is a time of exploration and that a few dates with one man doesn't mean he'll be staying around in your life.

The Preadolescent Period to Puberty
(From Nine to Twelve)

Although adults tend to believe that experiencing divorce from ages nine to twelve is easier for a boy because he is older, in truth it is just as hard as at an earlier age. The difference at this age is that boys may develop more serious behavior problems, which can cause their mothers to feel even more estranged and fathers to lose interest in being with their now-difficult-to-handle sons. At this age, boys tend to ridicule anything female-related and are more likely to get into trouble without firm guidance. One mother told us that when she and her husband separated, her son, who had never had problems in school before, began to find himself in trouble with his teachers. Another told us that her son, who was eleven when she and her husband divorced, refused to take any commands from her until they went to therapy together and began to work things out.

Aggressive behavior in boys as a result of divorce should be tolerated by both parents to a certain degree—they must see it for what it is: an outward manifestation of a boy's pain. A divorced mother should not try to handle this problem alone; if possible, her ex-husband should be involved in working with their son to get him to talk about how he is feeling. The use of a professional therapist may also be indicated. Of course, this is easier said than done—usually parents who get along well don't separate in the first place. In the best interests of your son, it is worthwhile to try to resolve your differences with his father at least in matters regarding his welfare.

In **extreme cases** some experts suggest that boys of this age may benefit from living with their fathers if the situation is out of control. This may be especially true if a mother has remarried, because boys at this age often find it difficult to accept stepfathers and so have a particularly strong need to maintain their relationships with their fathers. We don't think a mother should give up custody of her son unless both parents agree the son will be better served; even then, the situation can be reviewed periodically.

Puberty

Studies show that until adolescence, divorced dads spend more time with their sons than their daughters, at which point the balance swings the other way. Adolescent males, even though they would seem to be better able to handle divorce because they are older, still suffer tremendously. Boys who are at this stage of development are in an awkward and sometimes painful period of time under normal circumstances, and through divorce they "suffer a loss of permanence and stability," according to Dr. Stuart Berger, author of *Divorce Without Victims.* This can "be very difficult for an adolescent—perhaps even more damaging than to an Oedipal-stage child."

What Can a Mother Do?
Both mothers and fathers can play important roles in helping their sons to cope with divorce and loss of the father in the family home. Fathers need to make certain they see their sons often, listen to what they are saying, and don't place blame on the boys' mothers for the divorce, at least in front of the son.

Mothers too should strive not to make negative statements about their sons' fathers, or about men in general, for this can contribute to a boy's fear of identifying with the male gender. A divorced mother who retaliates against her ex-husband by trying to sabotage the father-son relationship never accomplishes anything positive. She ends up hurting her son and may drive his father away—a no-win situation for everyone.

"My son stands in front of the television as if he is mesmerized," say Mary, the divorced mother of a six-year-old. "He doesn't answer me when I talk to him and it drives me up a wall. But I get angry in a way that is out of proportion to what he is doing. I know it's because his father always did the same thing to me."

This is another trap that divorced mothers need to avoid. It's easy to transfer hostility for ex-husbands onto males in close proximity—their sons—especially if there is a physical resemblance or similar personality traits. This also can be quite self-defeating, as it will only alienate their sons.

Male Role Models—a Boost for Single Moms
Most mothers worry about their sons overidentifying with them—for single mothers, this fear may be magnified. If they don't try to overcompensate for their sons' loss of their fathers—trying to be both mothers and fathers—this fear is ungrounded. A mother **cannot** be both mother and father; it's not logical that a woman can teach her son how to be a man. However, if your son will be seeing his father only infrequently, or perhaps not at all, it is important that you find other male role models for him. While he may be deprived of observing a husband-and-wife relationship, he will have the opportunity to learn how to be like other men.

A mother should make every effort to involve other men in stable relationships with her son. This might be a stepfather, grandfather, or uncle, who would be of a more permanent nature; or men who might be involved for reasonable periods of time, such as teachers, coaches, religious figures, Scout leaders, or friends of the family. If such a male is not available, a mother can investigate having her son become part of a Big Brother program. She might joint a chapter of Parents Without Partners, which sponsors activities where her son can be exposed to single fathers or simply provides social activities for single-parent families. "Being around mostly intact families," says psychotherapist Dr. Irene Kaminsky, "can make the loss of a father even more stressful for a boy. If he can be in social or cultural situations where the community is mostly one-parent families, the boy won't feel singled out." There are even support groups of peers from divorced families in some communities, which might be useful for your son.

Mothers can support sons who don't see their fathers in another way as well. Regardless of how she feels about her former husband, she should make an effort to stress his positive aspects. This will actually enable her son to have better self-esteem—if he can feel good about the kind of man he has for a father, he can feel good about himself. A wonderful example of the way this works is President Bill Clinton. Although his father died when he was a baby and he had a poor role model in his alcoholic stepfather, he incorporated his mother's memories of his father into himself and reached manhood with his self-esteem intact. He even spoke of the father he lost in his address to the Democratic Convention that nominated him for the Presidency.

Working Together
The best thing that both parents can do for their son once they have made the difficult decision to divorce is to keep the lines of communication open. They should tell their son together about the divorce and what it will mean—that they will live apart but both will love him and take care of him, even though they are no longer in love with each other. Above all, they should stress that there is nothing their son did to cause the divorce. Both parents should try to maintain a civil relationship for the good of their son, and a mother must do her best to allow the father-son relationship to be maintained unimpeded.

If the divorce is predicated upon the father's homosexuality, a situation which is not as uncommon today as one might think, the son should be told if he is old enough (school age) to understand what homosexuality means. In *Divorce Without Victims* Dr. Stuart Berger says, "There is no evidence that educating your child about homosexuality exposes him to a greater risk of engaging in homosexual behavior." Family secrets are not good for children—they leave children living in a world based on false foundations.

A boy's self-image as a heterosexual male can stay intact even if he knows his father is homosexual. If the father is warm and caring with his son and understands his son's need to be like his friends and to express his heterosexuality, they will be able to work out their relationship. It is also helpful if the father is honest about how difficult a homosexual life can be and lets his son known it is not a choice he would make if it were something he could choose about himself.

As a mother, you should not disparage your son's father if he is homosexual no matter how you feel. You should also be aware that there is a possibility that your son may try to overcompensate in an attempt to prove his own heterosexuality and may exhibit exaggerated or macho behavior. This behavior would suggest the need for some counseling and might also be tempered by relationships with older heterosexual males (an uncle or a grandfather) in addition to his relationship with his father.

The Dilemma—Staying Together for a Son's Sake

Studies show that if a couple is having a volatile and turbulent relationship, it may take an even greater toll on their son than divorce. Interestingly, parents tend to fight more openly and for longer periods of time in front of their sons than their daughters. Although an intact family is ideally the best environment for a young boy, most experts agree that if parents are truly unhappy in a marriage, divorce may turn out to be the less damaging option for his development.

"The father is first introduced to the son by the mother," says Loren E. Pederson, author of *Dark Hearts: The Unconscious Forces That Shape Men's Lives.* "Her conscious and unconscious attitudes towards her husband as well as her own father shape the image of the father before the actual father can shape himself to his son. The mother's love and respect, resentment and hostilities or ambivalence are all conveyed to the son."

If a mother is unhappy in her marriage, her son may be confused about identifying with his father, the source of her unhappiness. Boys in this environment sometimes overcompensate by exaggerating their masculinity and becoming overly aggressive. There is also the possibility that the opposite behavior may result and a boy may become too passive. Paradoxically, many studies link parental fighting with behavior problems in children, and boys are more likely to be the culprits—from a young age they tend to get into more mischief and be more demanding of their parents.

There are other situations in intact families that are harmful to boys, not only the ones which result in fighting. "A skewed family," says Andre Bustanoby in *Being a Single Parent*, "produces males with gender-identity problems." For example, he describes a family in which the mother is a dominating person with a husband who is dependent on her and may therefore be in competition with his son. A boy being raised in this environment has trouble separating from his mother and will have trouble grasping his own sexual identity and will probably not identify with his father.

Even if only one parent is unhappy in the marriage, this is not likely to be a good environment for a young boy. A woman who is in an unhappy marriage may place all of her emotional investment in her son, which is too much for a boy to handle. If the father is unhappy or feels "trapped" in the marriage, he may treat his wife with anger and disrespect. This message will not be lost on his son; he will grow up believing that this is an appropriate way to treat women.

There are many other types of familial situations which are detrimental to a boy's emotional state and happiness, but we mention these few examples only to make a point. Although it is clear that divorce does have consequences for young boys, it may still be preferable to being in the midst of a bad marriage.

Divorce is not a pleasant experience and can cause some emotional hardships for young boys. With proper handling and guidance from his mother and his father, a boy can overcome the problems he encounters. As Dr. Berger writes, "I believe that with love, knowledge, and patience you can ease the inevitable tensions and distress of the divorce period for your child."

If You Are a Widow
A widowed mother of a son may have some unique problems to cope with in addition to the problems we've discussed earlier in this chapter when fathers are not around. She may be so steeped in her own grieving that it may be hard for her to focus on her son's grief. Joining a support group for widowed people may help in working through this problem, but only time will help her heal.

A widowed mother must help her son not to overidealize his father, or he may create an image of his father that he can never measure up to—and may spend the rest of his life trying.

Strange as it may seem, unconsciously we see death as an aggressive act—the person we love has hurt us by leaving us.

A boy may respond to his father's dying by identifying with the aggressor—his father—and becoming aggressive himself. If this occurs, his mother can try to explain to him that his father would not have intentionally left them for any reason and can remind him how much his father loved him.

A mother also needs to be aware that her son may develop a fear of death when he loses his father; he may worry that he will lose his mother too, or that he himself will die. Try to be as reassuring as possible.

Widowed mothers will also have to be vigilant to make certain their sons don't feel they must assume their fathers' place in the family and take care of their mothers—a burden too great for children.

We recommend strongly that if your son loses his father through death, you seek therapy for both of you to help you get through the grieving process and to face some of the problems ahead. As we described earlier in this chapter, it will also be important for your son to have male role models in his life.

7

"Like Your Daddy": Fathers and Sons

"My husband travels a lot for business and my son is very angry about this. He takes it out on me by being a real discipline problem. It makes life very difficult at times."

—*Ann, mother of five-year-old Andy.*

"My three-year-old son was watching a video one day about different professions you could pursue 'when you grow up.' He expressed great concern to me that he didn't know what he wanted to be when he grew up. I explained to him that he had plenty of time to make a decision, and that he needed to see what all kinds of people did before he could decide. Still, he still seemed quite upset about it, and within an hour he came and told me he decided that he would be a doctor. Of course, his father is a doctor."

—*Sandy, mother of Ricky, age four.*

As we discussed in Chapter Four, a boy's mother is his first object of attachment. Through her he learns to trust and to experience first love, and through her he begins to build his self-esteem. But from his father a boy acquires his sexual identity. To many mothers the father-son relationship can seem mystifying and unpredictable and a world that only males can

70

share. A mother seeking to understand her little boy can profit from a thorough introduction to the psychological and emotional dynamics of their relationship, and this chapter will provide an overview.

If you as a mother appreciate the importance of a rich and varied father-son relationship, you can tender a less than perfect father-son bond into full bloom. This chapter will help you analyze your son's relationship with his father and will address weaknesses you may perceive as well as encourage the strengths. We will be touching upon a number of subjects related to father-son relationships, some of which will probably never be an issue between your husband and your son. However, as the mother of a son, you need to know the potential problems that might threaten this sometimes fragile relationship and what you can do to help.

Having a Boy in the Family

Take heart; research shows that marriages are more likely to stay together if there is a son in the family. On average, parents who have **only** sons stay married longer than parents of boys and girls or girls only. Consequently, 5 percent more boys than girls live in intact families. Some researchers speculate that this results in part from the fact that fathers tend to roughhouse and play more with their sons than their daughters and are more involved in child rearing—they change diapers more, eat more frequently with the family, and participate more in family events than fathers of all-girl families. If involved fathers make for happier marriages, it would seem that having a son does affect your relationship with your husband as well.

But don't be misled by the rosy picture we have just painted—the father-son relationship may be fraught with confusion and tension. Even at its best, it is complicated.

In Chapter Four we spoke of the psychologist/pediatrician D. W. Winnicott's description of the mother and new baby as being a unit. While the description is apt, it overlooks a critical component of a baby's world—his father. Right from the start, fathers can provide experiences for babies that are different from those of mothers. They smell different, feel different, have deeper voices, and tend to play differently than mothers. For example, a father may toss his baby in the air, while the mother will coo or snuggle with her baby. It is a given that a boy's father will become a role model for him; whether he is a good one or not depends on the father.

The Importance of a Father's Early Involvement
A father's relationship with his son from as early as infancy
will reflect on their future relationship. Studies have shown
that at only eight weeks old, babies handle stress better when
they have fathers who participate in bathing, feeding, and
dressing them. At six months, babies with actively involved fathers score higher on some tests of mental and motor development.

This is why it is **never too early** for a father to be a part of
his son's life even **before** birth by attending childbirth classes.
Unlike previous generations, 90 percent of fathers are present
at their children's births today, which is the perfect way for
intimacy between a father and son to get a jump-start.

"My husband was ambivalent about having children, and
wasn't very emotionally involved in my pregnancy," Rita confided in us. "But during my labor, my son was in fetal distress—his heart rate was dropping and my husband was really
frightened. When they finally put the baby in my arms, instinct
took over and I immediately said to my husband, 'Do you want
to hold him?' His answer 'Yes' was so full of longing, I knew
then that they were going to be fine together."

In the first few years of a boy's life the father is important not
only because he provides a different experience for his son but
also because he adds to the child's sense of security. "The father's role in helping his son differentiate self from mother,
mother from other, maleness from femaleness, femininity from
masculinity, continues to be decisive throughout childhood,"
writes Louise Kaplan in *Oneness & Separateness: From Infant
To Individual*, "but especially during the first years, when differentiation is the central thrust of life."

Beginning sometime between ages three and six, the father's
role in his son's life takes on added significance. In Chapter
Four we discussed the need for a boy to separate from his
mother fairly early in his young life in order to identify with
males. We also described the Oedipal phase a boy goes through
when he "is in love with his mother" and subconsciously wishes
his father would go away. Simply being around a father helps
a young boy come to grips with this phase, because at some
point the boy realizes his mother and father have *the* romantic
relationship and if he can't have his mother, he may as well
become like his father.

From this point on, a boy will measure himself against his
father for the rest of his life. If his father or another male role
model isn't in his life, a boy could become stuck in the Oedipal
stage. He needs to identify with that which is masculine so that

it is familiar and so that he may become secure in his own sexuality.

"What the presence of the father does is to help the son avert being lost in the maternal orbit," say Gregory Max Vogt and Stephen T. Sirridge, authors of *Like Son, Like Father.* "The father buffers and protects the son from being swallowed up by the force of togetherness and undifferentiation, that pole of dependency, that movement toward union."

The son needs his father in another way as well. If a father were not present, a boy's mother might feel she had to overcompensate in order to be both mother and father. An overly involved mother could potentially cause psychological harm to a boy, ranging from his rejection of all that is feminine to the other extreme, in which he rejects all that is masculine. When a father is not present, other men, such as an uncle, a grandfather, or a friend of the family, can help a mother maintain her balance as a parent.

Why Boys Need Their Fathers

Although the mother is the only person who can feed her baby if she chooses to nurse, fathers have just as much ability to nurture in every other way. Yet it is often difficult for men to develop parenting instincts, for a number of reasons. The underlying causes for this dilemma are diverse: many men have jobs that keep them away from home; other men, probably a majority, did not have fathers who nurtured them and simply may not know how to be intimate with their sons or may as a result harbor an inexplicable fear of getting close to their sons. In some cases their wives unconsciously make it difficult for them to get involved with their children.

"I fantasized about a daughter," said writer and father Chris Verner in an article in *Child* magazine, "because I feared a son. I was terrified that we'd carry on the sorrowful pattern of alienation and resentment that has marred so many father-son relationships."

This sentiment, unfortunately, is expressed by so many men and is a major reason they don't use their full potential for fatherhood. Our role models for parenting are our own parents, and as Samuel Osherson describes in his book *Wrestling With Love,* "Fathers are mysterious figures for boys; they often come and go, leaving home early and returning late, like the tide."

A Gallup poll commissioned by The National Center for Fathering found that one-third of the men surveyed felt that their work responsibilities were the reasons that they were not better fathers. Today, most fathers work an average of fifty-one hours a week—a good deal more than the forty-hour work week of the past. Even when mothers are working outside the home, studies show they still spend one-third to one-half more time with their children than the fathers do.

The actual hours a father spends with his son are only a part of the problem. Jean Curtis, author of *Working Mothers,* has coined a term, the "psychological parent." She explains in her book that although the mother may also be working, she still assumes "direct personal responsibility for the whereabouts of the child . . . . knows the child's shoe size . . . . knows what diseases he has been exposed to. . ." Few fathers queried on this point disagreed that the mother was the "psychological parent." Again, it may seen natural for fathers to relinquish many of the responsibilities because they never saw their own fathers performing tasks such as taking children for medical checkups and carpooling.

Robert Bly, author of the best-selling book about men, *Iron John,* claims that the "love unit most damaged by the industrial revolution has been the father-son bond." By this he means that prior to the Industrial Age, when most societies were primarily agrarian, father and son worked on the farm together or the father had a business at which his son apprenticed. A father and son spent a great deal of time together every day, allowing the father-son relationship to grow and giving the boy a chance to get to know his father and emulate him. Most fathers today leave their sons to go to work and seem to be at work most of the time.

The ideal solution to this problem would be for Dad to cut back on his work hours and try to be home more often. In the real world, this may be out of the question. It seems to take long hours or even two jobs just to make ends meet. One approach that is somewhat realistic is to encourage your husband to take your son to work with him on occasion or on the weekend when he is old enough to understand what his dad does. This will help your son to be able to think about his father and picture what he is doing and where, rather than viewing his daily disappearance as shrouded in mystery. It is also another way a father can share a "piece" of himself with his son, and provides an opportunity for a father to show his son how proud he is to introduce him to his fellow employees.

Most working mothers have developed their own way of reaching out to their children to compensate for their daily absences. They set aside special nights for the family to be together, take trips to special places with their kids, and make up for lost time on weekends. Dads could certainly benefit from the same strategies.

Why not try suggesting activities your husband and son can do together, preferably things they can do alone? If a new exhibit has opened at the museum that you know your husband would enjoy explaining to his son, mention it. Make a point of having plans of your own so that your son's father will need to spend time alone with him, and don't give too many instructions before they leave—make Dad feel like you know he can cope without your advice. You should also get your husband to share the responsibility for school events, parent-teacher conferences, etc.

Fathers Who Have Not Learned Fathering

Men whose own fathers were uninvolved with them may **want** strong relationships with their own sons but are uncertain about how to be loving and show their emotions. They may pass on the "hereditary silence," as Guy Corneau, author of *Absent Fathers, Lost Sons*, describes it, because they have not seen their fathers or other men express their feelings and so don't know how to do so with their own sons.

In general, our society does not allow men to express emotion openly. When they do, we label them weak or effeminate; we want men to be **masculine.** Dr. Kyle Pruett of the Yale University Child Study Center points out in his book *The Nurturing Father* "that 'masculine,' of course, does not mean male. It really means only the traits, behaviors, expectations and appearances shaped by a society and its institutions that are publicly linked to maleness." For a boy to reach adulthood feeling that he knows his father, his father must allow his emotions to be visible—hardly an easy task when most males grow up being either subtly or openly taught that this is not acceptable behavior. A father must teach his son that masculinity *and* feelings can go hand in hand.

If a father always seems strong and never shows "weakness" or disappointment, his son will grow up with a false image of what it means to be a man. It is more important for a son to see that a father can be sad, have setbacks, and face problems in life which are overcome, so that the son will learn by example that he too will be able to handle what life brings his way. Trying to live up to the false image of a father who appears to be an invulnerable rock can place a boy in a precarious position when his own life issues arise.

In Chapter Five we discussed the concept of the good enough mother versus the too good mother. In fact, the same ideas

apply to father-son relationships. A good enough father will
open up to his son—he'll let him know about things that upset
him and may help his son to confide similar feelings, which will
foster their relationship. A too good father will meet his son's
every need (and then some) and never let his son see his vulnerability.

"As long as fathers do not incorporate the other side of the
masculine, the side that is capable of love and tenderness,
there will be no significant change in the male community—or
in relationships between men and women," says Guy Corneau.
Although women are traditionally expected to teach their children intimacy, a father is perfectly capable of teaching this as
well. Boys also need to have their fathers tell them they love
them, which they usually hear only from their mothers, and to
have their fathers show physical affection for them. You as a
mother can urge your son's father to let his son see "all" of him
and to let his son know he loves him.

No Room for Father
What else can you as a mother do if you see that your husband
is not involved with your son or that he simply isn't around
enough? First, talk to your husband and make certain he
knows how much his son needs him. Sometimes mothers seem
so capable of taking care of their children that fathers don't
feel needed or can't figure out what their role should be. You
may literally have to tell your husband the ways in which he
can be involved with his son.

Even with so many women working today, it seems that most
couples still assume traditional roles in which the mother is
responsible for most child-related needs. When a father does
try to get involved, mother are sometimes unconsciously re-
sentful, or feel their role is being usurped, and so become critical of how their husbands handle their sons, causing fathers
to retreat.

If you harbor fears that your husband can't handle child-
care responsibilities, a study done at the Yale University Child
Study Center by Dr. Kyle Pruett might put your fears to rest.
Dr. Pruett followed seventeen families for a number of years in
which the father stayed home with the children while the
mother went to work. The conclusions he drew from his study
were reported in his book *The Nurturing Father:* the children in
the study showed no signs of intellectual or emotional problems
and appeared to be more flexible in terms of their ideas about
masculine and feminine identifications and roles.

"I remember the first time I asked my husband to watch my son all day," reminisced Arlene. "I wanted to go to a seminar. He actually said to me in surprise, 'You trust me with him?' When I responded, 'Why wouldn't I?' I could tell my husband was pleased."

Try to examine your own motives if you are insisting on doing *everything* together as a family without letting your husband have his own time with his son. If decisions need to be made for your son, or problems with behavior arise, don't handle them by yourself—get your husband to share in the process. Particularly if the issues are "male-oriented" problems such as getting into a fight in school, not making "the team," etc. Ask for your husband's perspective as an expert in a world in which you are only a visitor.

It is also important that you agree on how to discipline your son, and if you can't agree on issues in front of him, at least agree to discuss them in his absence until you reach a compromise position (see Chapter Twelve).

We may have made it sound as if a mother needs to work hard to encourage a good father-son relationship, but this is not always the case—most just happen of their own accord. Our intent is to suggest that mothers be on the watch to see if their help is needed.

As Boys Grow Older

As boys get older, their fathers are often their first heroes, which is another reason it is so important for a father or another male to be around for a boy. If the father were not present, a boy might idealize the father he doesn't really know, thereby creating standards no one can live up to, including himself. Simply put, a present father who is human and makes mistakes is a better influence on a boy than the memory of a father who seems infallible.

A father's example also helps to keep a boy out of trouble. Juvenile delinquents (regardless of socioeconomic background) are far more likely to come from families in which the father shows no interest in his son and therefore the son feels his father doesn't love him, rather than those in which the relationship thrives. "Mother alone is not enough," says psychotherapist Dr. Irene Kaminsky, who works at an adolescent-male residential treatment center in New York City. "A boy needs to identify with males. He needs a 'mirror,' someone to look at and be able to answer the question 'Who am I going to be when I grow up?'" Kaminsky says that as boys approach the preteen years, peer groups begin to grow in importance. A good relationship with a father keeps a boy from being pulled too much into the peer group, where he might get pressured into trying drugs, shoplifting, and even more serious trouble.

Preadolescent and adolescent boys who are connected to their fathers will also be more comfortable with their sexual identity and the changes that puberty brings. They need to have the presence of their fathers' bodies in order to have a positive feeling about their own. If this opportunity is not afforded to a young boy, he may grow to feel negative about female bodies (his way of rejecting his mother), rather than feeling good about his own male body. When boys begin to feel awkward about their bodies and unsure of themselves as they near the threshold of manhood, which they often do, an involved father can enhance a son's self-esteem and encourage his maturity.

Boys at this age often spend more time watching men on TV than being with their own fathers. Since we learn by imitation, when the primary male models available to them are TV idols, this only causes boys to exaggerate stereotypical masculine traits. They need to be "tougher," more macho, more daring, etc. The image of masculinity they get from TV—which features violence, risk-taking, a lack of emotional involvement, and womanizing—gives boys the wrong message about what it means to be a man. The more time a boy spends with his father, the better he can understand that this TV image is not real.

Boys also take their cues from their fathers about relationships with other men. Men are more likely to have male friends when they reach adulthood if they grow up seeing their father having friends. Psychotherapist Rene Bouchard says that "most men are hungry for connections with other men. They don't have them because they didn't learn to have them from their fathers." Most men have superficial relationships with other men. A boy isn't likely to see his father go out with friends as often as his mother does or chat with his friends on the phone regularly. A father should make a point of bringing his son along when he does go out with male friends or relatives, and show his son that men can be comfortable around each other and enjoy each other's company.

What Women Can Do
A man who is estranged from his own father may have difficulty parenting a son. Or alternatively, he may try to relive and change his own childhood by pressuring his son to behave in a manner that may not be good for the boy. If this is the situation with your husband, do your best to get him to come to terms with his relationship with his own father. If he harbors

feelings that his father wasn't there for him, show him that he may be re-creating this problem with his own son, and that he has the power to break the chain of silence. Do your best to get him to explore his relationship with his father and how it may be affecting his relationship with his son. You might suggest he consider therapy or join a men's group to help him unlock inner feelings he is afraid to face.

But frequently women wield a double-edge sword when it comes to the men in their lives. While women say they want sensitive, caring husbands who are not afraid to talk about their feelings, some women get frightened when their husbands appear to be vulnerable or insecure and fear their spouses are not "man" enough to weather a life crisis if it comes. You can help the relationship between your husband and son by examining whether you deliver mixed messages to your husband. Try to sort out your feelings so you can be consistently supportive and not operate on a double standard. Verbally reinforce to your husband how happy it makes you feel to see him share tender moments with his son and to see them spending time together. Mention how your son waits for him to come home every day and looks forward to their time together. Let him know in as many ways as possible how important he is to his son.

"My husband never planned on doing very much in the way of child care when our son was born," Sheila, one of our respondents, wrote. "But from the day we brought Jonathan home from the hospital, he started changing diapers, doing his laundry, and making up formula. I know that they have a stronger relationship today than they would have if my husband had sat back and watched me take care of everything. Now they go everywhere together!"

You can aid your husband in teaching your son to incorporate his so-called feminine and masculine traits into his personality by suggesting more than just that he talk about his feelings. Tell your husband that if he lets his son know it's okay to play with dolls *and* trucks, he will give him a very clear message. Even better, propose to Dad that he make a point of doing things normally associated with women in view of his son—cooking, cleaning, doing the laundry, etc., so that his son won't think these activities are "unmanly."

Many men maintain a physical distance from their sons, especially as their boys get older, sometimes due to an unconscious fear of latent homosexuality. The unconscious fear is in concert with the fear of appearing to be too sensitive or too gentle. If you tell your husband that the gentle side of him is one of the factors that attract you to him, you'll be imparting the message that sensitivity and warmth are sexy and appealing, and he may be able to allow himself to feel masculine while his emotional side is in view. He then will be able to pass this message on to his son.

Brad Sachs, a psychotherapist and director of The Fathering Center in Baltimore, Maryland, suggests that even fathers who have not learned from their own fathers how to be in touch with their emotions are still not at a total loss. "Your ability to be a nurturing, caring father," says Sachs, "comes from wherever you can get it. You don't just learn about it from your father—but from all the people in your life— there is a matrix of influences. A man should try to remember how he felt when he was given attention by adults in his life and provide the same opportunities for his son." Men can also learn from observing other "well-adjusted" fathers and reading books and materials on parenting, or even taking a parenting course.

Sachs also suggests that *not* all fathers will be comfortable doing *all* things with their sons, and they should find those activities with which they are comfortable and build on that strength rather than worrying about what they *can't* do with their sons. A mother can help foster these strengths by noticing where they lie and encouraging them to be shared by father and son.

For example, if your husband likes to build things, suggest he make a treehouse or a toy box for your son so that he can turn something he excels at and is comfortable with into a shared experience with his son. At the same time they are spending time together, your husband will also be sharing a "piece of himself" with his son, which the boy can incorporate into himself. Someday he may grow up to have warm memories of himself and his dad down in the basement, using a hammer and saw and admiring their handiwork. This will also be an activity that Mom is not part of, just the "men."

Sports and Dads
"My husband is not interested in any sports," Allison fretted when she filled out her questionnaire. "Who is going to teach my son to play baseball, and other sports that boys like to play?" This question goes to the heart of an important link between many fathers and sons. Most find sports an activity they are at ease sharing with their sons. For one thing, it is an acceptable way to be physical with other males. Also, it has a defined atmosphere—there are definite rules and regulations—and men are willing to participate in activities with other

males that have parameters. It is a permissible activity as well because it encompasses aggressiveness, a trait equated with masculinity.

There is, however, a danger when sports are the primary link between father and son. In some instances they may become competitive, which is not healthy for their relationship. The son may feel he can never be "as good as his dad" or that if he is as good, his father may harbor resentment against him. A father may try to relive his youth through his son, and to make his son better than he was. We see this all too often in fathers who begin pushing their sons as very young boys into training to become professional athletes and who devote their lives to this goal at all costs. Or a father may be disappointed in a son's lack of athletic prowess, which can cause a permanent rift between father and son. We discuss the issue further in Chapter Ten, but we raise it here primarily to point out that while sports activities are useful for fathers and sons to share, they may not be without a cost, and there are many other ways for fathers and sons to relate to each other. The important thing is for a father to follow his son's lead in the areas in which he shows an interest. Just watching sports events on TV together provides father and son with something they can share.

On the flip side, a father who is not athletically inclined can still show an interest if his son has talent or an interest in a particular sport, by attending games or events, talking with his son's coach, and discussing his strategies with him.

Abusive Fathers

Fathers who are abusive have a devastating affect on their sons' lives. Most mothers will read the above sentence and believe that this section does not apply to them. We hope it doesn't. But abuse comes in many forms and knows no socioeconomic or ethnic boundaries. It can happen in any family and you should know how to recognize the symptoms of a child who is abused.

Emotional Abuse

It seems like innocent teasing. . . .a father constantly makes "fun" of his son because he is afraid to play football or isn't tall enough for basketball. But it's not fun to his son—it is an attack that makes him feel ashamed.

The most common form of abuse is verbal or emotional abuse. This is the kind that can "break" a child emotionally and cause a boy to grow up feeling angry, helpless, and full of self-hatred. Fathers who abuse their children emotionally were often brought up that way themselves, and it is the only way they know how to relate to their sons. A father who calls his son names, constantly makes critical comments, blames the child for problems that are beyond the boy's control, and administers cruel discipline is for all practical purposes an abusive father. This type of father may expect his son to be perfect, will constantly make him feel ashamed for his behavior, and may wind up abandoning him emotionally, leaving a wide gap of distance between them.

The diagnosis of an emotionally abusive father can be hard to make. How much criticism is too much? When are words teasing and when are they hurtful? If you feel your husband is too hard on your son, you should pay close attention. Your clue that something is wrong may be in the way your son reacts—does he look hurt, does he mention to you the things his father says, is he withdrawing from his father? If you feel your husband's behavior is extreme, you must intervene. You can try discussing the problem with your husband—perhaps he is not aware of what he is doing. You can suggest he get professional help to deal with his behavior (and your son may need some to help restore his self-esteem). In severe cases, you should consider removing your son from this environment.

Physical Abuse
Some abusive fathers step over the line and physically exploit their sons. Because of all the media attention in the past few years, this phenomenon seems to be something new; but in fact, the term "battered-child syndrome" was coined a long time ago. Frequently, such men were abused children themselves. Outside circumstances may also contribute to child abuse, including an unwanted pregnancy, a premature birth, a child who is born with a chronic illness, low intelligence, or even a child who cries constantly. This can be particularly stressful if a father is too young or unprepared for fatherhood. Poverty may also put added pressure on a family.

In New Rochelle, New York, a young father recently drowned his infant son in the bathtub. Neighbors were shocked—they had always seen the young father proudly pushing the baby in his stroller. They also observed that the father always left his apartment to go into the hallway to smoke cigarettes so that the smoke wouldn't bother the child. The unfortunate incident occurred not long after the father lost his job.

We know you are probably saying to yourself, This could never happen in my home, and the odds are it won't; but you should know that in 75 percent of fatal child-abuse cases, the guilty party is a parent. As a boy's mother, you need to know the facts. If your husband is hurting your son physically, you must intervene.

An episode of the popular television show *L.A. Law* portrayed a family in which the father was intentionally causing his son to have accidents in order to collect insurance claims. The mother, who clearly loved her son, did not suspect her husband was abusing her son for quite a while, because the injuries looked like accidents. Of course, this is purely fiction, but the point is well taken. Physical abuse in its early or less extreme versions may be tolerated by a mother who can't bring herself to acknowledge what is really going on.

A wife may see her husband's behavior as just a severe form of corporal punishment. Although she may feel it is harsh, she may not be willing to get in the middle. Signs of excessive physical punishment—multiple lesions in various stages of healing—are one of the indicators doctors look for when suspecting child abuse.

Some of the earliest symptoms of physical abuse, outside of visible injuries, include a child's failure to thrive (gain weight and grow), passiveness, developmental problems, and a negative self-image. Physically abused children can exhibit a lack of trust and are often negative, aggressive, and hyperactive.

We won't spend too much time here going into reasons why a parent may become physically abusive—this is a big subject and we recommend several good books on it in the back of this book. Our intent in covering the subject is simply to impart a message to mothers whose sons are being physically abused by their fathers. Therapy and other forms of professional help may provide a good, long-term outcome to this problem if your husband is willing to get help. It may be necessary to remove your son from the home until the situation improves.

Physically abused boys can grow up to be abusers. Also, they can be impotent, and unable emotionally or sexually to invest in another person because they are so traumatized from their experience. The abuse is often suppressed in their minds, and they suffer from psychological problems such as depression and anxiety without knowing why.

Sexual Abuse
Between 45,000 and 90,000 boys are sexually abused each year. Four out of five boys are abused by a member of the family or someone they know. As unbelievable as it sounds, sometimes it is a father or stepfather or a mother's live-in boyfriend who is the molester.

Many women would say that sexual abuse within or even outside the family is something they never encountered as a child and they can't imagine it could ever happen to their own children. One of the authors of this book thought so too. She comes from a nice middle-class family and remembered no such traumatic events in her life. But after a great deal of thought, she recalled that her teenage stepbrother threatened to fondle her breasts—a request she squashed by warning him she would report his illicit smoking habit to his father. It was shocking to realize this memory had lain dormant for so many years.

Statistically, it is unlikely that your husband or another man known to your family will molest your son—but it is not impossible. Again, we will not attempt to discuss the reasons in detail, but we will provide you with the symptoms that might suggest sexual abuse. (The perpetrator could be a father, another relative, a baby-sitter, a religious figure—male or female). If you observe the following groups of behavior in your son, seek help.

Under age five:

- night terrors
- clinging behavior
- developmental regression

School age:

- anxiety, fear, depression
- insomnia
- hysteria
- sudden weight loss or gain
- sudden school problems, truancy
- running away from home

Adolescents:

- strong defiance of parents
- chronic depression
- social isolation
- running away from home

Some say boys suffer more damage by incest than girls—if abused by a role model, a boy begins to act differently. In the book *Child Abuse,* authors Ruth S. Kempe and C. Henry Kempe state, "Incest seems to leave boys with such severe emotional insult as to block normal emotional growth."

A boy who is sexually abused may begin to hate his body. He may suffer from fear, guilt, shame, anger, or depression. A molested boy may avoid contact sports because of his fear of males. In very young males, excessive masturbation is a sign of abuse, as is inappropriate sexual play, bed-wetting, and gender-role confusion. Older boys may suffer from headaches and addictive disorders, practice self-mutilation, and even try to commit suicide.

Even if a child is put into therapy, the sexual abuse may have long-lasting repercussions. It's possible that when a boy reaches puberty he may fear he is a homosexual because he has been in an intimate sexual relationship with a man. He could have trouble with physical intimacy, and the events of marriage and new fatherhood might cause him to revisit his trauma.

In many cases a boy will not tell his mother if he is being sexually abused by a father, family member, or someone outside the family. He may be too ashamed or too afraid. If a mother recognizes any of the symptoms we have described, she should question her son and seek qualified help. Sexually abused children can be treated with medical attention, psychotherapy, and play therapy. If a mother suspects her husband is the abuser, she must confront him, try to get him into treatment, and remove her son from the immediate danger.

In Chapter Eight we discuss how you can teach your young son that his body is his own and no one has the right to touch it without his permission.

Fathers and Addictive Behavior

Men are four times more likely to be addicted to alcohol than women, so there is a greater likelihood that a father will be an alcoholic, rather than the mother. Alcohol and chemical dependencies often go hand in hand with the kind of physical and emotional abuse we've described. Addictive personalities also tend to have a problem being intimate with other people, which may further complicate the father-son relationship.

Our advice for mothers of sons who live in homes in which a father is an alcoholic or a drug addict is much the same as for those in which the father is simply abusive. Do your best to get your husband to seek help, but if necessary, remove your son from the home to keep him out of danger. The danger is twofold. The most immediate risk is that your son may be harmed physically or emotionally by his father, who is drunk. The more long-term threat is that the predisposition to chemical dependency is believed to be inherited, which puts boys of fathers who are chemically dependent at higher risk to be addicted as well.

A father who is a good role model to his son—avoiding the use of alcohol and drugs, even cigarettes—may help to thwart his son's usage. A father who is actively using drugs and alcohol in front of his son is inviting him to imitate what he has seen in his own home. Remember, the message a child receives at home is stronger than the messages he receives outside the home. So a father's example in this area can be significant.

It must be clear to you by now how essential a boy's father is in his life and how the nature of the relationship can shape a boy's character. As a mother, you cannot control this relationship, nor should you try to do so, but you can be encouraging and do some cheering from the sidelines. Solid relationships with fathers help boys grow up to be men who are happy with themselves—something we all wish for our sons.

8

A Boy and His Penis:
On Boys' Sexuality

"I was sitting around a table with several family members and my twenty-six-year-old son," relates Elaine. "In the course of the conversation I said the word 'penis.' My son got very upset. He said he didn't care how old he was, he didn't want to hear his mother say *that* word. We all had a good laugh at his expense."

Just saying the word out loud makes a lot of people uncomfortable—sometimes it's sons with their mothers, sometimes it's the other way around. Yet there was a time when this was not so. In ancient Egyptian times, the penis in the form of the phallic symbol was not only discussed but worshipped because of its magical role in reproduction. Lavishly depicted in drawings and statuary, many gods were shown with exaggerated penises or even with more than one penis! Not until the sixteenth century, when syphilis became rampant, did sexual mores begin to inhibit open discussion of the male anatomy.

We have called this chapter "A Boy and His Penis," but here too the word stands for more than a bodily organ to include male sexuality in general. As soon as the doctor determines whether a newborn has a penis or a vagina, the first step is taken in the development of the child's sexual identity. Simultaneously, the bond between infant and mother takes on a new definition. In this chapter and the next, we hope to broach some of the issues many mothers often find difficult or even impossible to talk about.

Sexual Exploration

Two out of three boys either masturbate another boy or vice versa in the preadolescent years.

By age five, 50 percent of all boys will have sex play with another child.

Almost one-half of preadolescent boys will try to have intercourse with a girl. One-quarter will at least partially succeed.

The above statements are all true. One goal in relaying these factors is not to shock or frighten you as a mother, but simply to make you aware that your son has or will become a sexual being in childhood. In fact, your son's sexual awareness may have even begun in the womb. Ultrasound has produced clear photographs of erections in male fetuses.

Dr. June Reinisch, former director of the Kinsey Institute for Human Sexuality, in the book *The Kinsey Institute New Report on Sex* suggests that these early signs of sexual functioning may be "the brain's way of checking all the circuits to make sure that the brain, nerves, blood system, muscles and organs are in working order."

You may very well notice your son having erections almost as soon as he is born. Babies as young as four months old can have orgasms, although ejaculation does not occur until adolescence. Before the age of one, however, orgasms are not likely to be caused deliberately by the baby. Almost from the time boy babies learn to coordinate their hand movements, they begin to explore their sexual organs and discover that it feels good to do so. But even when they are not touching themselves, they are likely to have erections. Most baby boys experience them regularly during the night when they are sleeping, and many other commonplace occurrences can cause erections in babies and young boys—nursing, cuddling, bathing, cold, excitement, fear, tight clothing, straining for a bowel movement, the need to urinate, or merely waking up in the morning. Just about anything, it seems, will trigger one!

Mothers of boys, particularly those who grew up without brothers, are often surprised to observe this phenomenon in their little boys. "I was helping Jon, my three-year-old, get into his pajamas the other night," related one mother. "When he took off his underpants, he had quite an erection. Even I was amazed at how large his little penis suddenly looked. Although he had had erections before, this one surprised him as well as me. He stared at his penis for a few seconds in amazement, and then turned to me and said, 'Mommy—what's in there?' "

An erect penis may look a number of different ways or lean at different angles, and all are normal.

Erections and masturbation go hand in hand (if you'll excuse a pun). Boys learn to give themselves erections and masturbate as soon as they have the motor skills to coordinate the activity. However, the amount of interest in masturbation varies greatly from one boy to another; some will stimulate themselves quite frequently from a very early age, while others may not really be interested until puberty. Both ends of the spectrum are normal, and neither should cause maternal alarm.

Many mothers of seven- or eight-year-old boys who answered our questionnaire reported they had yet to see any indication that their sons had begun to masturbate. Indeed, their children might not yet be engaged in this activity, but they also might be masturbating privately. One mother wrote that, to her knowledge, her eight-year-old had not begun to masturbate and she had never discussed the subject with him. But he came upon our questionnaire on his mother's desk and asked her, "Mom, what does mast-ur-bate mean?" She turned several shades of red and, after thinking for a minute, said, "You know, it's when you, uh, play with yourself." "Oh, **that**," he replied and ran off to play, leaving his mother to wonder if perhaps he was more enlightened than she had believed. Other mothers reported the following:

"My boys are masturbating constantly."

"I come into the living room sometimes and find both my son and my daughter watching TV with their hands in their pants."

"When my son was about six, he started touching himself a great deal, and it suddenly seemed he didn't let go of his penis for about two years!"

Although one mother mentioned her daughter's masturbation as well, in general, boys tend to masturbate and touch their genitals than girls do—mainly because their sexual organs are more prominent and they become aroused more quickly than girls.

If you have any concerns about your son masturbating, we'd like to put them to rest. Doctors and psychologists all agree that masturbation is an entirely normal and healthy activity for a child—there is absolutely no reason to stop a boy from this form of self-exploration.

One reasonable concern is that children learn that masturbation is a private activity. As soon as a boy is old enough to understand, it is time for a mother or father to explain to him that it is perfectly all right to touch and "play" with himself, but only when he is alone and in his own room. This advice serves two purposes: it prevents embarrassment to others and possibly to himself, and it teaches him from a young age that sex and privacy go together.

Occasionally a mother will have difficulty in convincing a boy to stop masturbating publicly. If you find yourself facing this problem, the best recourse is to discuss this matter fully with your son. If nothing seems to work, it may be time to seek some professional help to address the question of why he is seeking attention this way. One mother told us that as a small child, her adopted son masturbated much of the day. He might have done this to comfort himself, just as a child would suck his thumb, or it might have been a sign that he had been sexually abused.

We'd like to tell you about one last, little-known fact about masturbation—one that is definitely not discussed at cocktail parties! Strange as this may sound, according to the original Kinsey Report published in the 1940s, more than 25 percent of American males have masturbated an animal while masturbating themselves. This is most likely to happen with preadolescent and adolescent boys (with the greatest proportion presumably living in rural areas; because we've become more urbanized since this study was published, this number may now be considerably smaller). While we personally don't know of any mothers who have ever discovered this happening, apparently it too is within the realm of normalcy. If you find your son and your family pet together, don't panic. It may scare you, but it doesn't mean your son is headed for trouble.

Mothers and Physical Contact with Their Sons
Mothers naturally hold, stroke, bathe, and diaper their sons when they are infants and toddlers, and many engage in that most intimate act between mother and child, breast-feeding. All physical contact between mother and son in the first few years of their relationship goes unquestioned. But at some point, many mothers begin to wonder if physical closeness with their sons has become inappropriate. The strong taboo against incest in our society can make us doubt our own motherly instincts and good sense.

The fear of mothers touching their children does not reach back forever in history. In the 1500s, for example, playing with a child's genitals was extremely common. Even today, cultures differ in their attitudes toward mother-son contact. One mother who answered our questionnaire told us that when her children were very young, she lived in Brazil. She found it was common for Brazilian women to rub the genitals of a crying baby to soothe it, even in public. With four small children close in age, she said she was tempted to follow the custom, but her American upbringing inhibited her. In this country we have been taught to believe that even cuddling and holding our sons may be wrong as they get older, and we become fearful of any feelings of sensuality that physical contact might evoke in us.

"I look at my son and see this adorable little boy and know that he will grow up to be an attractive young man," Maria told us. "I imagine how girls will see him when he is older. I guess you could say I look at him sexually, but I don't think there's anything wrong with this."

Two recent articles in women's magazines have focused on the writers' awareness—both were fathers—that on some level, they were sexually attracted to their daughters. As David Leonard wrote in *Child* magazine, "There is a secret subject that child-rearing books never get around to talking about. The secret is that parenting sometimes involves sensual feelings toward the child, and vice versa. . . . I know from talking to women as well that men are not alone in struggling with these sensual feelings."

And in *Glamour* magazine, Christopher Hallowell noted, "Perhaps there is no perfect answer to such a complex question as where the boundaries of sexuality lie. [But I was] aware of the artifice of the separation of sex and sensuality that so many adults adhere to, and that Maggie so far was innocent of. To her, still a child, both are one."

One respondent to our questionnaire recounted a phone conversation she had had with a friend who had a young son when she herself was pregnant. Her friend told her, "Having a little boy changes your life. You'll even find you don't need as much physical contact with your husband, because you'll get a lot from your son." Although this mother was talking about the simple joy of child-given hugs, she was acknowledging their sensual aspect.

Our relationships with our sons *are* sensual in their own way. What could be more beautiful than the sight of the child you gave birth to lying peacefully asleep, unaware that you are watching him? What could smell more delicious than your little boy's clean skin after his bath or feel warmer than his little hand in yours? And what could be sweeter than the pure kisses your son gives you—a sensuality that can't be re-created, because adults don't love unconditionally as children do. You are the first love of your son's life!

Responding to her son's tenderness is a mother's rightful work. Boys learn through their mothers about love and how to relate to the opposite sex. Therefore, a good physical relationship between mother and son will be a positive reinforcement for the boy's future relationships. Feeling an underlying sensuality in this relationship is perfectly normal for the mother—it means she is responding to her son's love and affection.

According to Aileen Goodson, author of *Therapy, Nudity & Joy,* "Evidence shows that people that have cutaneous (skin) stimulation by a loving mother during infancy and early childhood are more adept and comfortable in all tactile relationships, including sexual behavior."

There are no rules that say that a mother should reduce her physical contact with her son at a certain age. Most experts agree that this is a matter of personal choice, based solely on the comfort level of the individuals concerned.

However, there was a general consensus among respondents as to when they thought it was time for their sons to bathe alone. Of the mothers who answered this question on our questionnaire, 91 percent said they stopped bathing their sons by age six or seven. This seems to coincide with the age at which boys should be able to start bathing themselves. Given this general agreement, it appears that mothers need not worry about when they should curtail physical contact with their sons, since nature will take its course. Prepubescent boys may feel very self-conscious at being seen naked by their mothers, and many will even start wriggling out of their mothers' embrace, thus eliminating the need for a mother to decide whether the time has come.

While we don't suggest pulling away physically from your son unless you are personally uncomfortable, we also don't recommend encouraging inappropriate behavior. For example, Maureen, the mother of a three-year-old, told us that her son decided one day that he wanted to pretend he was a baby and drink milk from her nipples. Although he did this in a "pretend" way—he did not actually touch her nipples but put his head close to her chest and made sucking noises—he became quite persistent about playing this game frequently. Maureen felt uncomfortable about this behavior and discouraged the boy from continuing—a good decision. Not only was he playing out a fantasy of not growing up and was holding on to a previous stage of infancy in his relationship with his mother, but ironically, he was mimicking adult sexual behavior. Had the mother allowed the sucking to continue, it might have been confusing for both of them.

What is appropriate? A child fondling parts of his mother's body is not a good idea; allowing this to occur is encouraging a sexual relationship, which will only confuse and possibly frighten her son. Likewise, a mother should not fondle or kiss her son's genitals or touch him in a sexual manner, or else she is betraying his trust. Even intentional frequent or prolonged provocative exhibiting of her body is a form of sexual abuse that is unhealthy between a mother and son, particularly after the time he reaches school age.

When he is old enough to dress and wash himself, a mother should not insist on doing this herself; again, this is an inappropriate interaction.

The matter of breast-feeding is in and of itself an interesting subject. While most women don't refer to breast-feeding as a sensual experience, in fact, for many women it is. We had one mother report to us that she had an orgasm while she was breast-feeding her son and felt terribly guilty about it, although there was no reason she should have.

We believe that breast-feeding beyond the age of two is not a good idea—it signals a mother's unwillingness to let her son go through the stage of rapprochement (see Chapter Four) and keeps her son a baby when he is too big to be suckling at her breast.

Mothers, Sons, and Nudity

Another, related subject concerns when sons should stop seeing their mothers undressed. Although many respondents to our questionnaire indicated that nudity had never been an issue they worried about in their homes, the majority of those who said it was an issue stopped allowing their sons to see them unclothed when the boys reached age five. Again, the experts agree that there is really a matter of family choice. There is no rule of thumb that after a certain age it is "dangerous" for a son to see his mother nude.

As one mother explained it, nudity had never been a problem in their house, because they just never worried about it. One day her eight-year-old son happened upon her getting dressed, took one look at her, and said, "Mom, yeccchh!" She took this as her clue to avoid being naked around her son in the future.

Lest we get overly sensitive about the nudity question, we should remember that human beings did not always wear

clothes and that in many societies today, nudity is still acceptable. Any discomfort we may feel stems solely from our cultural
upbringing. Anthropologists believe that humans began wearing clothing for two reasons—neither of which pertained to psychological impact. The first reason was for protection—in cold
climates people began to wear clothing for warmth, and in the
warm climates for protection from insects and injury. The other
reason was for decoration—clothing was designed to *emphasize,* not hide, the sexual organs, thereby making them more
appealing.

Still, we don't suggest you actively promote nudity in front
of your son. In fact, if a mother intentionally presents her son
with a close-up view of her nude body on a regular basis, this
is a form of emotional abuse. The result may be that her son
grows up to feel guilty about having a relationship with another
woman. We know of a grown man who was raised in a nudist
family and now has a great deal of anger toward his parents
because he is unable to have a relationship with a woman. His
memories of constantly seeing his mother's body make him
uncomfortable, and he projects this discomfort onto other
women.

But if you teach your son that seeing a woman's body is bad,
he may carry this belief subconsciously into adulthood. It is
important to let him know that the human body is not something to be ashamed of and that seeing the bodies of people
close to him should not be upsetting.

Many psychiatrists and psychologists suggest that allowing
your son to see you naked until age ten or eleven is fine, although from our questionnaire it appears the majority of mothers feel that the cutoff should be earlier. Many started limiting
exposure before their boys were five.

Richard Green, M.D., J.D., professor of psychiatry at the Department of Psychiatry and Bio-behavioral Sciences, UCLA
School of Medicine writes that he believes that nudity in the
family is a source of learning: "Anatomies teach. An earliest
possible signal directing a child to correct self-placement [is
witnessing the 'anatomic distinction between the] sexes' (as
Freud elegantly put it) [and to compare its own genitalia] with
a male and with a female. Thus, a parent's level of comfort with
household nudity, the opportunity for a child to see a parent
disrobe occasionally, or the opportunity to bathe or shower
with a parent or a sibling can be an important early cue in
establishing this first component of sexual identity."

Ronald and Juliette Goldman, well-known Australian educators, in their book *Show Me Yours* recommend the following:

- A healthy openness to nakedness within the family in the early years, especially at bath time, during the summer, and at the beach;
- a need to see the sex organs as normal functional parts of the body which we need not be ashamed of;
- a gentle induction, free from repressive associations, about the need to respect others' feelings, explaining why older people, relatives, visitors may be concerned at seeing nakedness;
- within the family, an acceptance of the need for privacy, especially when and if requested by siblings of the other sex.

Your Son and His Sexual Education

"Joey asked me where babies come from today," one questionnaire respondent told her husband at dinner.

"Did you tell him they are found under a cabbage leaf?" he asked, amused.

"No, of course not. I told him the truth," she replied. "I told him the stork brought them."

Of course, this mother was teasing her husband, but the truth was she had realized how complicated the issue of sexuality and little boys can be. It is just this complexity and the opportunity for misinterpretation that make it necessary for you to begin your son's sexual education at a very early age.

We all remember the sitcoms that showed Dad having "the talk" with his son about "the birds and the bees." In reality, mothers share equally in the responsibility of providing sons with an education about sex. After all, moms are in a better position to tell their sons all about girls.

Providing a boy with a jumping-off point for discussion may be the most comfortable way to initiate this education. A number of good books, even for young children, begin to teach about anatomy, physical differences between the sexes, and the basics of reproduction. The coming of a new baby in your own or a relative's family serves as an excellent opportunity to introduce the subject.

As never before, mothers today fear what their sons could be exposed to when they become sexually active. Our questionnaire respondents indicated that one of the greatest fears mothers have about their sons' futures was that they might contract a sexually transmitted disease. With the killer AIDS a very real threat and venereal disease at an all-time high, this is not the paranoia of overprotective mothers; it is a very frightening reality. But AIDS and sexually transmitted diseases are not the only problems. U.S. teenagers have the highest rates of pregnancy and abortion in the developed world, and only a small percentage of sexually active boys use condoms.

We need to educate our sons about sex at home. We can't wait for them to learn what they need to know in sex education classes at school—they will be too old by then. Lessons begun at a young age and repeated throughout childhood will be learned far better than those introduced for the first time in preadolescence, when boys tend to take such lessons lightly.

Teaching our sons about responsible sex is our best hope, for both protecting them against the dangers of sexually transmitted diseases and enabling them to have satisfying relationships. If boys learn that responsibility—to one's self and to one's partner—is an integral part of a sexual relationship and that a sexual relationship is an expression of deep feelings, not a form of recreation, they will grow up protected on all fronts. If they don't learn these facts from their parents, they may learn half-truths from less trustworthy sources—namely, other children. Another important reason that our sons' sexual education must begin early is because there is no guarantee that puberty will coincide with the double-digit years. Some boys can begin showing signs of puberty as early as age eight. Nothing could be more frightening to a young boy than to discover sudden changes in his body without being aware of what they mean.

You can begin your son's sex education as soon as he is old enough to talk by teaching him the correct names for the body parts, just as you teach him to name the parts of his face. By age five, he will be able to understand a simplified version of how babies are created and born. By the time he reaches prepuberty, no later than age nine, he should have a pretty clear understanding of sexual intercourse, pregnancy, birth control, protection against sexually transmitted disease, and the role of love in a sexual relationship. And he should have a clear understanding of how his body will change in puberty and of the significance of those changes for his behavior as an adult with the ability to make love and create babies.

We find ourselves talking to our babies about making babies of their own someday—and this makes us realize that we are sexual beings from birth and throughout the rest of our lives.

From the first time we change our new babies' diapers to the time we notice their first facial hairs, we are aware of our off-spring's maleness. By helping them feel at ease with their roles as boys and as sexual beings, we will be paving the road for them to grow into happy teenagers and secure men.

9

"Mom, When You Were a Little Boy ...": Gender Identity

"Mommy, were you a little boy when you were young?"

"Was I a girl when I was a baby or a boy like I am now?"

"Do boy zebras have penises?"

These questions, asked by very young children, illustrate that even though they recognize the obvious differences between boys and girls, they aren't quite sure what it all means.

Although a boy is born with male genitals and is thus declared a boy by the attending physician, his gender identity—his sense of himself as a boy—takes time to form. At some point between birth and age three, a boy begins to think of himself as a boy and becomes aware that he is going to be a boy for the rest of his life. His gender identity evolves not only from his biological orientation (seeing that he has male sexual organs) but also from his environment (his perception that he is treated as a boy and his observations of how other males behave).

That a boy learns about gender from his environment is born out by studying children who are born as hermaphrodites. In this highly unusual condition, a child is born with ambiguous sexual organs—for example, the child might have a prostate

98

gland internally (a male organ) as well as a vagina. Often such children eventually have surgery to make them more like one sex or the other. But it is usually the sex they are deemed to be at birth and during childhood with which they identify, regardless of what they look like physically—clear evidence that environment is a strong factor in gender identity.

However, *gender* identity is not the only component of a person's *sexual* identity. In *The Kinsey Institute New Report on Sex,* Dr. June Reinisch and Ruth Beasley actually describe nine different components of a person's sexual identity:

(1) Chromosomes—a fetus with an XY pattern of chromosomes becomes a boy; one with an XX pattern becomes a girl.

(2) Gonads—boys have testes.

(3) Hormones—boys have more androgen-type hormones than girls do.

(4) Internal organs—boys have a prostate gland.

(5) External organs—boys have a penis and a scrotum.

(6) Brain—boys and girls have different levels of the brain chemical and structures related to sex.

(7) Birth assignment—the doctor says, "It's a boy!"

(8) Gender identity—a boy says, "I'm a boy."

(9) Sexual orientation—a male is attracted to a woman or to another man.

As you can see, although *gender identity* is one of many factors determining sexual identity, it is the only one that can be influenced by environment. People learn their gender identity in a variety of ways—for a boy, by imitating his father and other males, learning how the other sex acts through his mother and sisters, and learning what goes on around him through books, television, and direct observation. A boy who lacks appropriate male models may have trouble integrating his gender identity into his sexual identity. Problems might also arise if he is treated differently from other boys—for example, if he is prohibited from participating in all sports. Such problems could range from an inability to identify well with other males to overidentification with females—issues we will cover later in this chapter. But when a boy's gender identity evolves normally, he moves on to another stage in exploring his sexual identity.

"Look at Me! I'm a Man!"

As boys learn more about their gender identity, they become more interested in the differences between the sexes, and, not surprisingly, in sexual exploration with other children.

On the popular television show *America's Funniest Home Videos*, the winning (funniest) video one night showed two very young children who interrupted the best man's toast at a wedding reception by drawing a great deal of attention to themselves. The little girl in her lovely party dress and patent leather shoes lay on her back on the dance floor while the little boy in his grown-up suit lay directly on top of her. The two held each other in a serious clench.

Many viewers might have wondered if the display had been orchestrated for the purposes of producing a funny video, but by age two, it is not uncommon for children to climb on each other or to try to look at each other's genitals. Certainly by four or five, they are more interested in other children's bodies and may participate in some form of sex play such as doctor, Mommy and Daddy undressing, and so on. Also at this stage, they begin to get curious about where babies come from.

One mother wrote in her questionnaire that she usually spent a few minutes sitting with her son in his preschool class before she left him for the day. One day several of his friends cornered her to tell her the news—Kyle's mother was going to have a baby! Kyle told her he wasn't certain if his mother was having one or two babies, and Greg laughed and said her tummy would be too big if there were two babies in it. The mother explained that it *was* possible to have two or even three or four babies in a mommy's uterus (a different place than the stomach), although it certainly didn't happen that often. The boys agreed that might be possible: "Oh, yeah, dogs have a lot of puppies at one time!"

The boys then asked how the puppies get out of the mother dog's uterus, and the mother explained that when they were ready they just "sort of came out." You mean they just walk out?" the boys asked incredulously, and at that point the mother suddenly remembered she had left the iron on at home and left preschool in a hurry. She said she felt it was not up to her to teach sex education to other people's children. Nevertheless, she was fascinated by the questions the boys had asked. And later that day she described the birth process to her own son.

The greatest amount of sex play takes place between the ages of six and ten. This is also when children tend to restrict themselves to same-sex socializing—the stage of "I hate girls" and

"Girls are dumb." For this reason, it is not uncommon for boys to pursue their sexual exploration with other boys. While group masturbation among young boys is not quite a ritual like joining the Little League team, it is fairly common. The sight of a group of young boys masturbating in the rec room might unnerve a mother who stumbles upon it, but it is really quite normal—and not in any way an indicator of the participants' future sexual activities.

Bear in mind that sexual exploration for young children is an important learning process that contributes to the health of adult sexuality. As a mother, you can help your son through this learning process in a number of ways. Probably the most important is to stay calm if you come across your son and other children involved in sexual play. Although you may choose to put a stop to it, do so casually. Above all, don't make your son feel he has done something wrong or shameful.

Another important contribution to the health of your son's sexual identity is the open affection you express to his father. Show him that physical contact between people who love each other is a good thing. And be affectionate with your son as well—children who don't get physical affection from their parents may go elsewhere for it.

The only time that sexual play can be detrimental to your son's development is if an older child forces undesired attention on him. There's no way you can prevent this from happening except by encouraging your child to play with boys close to his own age and teaching him to let you know if someone does something to him that he doesn't like. Teach your son as openly as you can that no one should touch his body or private parts if he doesn't want them to be touched, most particularly not strangers. He needs to understand that his body is his own and that any intrusion is something he needs to tell you or his father about.

Nontraditional Sexuality

"My son likes to dress up in my high heels and jewelry. Should I be concerned?"

"My son is terrified of any game or play with other little boys in which he might fall down or get hurt. Is this normal?"

Mothers of little boys frequently ask such questions of therapists and psychologists. And in our interviews we uncovered mothers' deep concerns about their son's masculinity and its relationship to their future sexuality and sexual orientation. Of the mothers who answered our questionnaire, 15 percent were concerned that their sons would have a homosexual orientation as adults, 8 percent were concerned that their sons would not be masculine enough (although we did not define what *masculine* meant), and another 2 percent were concerned that their sons would be approached by homosexual men. These findings told us that mothers worry about the outward manifestations of their sons' masculinity, about their eventual choice of sexual partners, and about their sexual vulnerability.

Although in general, homosexuality is now discussed fairly openly, mothers rarely talk about it with respect to their sons and are not necessarily well informed about it. Nonetheless, many mothers wonder and worry about whether their sons could "become gay."

For example, Jill's nine-year-old son is healthy, active, plays well with other boys, and enjoy sports. She told us her one worry about her son was that he might become homosexual as an adult. Her fear arose from observing the boy's gentle side—he protects his sister, looks out for younger boys, and in general has a sweet personality. It's sad that this very desirable part of her son's personality should cause Jill so much concern.

Another mother, Ruthann, described how startled she was to come across her young son trying on her bra; had she found a daughter doing the same, she would probably have thought it amusing.

But this is a mother's dilemma: how do we raise sons who are loving, nurturing beings who will grow to be kind, caring men without suppressing their masculinity? Although we have already discussed ways in which a mother can help her son grow into a man who possesses a "feminine" side that is well integrated with his masculine traits (Chapter Four), we'd like to relate this now to the issue of sons' sexual orientation.

As we mentioned earlier in this chapter, a number of different factors determine our sex roles, one being our sexual orientation—are we attracted to a member of the opposite sex or of our own sex? Historically speaking, homosexuality and bisexuality have been accepted parts of most cultures; this is particularly well documented in the history of ancient Egypt and Greece. It was only much later, when Victorian prudishness was established, that homosexuality became unacceptable—as did any openness about sexuality, for that matter.

In fact, in all species of mammals a portion of the population engages in homosexual activity. This fact alone would seem to dispel the notion that homosexuality is "unnatural," as some would have us believe. Scientists and researchers do not believe that homosexuality is a choice people make, but rather that it is a part of their personality. We know that children's personalities are basically formed by the time they are a few years old, so it makes sense that their sexual orientation would be as well.

In this country, it has been believed for many years that 10 percent of our population is homosexual. More recently, some researchers are trying to prove this percentage is much smaller, perhaps closer to 3 percent. Regardless of the actual rate, there are still enough homosexuals in this country to constitute a considerable percentage of an enormous population. This suggests not a deviancy from the norm, but rather a subset of the population—a minority, but still a significant one.

No one knows what causes sexual orientation be it homosexuality or heterosexuality. Actually, our orientation either way may not be as clear cut as we'd like to think. In the 1950s, Alfred Kinsey, founder of the Kinsey Institute, developed a "scale" of sexual orientation that is still used by sex researchers. Simply explained, it rates individuals who have had only heterosexual experiences as "0" and those who have had exclusively homosexual experience as "6." Those who had had any combination of both fall somewhere in between, depending on the relative prevalence of the two kinds of experiences. Many researchers consider other factors as well, but to make a point we find it more useful to discuss this system in its purest form.

As a heterosexual mother, your first reaction might be, "Well, okay, I'm a 0." Yet when we urged our interviewees to discuss their sexual experiences in detail, they recounted homosexual experiences they had had when they were younger, even though they had never before identified them as such. For example, one woman remembered that at the age of thirteen or fourteen, she and a girlfriend had "practiced" kissing with each other so they would seem to be experienced when they actually got to kiss a boy. No doubt the girls were also curious about what it was like to kiss another girl, and in fact, kissing a girl probably seemed less threatening than kissing a boy. Technically, the kisses counted as homosexual acts.

Looked at in this context, it is easy to see that we all have the potential to experiment with homosexual experiences and that homosexuality is not so unrelated to our lives. In fact, fewer of us are probably "0s" than we might believe.

The best we can do here for mothers in clarifying this issue is to provide the *known* facts about homosexuality and the theories (all unproven as yet) surrounding it. We are not making a value judgment on whether or not mothers should be concerned about their sons' potential for homosexuality; nor are we hypothesizing about or suggesting what may cause it (because no one knows). We are simply presenting the information available at this time. If nothing else, we can help to clarify any misinformation you may have heard or read.

The consensus among experts is the following:

- Homosexuality is not contagious.
- It is not inherited.
- It is not a choice a boy makes—it is part of his personality.
- There is no test for it.
- It can't be predicted from childhood.
- Psychotherapy probably will not change a homosexual orientation.
- Mothers should not blame themselves if their sons become homosexual—a mother does not cause her son to become homosexual.

Dr. John Money, noted sexologist and professor at Johns Hopkins School of Medicine, writes in the book *Lovemaps* "Homosexuality, like heterosexuality, is not a matter of preference, choice, or voluntary decision. It is a status, like being tall, dwarfed, or left-handed, and is not changed by desire, incentive, willpower, prayer, punishment or other motivation to change."

Why, then, if homosexuality is simply a subset of the norm, does it frighten so many mothers? There is no simple answer to this question. A partial answers lies in the fact that our culture is only beginning to accept homosexuality as normal. In general, mothers don't want their sons to choose a lifestyle that will entail difficulty and pain. And for most mothers, facing the possibility that they will have no grandchildren may also be a keen disappointment.

From another point of view, most mothers are heterosexually oriented and may fear "losing" their sons to a homosexual relationship more than to a heterosexual one because the former is outside their own experience. But perhaps even more painful is guilt engendered by the well-entrenched myth that somehow by doing something "wrong," mothers can cause homosexuality in their sons.

In essence, the myth holds that an overbearing mother (usually in conjunction with an absent or distant father) can lead a boy to become a homosexual man. Dr. June Reinisch, former director of the Kinsey Institute, rejects this notion out of hand. She says in the *Kinsey Institute New Report on Sex*, "Simple explanations (such as having a domineering mother) do not hold true for most homosexuals. Homosexuals and bisexuals come from as many different backgrounds as do heterosexuals."

Again, the plain truth is that no one knows what causes homosexuality. Scientists, psychologists, and sex reseachers are quite divided on what *might* cause a homosexual orientation. Many believe the phenomenon has biological origins; others feel that the roots are psychological. Still others feel the explanation may lie in a combination of both. To date, there is no definitive answer, although much research has been conducted on the subject. To help you sort through the myriad theories and rumors on the origins of homosexuality, we provide an overview of this research. We begin with the studies that have focused on environmental, cultural, or psychological factors.

One significant body of research has centered around the "sissy boy." A sissy or feminine boy is defined as one who has some or all of the following personality attributes: he does not like to participate in rough-and-tumble activities with other boys; he often prefers to play with girls and toys usually associated with girls, such as dolls; he may like to dress as a girl; he may even express an interest in being a girl. These boys are labeled sissy by their peers and other adults—and sometimes by their own fathers—for failing to interact and participate with other boys in their activities.

In one study, researchers Saghir and Robins took histories from a sample of homosexual men and reported that two-thirds of the men indicated that they were considered feminine as young boys, while only 3 percent of heterosexual men in a control group had the same recollection. Studies by others showed similar results.

Another well-known study was conducted over a period of fifteen years by Dr. Richard Green and was reported in his book *The Sissy Boy Syndrome.* Dr. Green monitored two groups of boys: one that had been brought to therapy because their parents were concerned about their feminine behavior, and the other group possessing more accepted "boy" interests—dressing as boys, playing with trucks rather than dolls, and indulging in rough-and-tumble play.

Green's study showed that "feminine" boys are more likely to mature into homosexual or bisexual men than the general population of boys. Two-thirds of his original "feminine boy" group were interviewed after fifteen years: of these subjects, three-quarters were homosexually or bisexually oriented. In contrast, only one boy in the "masculine boy" group reported this orientation.

While Dr. Green's study found that "feminine" boys tended to have a distant relationship with their fathers, he did not find a commonality in their mothers' behavior—the so-called overbearing mother was not a factor. And he concluded not that the distance between father and son might contribute to the son's homosexuality, but rather that this distance was the *effect* of it—the child's feminine behavior drove the father away. None of these boys were close to other boys, and this plus the father-son distance caused what Green calls male-affect starvation. He suggests that the subjects' hunger for relationships with males as boys might have contributed to the desire to have intimate relationships with men as adults. He also concluded that as teenagers, feminine boys might not have been attractive to teenage girls, again causing them to seek homosexual relationships.

It's important to be very clear about what these data mean. They do not mean a boy who is unaggressive and who has a sensitive nature will become homosexual or that boys should be encouraged to be more masculine so they won't grow up to be homosexual. We all know many men who are gentle and/or nurturing—men who don't appear supermacho outwardly and who are clearly heterosexual—just as we know homosexual men who are quite masculine. The data indicate that boys who exhibit feminine behavior have a higher *likelihood* of growing up with a homosexual orientation than boys who do not. But we don't know why this is so—we still don't know what causes this behavior.

As Dr. Green himself concludes in his book *The Sissy Boy Syndrome*,

> By reporting the findings of this study, I could frighten some parents of young boys. The findings are easily misinterpreted. They should not be interpreted to mean that a boy's occasional dressing in girls' or women's clothes, playing with dolls, making believe he is a mommy, playing games with girls, or having no interest in rough-and-tumble play and sports are behavioral problems of childhood and/or harbingers of later atypical sexuality. The behaviors shown by these boys were well beyond the range of cross-gender behaviors shown by many boys, boys who are *not unhappy being male*. Indeed, if the "feminine" boys had been girls, they would have been traditionally feminine girls. Furthermore, the cross-gender behaviors were not found in isolation but together formed a consistent portrait of a cross-sex

identity, a syndrome. And even then, with the pervasive nature of the boys' cross-sex identity, not every one became homosexual or bisexual. For a given "feminine" boy, the answer to the question "Will this boy become gay?" must be, "We don't know."

There is a temptation and danger in translating these and other researchers' findings into advice on how to maximize the prospects of a heterosexual adulthood. The data do not tell us that. There is far too much variability. Even if they did, I would not argue to teach the "lessons" learned. There is far too much variability in the lives of men who also happen to be heterosexual or homosexual.

Dr. Green also found, and most researchers agree, that the intervention of therapy is unlikely to change a boy's orientation from homosexual to heterosexual. Still, there are those who think otherwise. Dr. John Money relates that in his own practice he noted that some fathers may actually subconsciously encourage their sons' feminine behavior to compensate in some way for something lacking in their relationships with their wives. Money feels that if a child in this type of situation can be relieved of the burden of filling the father's need, then his desire to be of a different gender orientation may disappear.

An article in *Parents* magazine supports this idea. It describes an actual case in which a four-year-old girl insisted that she was a boy and even crafted herself a clay penis, which she placed inside her pants. After attending family counseling sessions, the parents learned that because they were fighting so much, and the father appeared so much stronger and tougher than the mother, the little girl was afraid to be a girl and weak. As the parents resolved their differences over time and the fighting lessened in the home, the child became less resistant to being a girl, although she still acted tomboyish in some ways. A boy might respond to the same home situation in a different way—by identifying with the less frightening person, the mother. In the particular case of this little girl, therapy did bring about a change.

Sexual identity becomes "imprinted" on a child within the first few years of life. Dr. Irving Bieber found that homosexual men were often strongly attached to their mothers in childhood (as are most children), but he concluded that this was the result of poor relationships with their fathers, rather than overbearing mothers.

Many psychoanalysts believe that in order for a boy to acquire a masculine-gender identity he must "disidentify" from his mother so he is able to identify with his father. It has been postulated that a boy's inability to do this for whatever reason could cause him to continue to identify with the feminine gender. And once that gender is "imprinted," the child is unlikely to change. Even if this were true, the problem would not be that the mother was acting in an overbearing manner, but rather that the son was unable to separate from her. Theoretically, then, intervention therapy at a very young age—two or three—might change the course of gender identity. But it is unlikely that most parents would recognize the need to provide counseling for a child so young. And later, therapy would be of use only if the child were uncomfortable or unhappy with his gender identity, and in any case, would be unlikely to change this identity.

By the way, many psychologists believe that therapy might prove more beneficial to *parents* disturbed by their son's behavior, to help them to accept it. But unfortunately, many mothers of homosexual sons fail to seek therapy because they wish somehow to deny that their sons differ from their expectations of them.

Other mitigating circumstances might cause a boy to exhibit feminine behavior. For example, the birth of a sister might make him desire the same attention the new baby is getting. If the parents don't pick up on this cause of their son's behavior, psychotherapy could help to solve the mystery.

It bears repeating that we do not equate feminine behavior in boys with homosexual orientation. This distinction is relevant only within the context of the sissy boy studies, which seem to indicate that boys who exhibit *extreme* feminine behavior have a higher-than-average likelihood of being homosexual or bisexual.

As mentioned earlier, some scientists believe that homosexual behavior may have a biological explanation. Here is a brief overview of some of the most significant research in that area:

(1) As reported in the book *Male Homosexuality* by Dr. Richard C. Friedman, one group of researchers believed that homosexual men had depressed testosterone levels compared with those of heterosexual men. The results of their research failed to yield any proof that this was true.

(2) Other scientists felt that homosexuality might be caused by neuroendocrine influences. Promising research has suggested boys' and girls' brains develop somewhat differently owing to differing levels of sex hormones. These investigators postulated that a deficit of

androgens (male hormones) during the prenatal period of a boy's development might affect his brain development, therefore causing him to become homosexual rather than heterosexual as an adult. This theory was tested both in rats and by studying a group of boys. The studies showed only "possible neuroendocrine influence on homosexuality" in some subgroups (this study has the flaw of having only included boys who had an unusual physical problem.) Even *this* conclusion is based on very limited data.

(3) Related to research on the sissy boy syndrome, another study looked at the possibility that undue stress during pregnancy could limit "prenatal androgenization" of a baby boy, causing him to become homosexual. The results of this research were not definitive.

(4) Recently a controversial study was conducted by Simon LeVay of the prestigious Salk Institute in La Jolla, California. LeVay scanned the brains of forty-one cadavers including nineteen known homosexual males and determined that the area of the brain which controls sexual activity was half the size of that found in male heterosexuals. Critics point out there are a number of flaws with this study. First, the sample size is probably too small to have statistical significance. Second, there is no way of knowing whether the brains were like this from birth or whether this area got smaller later in life. All of the homosexual men whose brains were scanned had died of AIDS, which might also have been a contributing factor; some scientists believe the brain can change in response to experiences. Last, some of the other males whose brains were scanned might have also been homosexual, because their sexual orientation was unknown and only presumed to be heterosexual.

(5) Another recent piece of research was put forth by psychologist Michael Bailey and researcher Richard Pillard of the Boston University School of Medicine. By studying identical twins, they found that if one twin is gay, the other twin is three times more likely to be gay than the general population, a finding they say does not apply to fraternal twins, who did not start life from the same fertilized egg. Critics of this study suggest this higher rate of homosexuality might just as likely be from having been raised in the same environment as from a biological origin.

Clearly, neither biologists nor psychologists have proved any cause of homosexuality. As mothers, we can't worry about doing the right or wrong thing, because there is no known wrong thing to do. Some experts advise mothers not to keep their sons from doing what other boys do, since this might make them an outsider. No other useful advice is forthcoming.

Wardell A. Pomeroy, author of *Boys and Sex,* says, "The best way to foster heterosexual development is to understand that homosexuality is not completely separated from heterosexuality. Many boys have homosexual experiences . . . we are all capable of every act imaginable. Parents would do better to admit it exists and talk about it quietly, objectively, thoughtfully, and factually to their children."

If your son does have a homosexual orientation as he grows older, Pomeroy adds, "In any case, it's important to learn to love, no matter what the sex of the loved one may be, since this is a great deal of what life is all about, so those who happen to love someone of the same sex are having the same kind of necessary experience as those who love in the conventional way."

Transvestism and Transsexualism

When most of us hear the term *transvestite* (someone who dresses in the clothing of the opposite sex), we immediately conjure up images of female impersonators wearing wigs, heavy makeup, and padded breasts who appear to be larger-than-life Barbra Streisands and Carol Channings. While most transvestites are male, the majority of them are ordinary in every way, except that they have a predilection for dressing in women's clothes (commonly called *cross-dressing*).

For reasons that are not clear, some boys experience an erotic response to women's clothing. It could be related to having a close relationship with a mother or sister or some positive feeling about a female. Whatever the reason, when these boys become adults, they can have the urge to dress as women from time to time. Although this may seem like an extraordinary and decidedly unmasculine interest, the fact is that most of these men are heterosexual and lead quite conventional lives as husbands and fathers, apart from their desire to dress as women. While they do not usually do this openly in front of friends and family, the practice is common enough that there are organizations and magazines for cross-dressed men. The mother of a man who becomes a transvestite may or may not have found her son dressed as a girl when he was still a boy.

If you find your son dressed as a girl, stay calm; this behavior does not necessarily mean something is wrong with him. Children like to explore other roles when they're young and this may simply be all you are seeing. If the behavior persists, you would be wise to seek therapy, primarily to make you feel more comfortable with your son's behavior, which you may not be able to stop. You can't change who your son is, but if you try to stop him from doing something he feels compelled to do, you will make him feel guilty and ashamed. Above all, love your child for who he is, even if he deviates from your expectations of him.

Transsexualism, while often confused with transvestism, is a far more serious gender-identity problem, and one that is most likely to appear first in childhood. A person who is truly transsexual believes that he or she is really of the sex that is opposite from their body—they feel trapped inside the wrong body.

Perhaps you remember hearing years ago about Christine Jorgensen, an American male who went to Denmark in 1952 to have his penis surgically removed because he felt that he was really a woman. That was the first time this now relatively well-known surgery was ever performed. More recently, Dr. Renee Richards, a respected physician, was in the news because she was barred from participating in a women's tennis championship. When it was learned that she had previously been a man before having a sex-change operation, the officials concluded she had an unfair advantage in playing women's tennis.

Actually, the number of transsexuals is really quite small. And no one knows what causes a child to believe he or she is really a member of the opposite sex; there might have been some "mistake" of nature when a baby was developing, but this has yet to be proved. Most transsexuals are male with normal genitalia and chromosomes, and it is unlikely that more than one child in a family will have this gender disorder. Studies have shown that fathers of these boys are usually absent or emotionally uninterested in their sons, but whether this is the cause or an effect of the child's behavior has not been determined.

Little boys who are truly transsexual will often prefer to sit when urinating and will express the conviction that they are girls even though they know they look like boys. They may also state that they want their bodies to be female. As adults, some transsexuals actually do go through sex-change operations, although the great expense and the physical trauma of the surgery deter many.

If your son seems to believe he would rather be a girl, you should seek professional help. Boys who are true transsexuals may need help in dealing with their confusing feelings. In some cases, they may decide through therapy to give up their ideas of being the wrong sex and may learn to be comfortable with their own sex. If they cannot do this, then therapy will help them deal with their feelings and decide how to live with this problem. Their parents will doubtless need help in dealing with the situation as well.

Therapy probably will not alter a boy's gender belief if he is truly transsexual, but other factors could be causing a child to "act out" an opposite-sex role, as we mentioned before.

We've provided you with the most up-to-date information on nontraditional sexual orientation. Most worrisome to mothers is the possibility that their sons could grow up to be homosexual and that somehow their mothering contributed to their sons' sexual choice. We hope, through the overview we have presented, that we have put mothers' minds at ease; there is absolutely no reason to believe that homosexuality is caused by improper mothering, and no one even knows yet if its origins are biological or psychological.

The best advice we can give you is to love your sons unconditionally—if their sexual choice is for other males, this is only a small part of their makeup and does not totally define who they are. The greatest gift you can give your son is simply to love him and to let him know that nothing can get in the way of that love.

10

Rough-&-Tumble: Horseplay, Sports, & Aggression

"After spending twenty-five years as a pediatrician, I can sum up the difference between boys and girls in six words," says Dr. Stephen Boris. "Girls cry and boys break bones!" While this might seem like an oversimplification, it's actually not far from the truth—at least the part about boys.

From the time they are very young, most boys tend to get involved in what behaviorists call "rough-and-tumble" play.

"My son is more daring than my daughter and makes me nervous that he will hurt himself seriously!" wrote Jenifer.

"I try not to say 'Don't do this, don't do that, it's too dangerous,'" said respondent Marlene, "because I don't want to make my son afraid of everything. But when I see him climbing up a concrete wall or jumping down a flight of stairs, it's hard not to panic!"

Why is rough-and-tumble play more common among little boys than little girls? There is no simple answer to this question. Myriam Miedzian, author of *Boys Will Be Boys*, points out that boys are often overstimulated from birth. Studies suggest that mothers are more likely to encourage a baby boy's large motor movements than a baby girl's and that parents handle male babies more roughly than girl babies. We also know that fathers toss infant sons up into the air more frequently than daughters and that this sex-typed behavior continues as children get older and fathers engage in activities such as wrestling and roughhousing with only their sons.

One of our discussion-group attendees smiled knowingly when we introduced this subject. She had recently spent an evening with her husband and young son at the home of friends who had a three-year-old daughter. Shana told us that while at her friend's house, her husband was playing with her son. He held him upside down by his feet, which was a game the two often enjoyed at home. The little girl watched them and then asked to have the same done to her. Shana's husband obliged. At just that moment the girl's father entered the room and viewed his daughter dangling by her feet with obvious trepidation. "Be careful you don't drop her," he said briskly, and it was clear he felt this was not the suitable way to handle his little girl. The little girl, after being returned to an upright position, looked up at Shana's husband with obvious delight derived from this unfamiliar physical encounter and said, "Can I go home with you?"

Is this rough-and-tumble play by young boys simply a function of how they are handled by their parents, or is there some genetic trait in boys that makes them more open to this behavior? Psychologists and researchers have debated the "nature versus nurture" argument for years. There is still no definitive answer to this question, but the majority of experts seem to agree that boys are generally more active and display rougher behavior than young girls and that this results from a combination of predisposition at birth and their environment.

Most research studies have concluded that young boys are more active than girls. Almost all of the mothers we talked to found their sons interested in rough-and-tumble play from the time they were two or three years old. The following is only a sampling of what we heard:

> "My son was a monster when I would take him places—he was so 'hyper' and into everything!"

> "He almost walked before he learned how to sit because he was so anxious to move!"

> "All four of my children skied, but only the two boys got hurt. They just weren't cautious."

> "Boys are so much more adventurous than girls—they get into more physical trouble."

*"From the beginning they needed a lot more physical atten-
tion than my girls . . . it seemed like we were always taking
them to the emergency room."*

"They have so much energy . . . "

Boys engage in rough-and-tumble behavior for a variety of
reasons; as strange as it might seem, it is actually a method
they employ to build friendships with other boys. In a sense,
it is a form of communication at an early age when boys are
not verbally adept. In fact, some child behavior specialists feel
it also helps boys build self-confidence. Similarly, they use this
same form of play as a way to relate to their fathers and other
men, learning how to handle themselves by the way men interact with them. For example, they understand when it is appropriate to call "time out" and "time to stop" by following their
fathers' rules.

Mothers often have a hard time watching all this roughhousing because either they simply don't see the point of it or they
are afraid their sons will get injured. Some get really annoyed
with their spouses, who often initiate rough-and-tumble play.
Frankly, we don't see any negative side to this unless it becomes overly aggressive and one of the participants becomes
frightened or is in danger of being hurt. In fact, if for any reason
a boy's father is not consistently in his life or is not around at
all, we think a mother should encourage this kind of interaction
with other males she knows and trusts, such as family members or friends. Bridgette Peterson, writing on this subject in
Smart Kids magazine, offers some guidelines for adult/child
rough-and-tumble play you might wish to pass on to your son's
father (or to use yourself if you share rough-and-tumble play
with your son):

(1) Know when to stop. Your child will learn this ability
     from you.

(2) Never use roughhousing to break a child's spirit by
     being too rough or too overpowering. Let a kid win some-
     times.

(3) Don't continue when the laughter stops.

(4) Set the example for roughhousing without hurting.

(5) Don't roughhouse in inappropriate places and then ex-
     pect your child to know better.

(6) Avoid critical or sensitive areas of the anatomy like eyes
     and "below the belt," and teach your child the same.

If your husband is not interested in rough-and-tumble play and your son is, he may seek it with other family members such as an uncle or older brother. You needn't feel that you have to provide your son with this experience unless you are comfortable doing so. You can't compensate for your son's father—you can only be his mother. By trying to be a replacement for your husband, you become the too good mother we discussed in Chapter Five.

Where to Draw the Line
Presumably adult males will know how to set limits for rough-and-tumble play, but when two young boys are involved, it's harder for a mother to make a judgment call. If you're not certain when to "break it up" between your son and another boy, consider the following:

(1)   Do the boys seem to be having fun, or is this clearly an act of aggression? Does one or both seem visibly upset?

(2)   Is one boy much heavier or bigger than the other, giving him an unfair advantage?

(3)   Are they roughhousing in a safe location (on the grass or on a carpet), or is someone likely to hit his head accidentally and get hurt?

(4)   Are the boys just roughhousing or are they hitting and punching?

(5)   How well do you know the other boy and his personality? If you don't know him well, you won't have a good idea if he might actually try to harm your son.

One mother described to us the first time she came across her five-year-old son wrestling with his friend in his bedroom. Although they seemed to just be playing, she wasn't certain if their wrestling was completely innocent. Rather than force the boys to stop what was potentially a healthy interaction, she told them if they wanted to wrestle they had to do it the "right way." She had them shake hands and then "start wrestling when the bell rang." Whenever their clinches got too intense for her comfort level, she "rang the time-out bell" and sent them for a cooling-off period. The boys were very happy with the game and she felt in control—a good situation for all of them.

No Pain, No Gain
A more difficult assessment for a mother to make is when her son's impulsive or daring behavior may put him at risk of bodily harm—the dilemma may start as early as the toddler years. "My daughter tried to climb out of the crib *once*," Anna told us. "My son tried and succeeded *over and over again*." This mother was smart enough to realize she couldn't keep her son from continuing his bid for freedom, so she put pillows on the floor beneath his crib to cushion his daily tumble.

Climbing to the top of the jungle gym, going down the hill on a sled, or jumping from the top of the stairs is a more frightening example than a toddler climbing out of his crib. Yet just as the toddler's mother learned she couldn't stop her son, so must all mothers of little boys learn that boys need to do what they do.

All children have to take risks in order to develop self-confidence. They learn by their failures (and injuries) as well as from their successes. While it may be difficult for them to let their children be exposed to potential injury, mothers often have to contend with the realization that boys are more likely to put themselves in danger than girls.

Thus we constantly have to balance the need to protect our sons against allowing them the freedom to explore the world in their own way. Young boys tend to connect emotionally through physical activity. If a mother holds her son back from experiencing childhood the way that other boys do, she may be setting him apart from his peers, ultimately isolating him from boys his own age and causing a socialization problem for him that may not be easily remedied.

Of course, there are some activities boys attempt that simply defy common sense and should be prohibited. For example, you shouldn't allow your son to ride his bicycle without his hands on the handlebars or to go bungee jumping. Being a good mother means using your own judgment as to when to let your son take some risks that are appropriate for his age, developmental stage, size, and physical capabilities. You should not attempt to protect him from all potential risk. You might have to "hold your breath," keep your fingers crossed, and let him experience some independence and control over his own body.

Author Nick Gallo, writing in *Child* magazine, points out that anxieties about our children taking physical risks may be a result of our own childhood experiences. Charlotte told us that at age fifteen she was baby-sitting her young brother when the plate glass in a storm door fell out and broke over his head. With her brother bleeding profusely, she ran for her neighbor to drive them to the emergency room, where her little brother received a large number of stitches. This memory is never far from her mind when she watches her own small son at play. She admitted that it might color her ability to let him take physical risks.

Gallo also points out that some kids are "wilder" and "more reckless" than others, and this may be a genetic personality trait. Labeled as "Big T" kids (thrill seekers) by Frank Farley, a psychologist at the University of Wisconsin, these kids exhibit high energy levels and an independent streak at an early age, and enthusiastically pursue physical challenges. If these tendencies are suppressed by parents, a boy with this type of personality may find less acceptable outlets for his energy when he gets older, such as drugs, alcohol, or delinquent behavior. This personality trait is not necessarily a cause for alarm; if you suspect your son fits this description, you can help him use his energy level positively by finding an appropriate outlet for his energy—sports, hobbies, computers, karate, even video games.

Boys Who Avoid Playing Rough
Not all boys behave in the manner we have just described. Some boys prefer not to be involved in a lot of physical activity. They may be uninterested in rough-and-tumble play and unwilling to take physical risks. Should a mother be concerned? The answer is probably no.

If your son generally seems to be content being a boy, but just doesn't care for the physicality so many little boys thrive on, you needn't worry. Each child is born with his own distinct personality, and the predisposition for physical activity that boys are believed to be born with is at best only a possibility, not a probability. While his reticence to engage in this type of play may be part of your son's genetic makeup (even shyness is an inherited trait), remember too that a good deal of a young boy's behavior is learned from his environment. If his father does not promote or participate in rough-and-tumble play, but instead spends his time with his son pursuing calmer activities like drawing or visiting museums, his son may take these cues for his behavior from his father. As you can see that your husband has successfully negotiated the road to manhood, this should alleviate your fears about your son. You and your husband may want to get involved in whatever interests your son develops on his own. Although it isn't absolutely necessary to do so, it is important not to suppress any of his interests.

We add one caveat here: if your son seems **excessively** passive, you should consider getting a professional evaluation. By this we mean a child who doesn't wish to participate in any type of activity or be involved with other children at all. Or a boy who is interested in being only with girls and wants nothing to do with other boys at all. There might be some underlying causes for his lack of interest in participating in the world around him that go beyond his own personality. They could be the result of an unhappy family situation, difficulties in school, or other problems he is experiencing which you might not even know about.

While some fathers may lead their sons away from rough-and-tumble play, others may encourage it at all costs. Many fathers worry that their sons will be regarded as sissies or wimps and will try to push their sons into activities which they consider masculine whether the boys show an interest or not. Their sons may react in one of several ways: either these little boys will do what their fathers want and yet are clearly unhappy about it, or they will refuse to participate altogether. A third possibility is that boys will overcompensate and will work to excel at the activity to make their dads proud of them.

Any of these reactions is unhealthy, as they all will result in anger toward the father, conscious or not. In fact, the anger may not surface until many years later. The boys may also be angry at their mothers for not rescuing them from this plight. Some fathers may begin to withdraw from their sons should they refuse to participate in sports or other such activities and become disappointed because their sons are not acting more "manly." It is very important to address this issue should it arise between father and son. If you can resolve it by talking frankly to your husband, both your son and your husband will benefit, but if you can't you should consider some professional counseling for your son, your husband, and yourself.

Psychologists suggest that men who react this way are actually dealing with their own latent fear of homosexuality, which manifests itself as the worry that their sons might not be "real boys." They believe their sons are seen by others as a reflection of themselves. Mothers are less likely to be concerned about this so-called masculine behavior because they don't have the same expectations for sons as fathers do.

Psychologists overwhelmingly agree that a boy should not be forced into taking risks and participating in rough-and-tumble play if he is not interested—this can only result in emotional damage. A mother should try to encourage a boy to experience a variety of activities but not insist that he must participate in any. The real problem that can arise from a boy's choice not to participate in certain activities is not what it says about him, but how his peers will perceive him; he may have trouble making friends or be labeled a sissy.

To some extent, children have to learn to negotiate this social crisis on their own. There are possible solutions you can explore to make it easier for your son if he finds himself in this sort of situation. You can help build his self-esteem by praising him for the things at which he does excel. Encourage him to continue with them and look for others with which he is comfortable. If you enroll him in after-school classes for activities he is interested in, he may meet boys with similar interests. Try to find some common ground for your son with other boys you know—while he might not like to climb trees or skateboard with the boys in your neighborhood, they might all enjoy a trip to the miniature golf range as your treat. If the boys get to know your son in a different setting, they may find they share interests with him. If you have friends with sons close in age to your own, discuss your concerns with them—they may be able to suggest areas in which their boys can relate to your son. Above all, accept your son—whether he prefers to play rough or read quietly.

Boys and Aggression
It is not only rough-and-tumble play that characterizes boy behavior as different from girl behavior. Boys tend to hit more, kick more, insult each other more, and in general act more aggressively, even by preschool age. By age three, girls will ignore aggressive approaches from boys, while other boys will respond with physical interaction. By this age, boys are also more likely than girls to play in groups; this causes a domino effect: if one or two of the boys get excited, the whole group can get out of control. By age five, boys begin to wrestle, punch, and shout at one another.

Before we continue the discussion of this subject, we would like to be clear about the definition of aggression. We are not speaking of the word "aggression" in the sense it is widely used today when referring to an individual who pursues things he wants. For our purposes in this book, we define aggression as taking physical action intended to hurt another person.

As when they discuss rough-and-tumble play, the nature versus nurture controversy is also heard among behavioral experts regarding aggression in the male gender. Many behaviorists believe that boys are inherently more aggressive than girls due to their biological makeup. Some of this belief is based on research which shows that little girls who receive what amounts to an "overdose" of male hormones prenatally are more likely to become tomboys than other girls. Most other studies regarding testosterone's role in aggression in males have been carried out on animal subjects. Critics point out that the conclusions drawn from these studies are not valid or transferable to human males. Boys with higher testosterone levels tend to be more frustrated, impatient, and irritable, and these traits can lead to aggression. While it is known that males with excessive testosterone levels are likely to be more aggressive, it is uncertain why this is so. In boys with normal levels of testosterone the role of hormones is less clear-cut.

No one disputes the fact that regardless of whether a disposition for aggression exists, boys in most cultures do act more aggressive than girls. It is also clear that aggression is learned by boys from their families, their peers, television, movies, and other media. If there is a genetic predisposition for aggression, it seems it is only a contributing factor to a behavior that is largely taught to boys.

Children learn to be aggressive very young, partly because they haven't fully developed their verbal skills yet, so grabbing, pushing, and hitting often seem to accomplish their goals of getting what they want. By school age, girls have significantly decreased this kind of behavior, while in boys it can continue to escalate. Studies have shown that boys tend to have more aggressive fantasies than girls, are more likely to retaliate against aggressive behavior (which only serves as a negative reinforcement), and are more interested in dominating their peers than girls are. The greater their level of aggression, the more successful they are at dominating other boys.

As a society, we are more willing to allow boys to be aggressive. When two boys get into a fight, we shrug our shoulders and say, "That's boys for you . . . ", whereas if we see two girls get into a fistfight, we are genuinely surprised, if not critical. Most of us have observed parents who are actually proud when their sons engage in fisticuffs and feel it proves they have the "right stuff." If a girl tied up another child because they were "just playing," we'd probably tell her to stop, but when boys do it we think they are using their imaginations. One mother even pointed out to us that in her family she noticed that when her daughter wanted to be daring on playground equipment, she and her husband worried, but when their son did it, they considered it something "a boy had to do."

Another mother told us she was quite disturbed to have her five-year-old son bring home a note from his teacher, informing her he had been choking another boy. The note said, "Please tell Charlie that this is not a time for wrestling, but time to be paying attention to the teacher." The fact that her son had his hands around another boy's throat was not deemed of sufficient importance by the teacher for her to make a phone call to give this distressing news to the mother. In all likelihood, the teacher had seen so much aggression in young boys in her class that she treated it routinely. This attitude serves as a form of reinforcement to boys; it teaches them that when they act aggressive, it is accepted.

By now you are probably asking how you can prevent your son from being aggressive or, for that matter, if you should try to prevent it or accept it as part of his maleness. The answer is that you can't prevent it entirely but you can take steps to contain it and reinforce other, less aggressive behavior. Suzanne R. Sunday, a researcher at Cornell University Medical College, states in the book *Genes and Gender IV: On Peace, War and Gender* that "while aggression may be affected by biological factors, it is not biologically determined. Aggression is neither inevitable nor uncontrollable in human or subhuman species . . . at best the hormonal, genetic and sociobiological data indicate there is no simple relationship between biology and aggression among human beings." Sunday was one of a group of biologists who issued the "Seville Statement on Violence." This statement said that except for rare pathologies, males who might have a predisposition for aggression are still subject to nurturance and these two factors together are what determines their personalities. It seems obvious to us that finding alternative methods to physical expression of anger will be beneficial to your own son and to other mothers' sons. Boys who don't learn to temper their aggression may become bullies or, as adults, get into real trouble.

The first step toward limiting aggressive behavior is to examine what your son is learning at home. Studies show that boys who exhibit antisocial aggressive behavior were often encouraged by their fathers to be aggressive toward their peers and received reinforcement for "combative attitudes" and behavior. (The immediate family is not the only influence on a young boy—the more aggressive male models he is surrounded by, the more aggressive he may become. For example, if a boy grows up in a tough neighborhood, he may imitate the same behavior he sees all around him.)

Try to avoid hitting or spanking your son—you will only be reinforcing the message that physical violence is acceptable behavior. In fact, most parents who do spank find it is not a very effective form of punishment anyway; it doesn't keep kids from repeating the behavior for which they were paddled. An approach that is more likely to be successful is to maintain an open line of communication with your child; tell him when you are angry with him, explain what he has done wrong, and give him a suitable punishment for the crime. This might result in the loss of television privileges or the use of a favorite toy or game, depending on his age. If you show him that you are able to talk about what makes you angry (rather than respond physically), you teach him by example to do the same. You should also make it clear that you want your son to let you know when *he* is angry or upset. (We'll explore discipline at length in Chapter Twelve.)

Another mistake we often make with boys is telling them that "big boys don't cry." This admonishment will only cause a boy to bottle up his feelings and can lead to aggression. We're not suggesting you let your son constantly whine or that you respond to tears he turns on to get his own way. But if your son falls and gets a scrape or has his feelings hurt, allow him to cry and be soothed—we are all entitled to cry when we get hurt, whatever our age or sex. Crying it out is certainly preferable to punching it out!

If your son seems to need a physical outlet to relieve his aggression, find an acceptable one for him and let him know it's specifically for that use. You might consider a punching bag, a pillow he's allowed to throw around, or something of your own invention.

In Chapter Eleven we will discuss how violent television, movies, and videos as well as realistic "war toys" can contribute to aggression and violence in boys. For now, let us just say that we believe that mothers need to limit their sons' exposure to these influences. Telling your son how you feel about violence will help to balance some of the violent and aggressive messages he is bound to receive. You can also discuss with him nonviolent solutions to social problems, thereby emphasizing that there are other, more acceptable behaviors and resolutions.

Although we feel that aggression in young boys should be kept to a minimum and channeled into acceptable outlets such as sports, computers, the arts, etc., we need to point out that tempering aggression does not mean teaching your son not to defend himself when necessary. It is unfortunate, but in today's world there are times we all need to defend ourselves in one way or another, so we cannot teach our sons not to do so. By giving a boy suggestions for nonviolent ways to deal with social problems, we can at least have the hope that the aggressive behavior our sons use in self-defense will be kept to a minimum.

Myriam Miedzian offers hope that we can teach our sons to conduct their lives this way: "The fact that a majority of men lead essentially non-violent lives in spite of living in a society that applauds the values of the masculine mystique, testifies to the lack of any intense inclination towards violent behavior on their part."

The Overly Aggressive Child

Up until this point we have been discussing a general tendency for aggressiveness found in boys which can be controlled with proper guidance. We now turn to a discussion of a more serious problem—the boy who has a greater-than-normal level of aggression. As we mentioned previously, this might be caused by a high testosterone level or other physical conditions such as a head injury, some forms of epilepsy, mental retardation, Attention Deficit Disorder with Hyperactivity (ADDH), and other learning disabilities. (Please see Appendix for more information.)

An overly aggressive boy may also be reacting to emotional distress, to an abusive parent, or to a parent who is cold or distant. A boy who is given too much responsibility, as when a newly divorced mother relies on him to be the man in the family, can also exhibit aggressive tendencies.

An overly aggressive boy is characterized by his demonstrating aggression at times that seem inappropriate and often in a manner which is self-defeating, according to Lawrence Kutner, Ph.D., author of *Parent & Child.* The problem often appears to be inborn, as many of these children are restless as babies, have trouble sitting still, are impulsive and easily distracted. Kutner makes several suggestions for dealing with this behavior.

Parents should try to determine patterns which trigger these assaults and remove the child from these situations before an incident takes place. Kutner notes that a child with these tendencies requires structure in his life and a daily routine. When a child is older, Kutner feels that classes in assertiveness training might be useful; this is to teach a boy a more acceptable method for channeling aggression than physical violence.

Aggression may also interfere with school performance and social interaction. If a boy is overly aggressive, he may have trouble making friends. Even if the friends don't complain, their mothers may not allow them to play with him. Failure at school and/or socially can make a child even more aggressive, and an escalating cycle is created.

Childhood aggression is a predictor of adolescent aggression and Conduct Disorder, a psychological diagnosis made when a boy begins stealing, committing arson, running away from home, and exhibiting other delinquent behavior. While only a small percentage of boys have this disorder, the signs usually appear at a young age and will become magnified during adolescence, so they should not be ignored. If you believe your son has overly aggressive tendencies, we suggest you seek professional help immediately; treatment by a mental-health professional may be crucial if he is to grow up to be a happy and productive adult.

Boys and Sports

One way to direct a boy's high energy level and aggressive tendencies is to get him involved in sports. Sports participation can play an important and beneficial role in most boys' lives, but it can be problematical as well. It raises conflicting issues such as the risk of injury versus the health benefits, and the positive psychological impact versus the potential negative effects. We'd like to explore some of these aspects now to give you a complete picture of how sports participation can affect your son's life.

Benefits of Sports

In general, American children are not as fit as they should be. One study indicates that 33 percent of all boys ages six to twelve cannot run a mile at a rate faster than a walking speed. Dr. Kenneth Cooper, author of *Kid Fitness*, reports that 40 percent of children ages five to eight have at least one heart-disease risk factor—physical inactivity, obesity, elevated cholesterol, or high blood pressure—and that the overuse of television and video games as primary activities of leisure for children is a major contributing factor.

Without question, being physically fit is essential for your son's immediate and future health. Dr. Cooper recommends that children should have at least three thirty-minute exercise workouts per week at an endurance activity like running or bicycling. Exercise helps to strengthen muscles and flexibility, promote lean body mass rather than fat, and improve the cardiovascular system. It is up to you to see that your son gets some form of exercise when he is younger. You can expose him to a variety of activities, and as he grows he will lean toward those he enjoys most or at which he is the most skillful.

There are also tremendous emotional benefits for boys who are involved in sports. In particular, team sports help a boy build character, teach him how to be a team player, and give him an opportunity to bond with other boys while at the same time providing a valuable learning experience. If a boy performs well at a sports activity, this will also help build his self-esteem.

What's the Downside?

Sounds good so far, doesn't it? But there are some less favorable aspects to sports that must also be considered when guiding your son into participation. For example, a boy who is not good at a particular game but is pushed into it by one or both parents may be embarrassed and unhappy. One mother told us she had always wanted to play in Little League, and during her youth girls were not accepted. She encouraged her son to play baseball almost from the time he was big enough to hold a ball, but he didn't play very well when he got to Little League and he was miserable. She finally had to recognize that it just wasn't the game for him. He decided he would prefer soccer, at which he has excelled.

There can be other problems as well. Somewhere along the line, your son may have a coach who teaches him to win at all costs instead of teaching him the rules of fair play. While a physically fit boy will tend to perform better in school, one who gets too involved with sports may neglect his schoolwork. Last, but certainly at the top of a mother's list of concerns, is the possibility of injury.

Will He Get Hurt?

Perhaps the greatest fear mothers have regarding their sons and athletics is the chance that their sons may get hurt. This concern is not totally unfounded. Although on the one hand young children's bones are far more flexible than adults', they are still prone to injuries. From ages six to eight, when children are beginning to get really active in sports, they still have what is known as open growth plates. This means that the cartilage at the ends of the large bones is still soft and more vulnerable to fracture. Although only 6 to 8 percent of children involved in sports suffer fractures, these are the age periods they are most likely to experience them. By the time they reach the ages of nine to eleven, the bones have begun to mature, but the soft tissue is not fully developed, making boys prone to knee injuries.

The most common injury a boy may sustain is a contusion (or bruise). Sprains (a tear in a ligament) and strains (a tear in a muscle) follow next in order of frequency of occurrence. There are also several common types of injuries boys experience that arc specifically sports-related, but none of them are considered serious health threats. Primarily, the treatment for the conditions we are about to describe consists of resting the injured body part, taking aspirin, and doing stretching exercises.

Osgood-Schlatter disease is a below-the-knee injury linked to overuse or repeated pulling of the thigh muscle. A similar condition is Sever's disease, which appears as a pain in one or both heel bones and usually occurs between the ages of seven and fourteen. Pain on the inner side of the elbow is often referred to as "Little League elbow" because it was first diagnosed in Little League pitchers, but it can be caused by other sports movements as well. Some boys will suffer broken bones and more serious injuries, but the incidence for most sports injuries is relatively low.

To minimize your son's risk for injury there are a number of safeguards you can employ. Most important is to make certain that any sports activity your son plans to start is appropriate for his age, weight, and skill level. You need to do your homework about the specific sport to decide which one is best for your son. For example, young boys probably should not be playing contact sports much before the age of eight.

> **R.I.C.E.=Rest—Ice— Compression— Elevation to treat injuries**
>
> **(1)** rest injured area
>
> **(2)** apply ice (but not directly to skin) for about twenty minutes
>
> **(3)** wrap injured area in an elastic bandage
>
> **(4)** elevate injured area to reduce swelling
>
> **If a limb looks oddly shaped, swelling is over a bone, or a child can't walk the next day, see a doctor.**

Within the same age group, different rules for organized sports may apply in different parts of the country. As Lee Schreiber, author of *Parents' Guide to Kids' Sports*, points out, "Hockey America has recently introduced nationwide rules prohibiting the use of body checking in hockey until the peewee level which is for kids ages twelve to thirteen. However, there is still body contact when kids crash into each other by mistake." In the Pop Warner football league, seven-year-olds play tackle in full gear, but in your neighborhood league this might not be the case. Kids' leagues often don't agree with the belief held by many pediatricians and sports experts that children should not play regulation games on full-size fields until they are at least nine or ten years old. Before they reach that stage they should be playing a modified game, and unless you check out your local rules you can't make an informed decision as to whether or not to let your son play.

The fact is most kids don't have the physical or emotional maturity to be real athletes before puberty when their bodies begin to gain strength. Until that point boys should be playing for fun, not by adult rules, which may put them in jeopardy.

Before your child gets started in any strenuous sport or physical activity, it's a good idea for him to have a complete physical. You might mention to your pediatrician what your son's plans are and get his opinion on whether this is an age-appropriate activity. There are some medical conditions that might preclude a child from joining up for certain activities, although it is likely you would already be aware of this limitation. Some conditions, like asthma, wouldn't necessarily prevent a boy from any form of recreation, but proper medical management should be discussed with your doctor.

Injuries can also be minimized if your son learns to stretch, warm up, and cool down as a part of his athletic program. You can ask your son's coach or sports instructor if he or she routinely includes time for a warm-up and a cool-down. You might ask if boys are matched by age or by size, with the latter being the correct method. Also, check to see that the boys play on a clean surface free of obstructions. Proper shoe fit and the wearing of well-fitting protective clothing appropriate to the sport are also key to preventing injuries. (Please see our chart on pages 130–131 for more specific information regarding the appropriate gear for specific sports.)

Organized Team Sports
Before the age of eight, boys are not ready to participate in competitive team sports, either physically or emotionally, and even at that age they may still have some difficulty with losing. Problems may surface again around age ten to thirteen, when boys hit puberty and begin to feel awkward about their size and changing bodies.

Participation in organized sports can be an effective method for teaching boys how to be team players and how to win or lose without reacting to either out of proportion. However, these benefits can be derived only if boys are coached properly. A coach can make all the difference as to whether the experience your son has in team sports is a positive one.

A good coach will help boys build self-esteem and see that they have fun. He will promote cooperating as a team, with individual members supporting one another and working for the common good. His role is to get kids to play the best that they can, but not to teach them to "go out and knock 'em dead." If he is overly critical of a boy's performance or puts too much pressure on a boy to perform, he may discourage him from continuing to play and can lower his self-esteem.

Neither should the coach favor the better players. Parents should expect to have all team members get a fair chance at playing. Although not everyone can be on the first string, if a boy sits on the bench all the time, he may stop participating in sports altogether, and he will certainly not be getting the experience that team sports is supposed to be offering.

Teaching the fundamentals of good sportsmanship is also part of the coach's job description; boys should be taught to shake hands when they lose and not to make fun of other boys or call them names. Above all, a coach should never teach his team to cheat or use dirty tricks.

You can probably get a pretty good idea of how your son's coach interacts with his team and what his philosophy is by listening to your son talk about practice and by observing at games. If you believe your son's coach is exhibiting or promoting improper behavior, you have two options. Try discussing your concerns with him first to make sure you have read the signals correctly, and if this does not alleviate your concerns, consider switching your son to a different team.

What to Do
So how can a parent decide whether or not to let a son become a jock? The truth is that it's not a mother's decision alone to make. As in all aspects of your child's growth, you must let him choose his own way of exploring the world. If sports appeals to your son, you shouldn't try to stop him even if it means, as one mother of a young football player told us, "sending him out there to get killed." This same mother admitted that although she hated to watch him play, her son had actually begun learning some self-discipline and was doing better in school since he started playing football. What you can do to help your son make informed decisions and to take proper safety precautions is to educate yourself about the sport in which he is interested. But the rest is up to him. As long as he seems happy and you're convinced the sport he's involved in is age-appropriate and not

interfering with other aspects of his life, you may find your son's involvement in sports to be a wonderful experience for him.

As we have advised, though, a parent should not push a boy into involvement in sports he does not desire. If your son is not interested in organized sports, work with him to find some sort of exercise he can build into his life, even if it's just walking or bicycle riding. We'll discuss the issue in more detail a little later in this chapter when we approach the sometimes emotionally laden subject of fathers and how they feel about their sons playing sports.

Minimum Age and Safety Requirements for Popular Sports

Sport	Minimum Age	Safety Considerations/ Comments
Baseball	7–8	Main injury is Little League elbow; a moderately strenuous sport that should be played with breakaway bases (not anchored); boys should wear jockstrap, protective cup for catchers, helmet with clear mask, no metal spikes.
Basketball	7–8	Mostly hand and ankle injuries; has become a contact sport. Boys should wear jockstrap, protective goggles, and high-top sneakers.
Football	8–10 (touch) 14 (tackle)	The contact sport with the most potential for serious injury; sometimes referred to as a collision sport. Can result in contusions, sprained ankles, and fractures. In rare cases neck injuries have caused paralysis. Although helmets are supposed to protect from this kind of injury, they may actually encourage using the head as a battering ram.
Gymnastics	6–8	Can result in a number of injuries, particularly back problems; no special equipment.

Sport	Minimum Age	Safety Considerations/ Comments
Ice Hockey	8–10	Also considered a collision sport with a relatively high injury rate, especially when body checking is allowed. Can result in knee problems, contusions, and separated shoulders. Safety equipment includes helmets, shield for eyes or face masks, gloves, padding, and mouthpieces, also protective cup for genitals.
Karate and Judo	6–8	Injuries can include fractures. Boys should wear arm guards, shin guards, jockstrap, and, at more advanced stage, head protection.
Soccer	6–8	Safer than football and basketball, but there can be injuries; boys should wear protective cup for genitals, shin guards, mouth guard, soccer-style cleats.
Swimming	5–6	Goggles are optional.
Skiing (Alpine)	Old enough to take lessons	Helmets, proper-fitting binding and boots; boots should be well padded.
Tennis	6	May result in tennis elbow or Little League elbow; sports glasses can protect the eyes.
Track and Field	6	May result in some overuse syndromes; no special equipment.

Sports Burnout

The important thing to keep in mind is that boys should play sports to have fun. Sometimes parents and kids get so caught up in the competition that they lose sight of that fact. Boys who spend too much time at one sport may fall behind in other aspects of their life—socially or intellectually. Boys can get so stressed out from the intensity of a sport that they may begin to exhibit the same symptoms of stress that adults do: headaches, stomach problems, anxiety, and even depression. This can happen if a child is pushed into a sport he doesn't enjoy or if he is pushing himself too hard. Besides the obvious health dangers, a boy who experiences sports burnout may become turned off to all sports.

The way to avoid burnout is to let a boy make his own choice about which sports he'll play, and to let him know that winning doesn't matter as long as he enjoys himself. If you notice that your son is getting too intense about a particular sport, try to help him pace himself and suggest he balance his time spent on that sport with other activities. If competitive sports seems to be too much for your son to handle, encourage him to switch to a noncompetitive activity.

Getting Started

Children are likely to be interested in exercise by following their parents' example. The Framingham Children's Study shows that children with active mothers are twice as likely to exercise as children of parents who don't exercise, and those with both parents exercising are six times as likely to follow suit.

Still, you should not start your son exercising when he's a baby. Most pediatricians recommend avoiding infant exercise classes, as they are of no benefit to babies and in fact may cause them to have injuries. As your son grows from babyhood to being a toddler and a preschooler, he may enjoy playgrounds, bicycling, swimming, and participating in other noncompetitive events. Your son will develop physically at his own rate, so there's no need to push him. Let him choose a sport he prefers when he feels ready.

You can start introducing basic motor skills such as catching and kicking to preschoolers, but bear in mind that young children lack the eye-hand coordination needed to connect a bat or a tennis racket to a ball. Boys at this age often become extremely frustrated when they can't see immediate progress in their capabilities. To counteract this frustration try setting very small, incremental goals for your son so that he can experience a sense of achievement. Don't worry about whether you have any special sports acumen; little boys won't know the difference. Above all, make exercise or sports fun!

You can also begin to prepare your son for the emotional aspects of organized team sports by playing games at home. According to Ann LaForge, a contributing editor for *Redbook*

Playground Safety

Between 250,000 and 500,000 children per year get hurt in playground accidents. Here are some safety tips:

—Make certain playground equipment rests on absorbent rubber mats, wood chips, or sand.
—Check that equipment is solidly anchored to the ground.
—Rungs on equipment shouldn't be close enough for a head to get stuck between them.
—Clothing strings, loose clothing, and stringed items placed around the neck can catch on playground equipment and strangle children (especially on slides and swings). This includes strings on hoods and attached mittens.
—In the hot weather, always check surfaces of metal playground equipment to make certain they are not too hot. The Consumer Product Safety Commission reports that children have suffered second- and third-degree burns on metal stairs, decks, and slides.
—Outdoor play equipment with "cargo nets" can be dangerous. (These are sometimes found at fast-food restaurants as well as playgrounds.) Nets having openings with a perimeter length (sum of the length of the four sides) of between seventeen and twenty-eight inches could allow a boy to trap his head and strangulate.

magazine, learning to lose is important. She suggests encouraging your son to play for the sake of playing, not for the sake of winning, and try to play games with him without keeping score; awarding achievement as well as criticism puts the emphasis on the wrong aspect of playing. LaForge gives the following age-specific advice:

Ages three to six: Play loosely structured games; don't worry about rules.
Ages six to eight: Focus more on rules, but avoid an emphasis on winning.
Ages nine and up: Stress skill development, not winning; don't allow cheating.

If boys learn early to deal with the frustration of losing and understand that playing the game is more important than the outcome, they'll probably get more enjoyment out of sports.

Bicycle Safety

—Boys should not ride two-wheel bicycles before they are five.

—A bicycle should be the right size for a boy; when sitting on the seat with his hands on the handlebar, he should be able to put the balls of his feet on the ground and straddle the center bar with an inch for clearance.

—Boys under age eight should not ride in the street; from ages eight to twelve, they can do so only if they have an older companion with them.

—Rubber-soled shoes, pants clips, reflective clothing, and helmets approved by the American National Standards Institute or the Snell Memorial Institute should be worn. Helmets should have a hard outer shell, absorbent inner liner and adjustable pads inside for fit, and a chin strap; they should fit properly and be lightweight with good ventilation. Knee pads are also good for small boys.

—Teach your son the rules of the road.

The Danger of Steroids
While we clearly acknowledge that sports can be a healthy outlet for a boy's naturally aggressive behavior, obsession of any kind can be detrimental. It is estimated that somewhere between 250,000 and 500,000 U.S. children, many of them under fourteen, have used or are using anabolic steroids to improve their bodies, primarily for athletic competition or body build-

ing. Some boys use them to improve their appearance and physique, and others are pressured by athletic coaches into taking them to gain muscle size and strength.

Anabolic steroids are the synthetic derivative of testosterone, the male hormone. Although there is a legitimate use of steroids for individuals whose bodies don't make enough of their own, or for a number of medical conditions such as asthma, an athlete's use of steroids is illegal.

In 1980, the death of a member of the U.S. Olympic judo team was linked to the use of steroids. The following is just a sampling of the numerous potentially serious side effects: high blood pressure; prostate hypertrophy, which can result in blockage of the urinary tract; liver dysfunction; hepatitis; cancer; high cholesterol levels; physiological changes known as "roid rages"; acne breakouts; baldness; breast enlargement; decreased male reproductive hormones; short stature; and a reduction of the body's inflammatory response. In younger boys there may be penis enlargement and increased frequency of erections. Steroids are particularly dangerous for adolescents whose endocrine and reproductive systems are still developing and which may be irreparably damaged. A serious injury may also be masked by steroids because they reduce the amount of perceived pain one feels and can cause an athlete to push beyond the normal limits.

It may be hard to imagine that your little boy might ever consider the use of steroids, but a survey of twelfth-grade males determined that 7 percent of them used steroids and that two-thirds of them started the use before age sixteen. Another study estimates that between 5 to 11 percent of high school males use steroids, with the female usage rate being only .5 to 2.5 percent. Although not likely to be a problem before adolescence, if your son is a serious athlete and you begin to notice unusual and often dramatic changes in him, consider whether he could be using steroids. About the same time that you begin to discuss with your son the changes puberty will bring, you might also mention the devastating effects that steroid use can have on a young male body.

The Fathers, Boys, and Sports Triangle

"Sports can be so central to a father-son relationship that," Lewis Yablonsky writes in the book *Fathers and Sons*, "they can be as revealing as a Rorschach test in evaluating father-son relationships."

Sharing a sports interest can be a wonderful experience for

fathers and sons or it can be a double-edged sword. Men are more likely than women to become emotionally involved when it comes to the issue of their sons and sports. This emotional response can manifest itself in a number of ways.

As Dr. Yablonsky explains, "For most fathers, an infant son is an ego extension, and this feeling persists at least until the teenage years. A son's successes and defeats are felt deeply by the father. . . . Some fathers use sports to solidify the sons' role as ego extension. For this type of father, the sport becomes a kind of psychodrama in which he lives out his own need to win in life through his son, and any rejection the son experiences is personalized by the father." A father who has this kind of need can put an enormous amount of pressure on a boy. He may be insistent that the boy take up the same sports he played as a youth, or conversely, one at which he didn't succeed. Perhaps it is no accident that the offspring of so many professional athletes follow in their fathers' footsteps—did they ever have a chance to do otherwise? The sad part is that when this dynamic is set up, not only is the boy living his life in a way he hasn't chosen, but he becomes willing to do this to himself in order to please his father. This kind of father lets his son know that the boy's failures are a great disappointment to him. He may be overly critical of his son's performance and systematically begins to destroy the young boy's self-esteem.

Not too long ago, one of us overheard a father complaining to his wife while his family was on an outing at a local park. The father was furious because his son preferred to sit and read a book instead of going to play softball with some other boys in the park. "What's the matter with him, anyway?" he said to his wife. "Baseball was my life when I was a kid, and all he wants to do is sit on his butt. And when I can get him to play, he runs as slow as a girl!" Although he did not make the remarks within his son's hearing, which would have been painful for the boy, this was a good example of how men suffer embarrassment at their sons' lackluster performances.

Some fathers become competitive when their sons take up the same sports they themselves played. While the boy is still learning the sport, the father may take every opportunity to defeat him. This can make a boy feel that he isn't good at what he's doing or that he'll never be as good as Dad. If a boy should surpass this kind of father at his sport, the father may resent the boy and a distance grows between them that may never be bridged.

There are also fathers who become overly involved in whatever sport their sons choose. They go to games and harass other players by booing or making derogatory remarks and second-guessing the coaches. This behavior only serves to embarrass his son, puts undo pressure on him, and teaches him bad sportsmanship.

The final problem that may arise with fathers, sons, and sports is when dad decides to become the coach. For most fathers this is a supportive act and may work out pretty well. But there are some fathers who can't handle coaching their own sons and may end up being overly critical of their sons in front of the whole team in order to give a semblance of fairness. Fathers may also give too much praise or too many playing opportunities to their sons, causing a backlash from other players and parents.

Sharing the world of sports can be a wonderful way for a father and son to spend time together, but a mother may be able to spot potential trouble from her seat on the bleachers. If you do sense any rifts between your husband and son, talk to your husband about it. Often the reactions a father experiences through his son's participation in sports are felt subconsciously, and are acted on unintentionally. You may help him to deal with these feelings and better enjoy his time with his son.

So You Don't Know the Whole Nine Yards

If you're not interested in sports you may feel left out when they take your son away from you. Sometimes the situation is compounded if fathers and sons share a strong interest in sports. There is hope for peaceful coexistence in a family composed of both avid sports fans and dedicated non-fans and we'd like to offer a few suggestions on how to achieve this state.

Even if you don't know a strike from a home run your son will still be very happy to have you cheering for him at Little League games. You can also work in the snack stand (a traditional role for sports mothers). The important thing is to appear interested and excited about your son playing. Lack of knowledge may actually work to your advantage; you'll probably watch your son's performance less critically and expect less from him. Unlike his father, you are not likely to be unconsciously trying to relive your lost youth through your son.

Instead of viewing your husband and son's sports connection as a way of keeping you out of their exclusive club, try thinking of it as your ticket to freedom. If your husband and son think spending Sunday afternoon freezing in a football stadium is this side of heaven, we say pack them a lunch and a thermos

of soup and wave goodbye to them from the doorway of your
nice warm home. Enjoy your afternoon alone reading a good
novel or taking a long uninterrupted bubble bath or any activity
you enjoy; you can always get the score from the game on the
evening news.

11

"Bang, Bang, You're Dead": On Guns and Violence

Boys and War Toys

"We absolutely *never* bought my son a toy gun. We made a big deal of it—it was a house rule. But he was most inventive in creating one," says Lila, mother of five-year-old Jake. "He would use his fingers, discarded paper towel tubes, the cardboard that comes on metal hangers from the cleaners, toy instruments, you name it. The kid was gun-crazy from three on."

"You know, we have home movies of my husband when he was a little boy and he was dressed up as a cowboy, complete with a gun and holster. He's a very gentle man now, so it doesn't seem to have hurt him to have played with toy guns." These are the words of Heather, mother of a four-year-old boy.

These mothers symbolize two ends of the spectrum in a range of opinions on the issue of weapons-as-playthings. Psychologists themselves reflect this diversity of opinion—some assert that toy guns teach violence, while others argue that fantasy fighting is a healthy outlet for a boy's natural aggression.

"Young boys," says Dr. Anthony D. Pelligrine, professor of early childhood education at the University of Georgia, "no matter how pacifist their parents, usually enjoy vigorous physical contact, battles, wrestling, and shouting. Girls rarely play-fight."

Dr. Lawrence Balter, the popular child psychologist, tries to reassure parents in *Dr. Balter's Child Sense*. He says that whether a child plays with a toy gun or not is not that important. Children may use a gun as a symbol of power, which they desire because they are little and feel powerless; they don't really understand what it would mean to kill someone. The message you give your child about violence will be far more significant, according to Dr. Balter, than the kind of toys with which he plays.

However, we believe it is important to help your son distinguish between play and fantasy. By refusing to buy what is commonly referred to by educators and child psychologists as "war toys," you can relay the message that you don't condone toys that mimic real violence.

"My son asks for a toy gun almost every time we go to a toy store and I always say no," Charlene wrote in her questionnaire. "I tell him each time, guns are very bad and hurt people so I can't buy you even a toy gun. Last year a friend of the family gave him a gun for his birthday. He took one look and said, 'I'm not allowed to have guns, but thanks!!!' We quietly took the gun out of the house after he played with it a few times, without making a big deal about it."

Myriam Miedzian in her book, *Boys Will Be Boys*, speaks for many parents and behavior specialists when she says she is strongly opposed to allowing children to have toys that are replicas of those used in actual warfare:

"There is reason to believe that these toys encourage assault, murder, racial violence, and rape as well as a militaristic attitude. Boys who are not given violence toys to play with may nevertheless use sticks as pretend guns or pretend spears or arrows. They can make believe that snowballs are hand grenades. A truck can serve as a tank. There is an important distinction between this kind of play and violent play with violent toys."

Miedzian is acknowledging that it is almost impossible to keep boys from playing at shooting and fighting, but she does draw a distinction in allowing a boy to use his imagination versus giving him realistic-looking weapons. These toys, many experts believe, make it difficult for a boy to distinguish between fantasy and what is real.

Consider some of the following stories that have recently appeared in suburban newspapers:

—A police officer came a "split second" away from shooting a fifteen-year-old boy because he had a replica of a .45 caliber semiautomatic handgun. The elements were in place, a nighttime disturbance, a gun, a crowd running from the gunman, and the gunman pointing the gun at police. In reality, this was a group of boys playing a game in which they pretended to attack this boy and then he would pull the gun on them.

—A young man was seen by police going into a retail establishment wearing a mask and carrying a gun. This prank, carried out with a toy gun, could have cost him his life.

—Police received a call that a youth in a donut shop had a pistol tucked into his pants waist. When they arrived they discovered he had a 9mm automatic toy gun replica.

We decided to have a look for ourselves at exactly what type of "war" and "violence" toys are being marketed today. We visited our local Toys 'Я Us (the largest chain of toy stores in the U.S.) and here's a sampling of what we found:

- The Uzi Submachine Pistol with "real sound"
- A water machine gun with "realistic machine-gun sound"
- The Machine—hundreds of battle actions and sounds
- The FX Intimidator Gun, which looks like a machine gun
- The Assault Uzi Play and Knife Set
- Camouflage helmets and clothing
- Micro Machines Military Battle Fortress
- The Stealth Force Mobile Attack Cannon
- The FX Devastator Electronic Cap Gun

Viewing this array of war-related toys makes it hard to believe that kids wouldn't be influenced by what they represent. And when you consider that our sons can watch G.I. Joe cartoons on TV every morning and watch real wars on the news at night, it is easy to see how a boy's view of the world of men can become distorted.

One fact most teachers and mental health professionals agree on—play teaches children. So it stands to reason that violent play teaches a violent way of behaving.

By giving our children war toys we are giving them an inappropriate message. If toys related to violence are acceptable to adults as playthings, wc arc tclling our children that violence is fun, and, says Miedzian, it sets up an inappropriate way of dealing with anger and encourages the mind-set of having "enemies."

Not all experts agree on this subject. Some believe that playing war or other fighting games helps boys release aggression, but most concede that those games that use a boy's imagination are preferable to those in which the toys are tied to a TV show or movie providing an already "programmed" story for boys.

Others, like the late, renowned child psychologist Bruno Bettelheim, place no such caveat on playing with war toys and in fact feel that this type of play offers a "cathartic discharge of aggression" which is necessary for boys. Miedzian argues that when Bettelheim wrote about this subject as a man in his seventies, he had not seen the type of war toy on the market today and was most likely relying on his memories of childhood toys that were quite different.

There are those who suggest that perhaps one consideration should be a boy's personality. If the child seems to understand the difference between reality and fantasy, and he doesn't seem overly aggressive, they theorize that perhaps it's not so harmful—or at least not as harmful as it might be for a boy who already shows a propensity for violence and aggression.

It seems to us that playing with war toys in conjunction with the viewing of violent movies, violent TV, rock and rap music, video games, and the viewing of violent sports like boxing and wrestling can't help but give boys violent role models. No matter what their personalities, they'll begin to accept violence as part of life.

Even if you decide not to let your son play with commercially manufactured war toys, you'll face some problems, because you can't control his environment twenty-four hours a day. If you're serious about prohibiting your son from playing with war toys, we suggest the following:

- Be firm when your son asks for toys from this category. If you give in some of the time, you'll be giving him mixed messages. Even if you are consistent, you won't be able to stop his violent play completely, but at least he'll know you regard violence as unacceptable behavior.

- Decide what toys you are comfortable with and where to draw the line; some parents feel swords are okay because they don't simulate real-life violence. After all, you don't hear of robberies at sword point these days!

- Tell relatives and friends not to buy war toys for your son. If they do, ask them if they would mind letting you exchange the gift for something else.

- If your son is going to play at another boy's house, tell the parents you don't allow war-toy play and ask them to honor your wishes while your son is in their home.

This last point is hard to enforce, so even if you chose to ban war toys from your son's toy chest, you'll need to sit him down and explain why. You should also be specific about what toys he is allowed to own so that you don't have to revisit the issue every time you go to the toy store. For example, let him know if a water gun shaped like an animal is okay and a realistic-looking shotgun is not.

We do not feel that playing with toy guns and war toys serves the best interests of little boys. To reinforce the message of violence, which is so pervasive in our society today, cannot possibly be beneficial. But we turn now to an even more serious subject which should be of great concern to mothers of sons, and that is the attraction for young boys to **real** guns.

Boys and the Real Thing

Letting a boy have a toy gun may be considered controversial. The danger of having a real gun in the home is not. A recent article in *Parents* magazine, "Children and Guns: A Fatal Attraction," suggests that this problem is becoming more profound, with 500 children per year killed by gun accidents every year in this country.

One of our questionnaire respondents tells of how her father always kept a gun hidden in his underwear drawer. None of the four girls ever touched it, but her brother found it and took a few shots one day. Luckily no one was hurt, but the incident shocked the family into reconsidering the wisdom of keeping a gun in a home where there were young children.

Every day in the United States ten children are killed by guns, thirty children are wounded, and 135,000 kids bring a gun to school. Today, more teenage boys die from gunshots than from all natural cases. While these numbers relating to guns and boys are incredibly frightening, what is most amazing is that 80 to 90 percent of guns seized at school **come from the home.**

The danger of guns in the home cannot be underestimated. Boys have a natural attraction to guns, particularly between the ages of four and ten. A toddler who doesn't even know what a gun is can pull a trigger out of curiosity. A school-age child may know what a gun is but still doesn't understand the danger because he doesn't know the difference between fantasy and reality. A preadolescent or an older boy may help himself to a gun to "be cool" or because he actually intends to use it. He may think he can handle a gun when he doesn't know anything about gun safety. Teenage boys are four times more likely to be successful at suicide than girls because of their access to guns.

We cannot emphasize strongly enough the wisdom of keeping guns out of the home if there are children present. If you have a gun for recreational purposes, consider keeping it at a gun club. If you or your husband feels you must have a gun in the house, the American Academy of Pediatrics recommends the following:

• Remove guns from areas in which children live and play.

• Keep guns unloaded in a locked cabinet and out of the reach of children.

• Keep ammunition locked up separately from the guns and don't let your children see where you put it.

• When a child reaches the teen years, enroll him in a gun-safety course.

> **B**B guns are not toys—they can kill. High-velocity BB guns, which have muzzle velocities higher than 350 feet per second, can increase the risk. Since 1980, the U.S. Consumer Product Safety Commission has had reports of twenty-five deaths by BB guns or pellet rifles. It is recommended that children under fourteen not use BB guns, and then only with adult supervision.

Added safety precautions would be to equip guns with trigger locks and **never** demonstrate unsafe gun behavior in front of a child.

But guns that accidentally fall into the hands of boys from home are only a part of the problem. "Teenage boys have always been violent," states psychiatrist Dr. Willard Gaylin. "We've moved up from fists to guns." According to the federal Centers for Disease Control, one student in five carries a weapon of some kind, and one in twenty carries a gun. In the inner cities boys can easily buy a stolen gun on the street for a very small amount of money, as little as $25.

We discussed in the previous chapter why some boys become excessively aggressive and even violent. To exacerbate this condition, guns today are readily available and more prevalent as drug-related crime rises. "While big-city schools are the primary battleground," according to *Newsweek* magazine, "the problem is creeping into the suburbs as well." We feel all parents should heed this warning and do all they can to promote gun control for the sake of our sons' futures.

The most important step you can take to protect your son

from guns is not to keep one in the home, but that's not all you can do to fight the rise in gun availability and the danger they might present to him. When he is old enough, you can discuss with him exactly what to do if he ever encounters a gun:

- Never touch a gun under **any** circumstances.
- Contact an adult immediately and report the gun.
- Persuade other children present not to touch the gun either.

If you are aware of anyone who has illegal firearms, you can call 1-800-AFT GUNS to report the situation anonymously to the Federal Bureau of Alcohol, Tobacco and Firearms, which will pass the information on to your local police. You can write to your congressmen and senators to urge that they vote for gun control laws. You can also contact the following organizations for more information and to lend them your support.

> **C**APS for toy guns are dangerous. If children carry ring caps, paper roll caps, or strip caps in their pockets, friction can ignite the caps and burn the child. They contain a small quantity of pyrotechnic material which can ignite when hit. They can also create a noise hazard if fired closer than one foot to the ear.

Center to Prevent Handgun Violence
   1225 Eye Street, NW
   Suite 1100
   Washington, DC 20005
   202-289-7319

Educational Fund to End Handgun Violence
   Box 72
   110 Maryland Avenue, NE
   Washington, DC 20002

Gun Responsibility in Every Family
   Box 743
   Naugatuck, CT 06770
   203-729-3636

Handgun Control, Inc.
   1225 Eye Street, NW
   Suite 1110
   Washington, DC 20005
   202-898-0792

Boys, Violence, and TV

Where do boys learn about using guns? Primarily they learn from watching television. Americans watch more TV than any other population in the world, so it would probably be fair to say that American boys watch TV more than any boys in the world. We know for certain that boys watch more TV than girls; after years of study, it has become an established fact that watching violence on TV makes children more violent. The quantity and quality of TV your son is watching clearly are areas which demand your attention.

A recent issue of *TV Guide* defined violence on TV in the following way: "Any deliberate act involving physical force or the use of a weapon in an attempt to achieve a goal, further a cause, stop the action of another, act out an angry impulse, defend oneself from attack, secure a material reward or intimidate others." Unfortunately, this definition applies to a great many shows on TV, including some of those specifically produced for children.

Too much TV viewing has multiple negative effects on children, including lack of sleep, limiting family interaction, and stifling imagination. Children who watch an excessive amount of TV tend to produce a lower quality of schoolwork because they are sleepy and have a short attention span. But exposing boys to violence and sex (usually interrelated on TV) is the most damaging aspect of heavy TV watching—it teaches boys values that fly in the face of what we as parents wish to impart on them.

Studies done at the Family Television Research and Consultation Center at Yale University indicate "there is a strong relationship between the viewing of action-detective shows and aggression." These studies show that even seemingly benign "fast-paced" programs such as game shows and variety shows can make a kid excited. They also found that children in grades three through five who watched "fantasy-violent programs" were less cooperative, less successful in interpersonal relationships, less happy, and less imaginative.

Many other studies link heavy TV watching to more aggressiveness, including several by the highly regarded Australian researcher Grant Noble. He found that children's play was less constructive after they viewed realistic aggression but, interestingly, "more constructive after seeing very artificial or ritualized aggression such as 'cowboy shootouts.'" This observation seems to dovetail with the theories on children's play with violent toys, e.g., that using a stick for a gun instead of a replica of a machine gun is healthier play.

Boys are at more risk for watching violent TV than girls because they are more likely to imitate antisocial behavior from TV—most of the lead and violent roles are played by men, and TV makes violence look exciting. Girls tend to feel TV is less realistic and overall have less interest than boys.

The negative effects of watching violent TV on boys can be seen at a very young age, for even at the tender age of two, boys can imitate what they see. In a study of nursery-school boys, those who watched action shows were observed to be more likely to get into fights.

Research done over a period of many years by psychologists Monroe Lefkowitz, Leonard Eron, and L. Rowell Huesmann, and published in the 1980s, provides some startling information. These researchers followed a group of boys who were watching a great deal of violent TV by the age of eight. After interviewing friends and neighbors when those boys were eighteen, the doctors learned that overall as a group, the boys were considered more aggressive than normal; by age thirty, many of them were involved in criminal activities.

There are other undesirable results of too much TV viewing of inappropriate programming besides learning violence. Boys who watch a lot of television tend to be more biased about male/female roles, since women are still not reflected as having equal footing in the world—the male characters are usually the stronger or in a more powerful position. Violent TV also teaches children prejudice, as blacks are often the villains or the victims in a show.

A survey in *Child* magazine in 1991 showed that in the Fall lineup of kids' shows, there were sixty-four male stars and only sixteen female.

It is not only violent police procedurals, detective, and other shows of this nature that are the problem. Even cartoons are filled with guns, head-bopping, chasing, characters being shoved off cliffs and buildings, etc. Cartoons create a more insidious situation because most parents will monitor adult programs for kids but will leave their young children "plunked down" in front of the TV watching cartoons, without concern.

One mother told us that every morning her son announces to her which cartoon superhero he will be that day. "I don't know whether to be happy he has such a great imagination or worried that he's carrying these cartoon characters around in his head," she says. We think superheroes are okay as long as a boy isn't imitating violent behavior.

The networks readily admit that children's TV programming is geared to boys. This is because boys are heavier TV watchers and because girls are willing to watch "boy" programs, but the reverse is not usually true. This is why we see a proliferation of superheroes behaving in a fairly violent mode on Saturday morning TV. These superheroes are far more realistic than those of our childhoods—for example, X-Men are more real than Mighty Mouse—so kids identify even more strongly with them.

In the book *Use TV to Your Child's Advantage,* authors Dorothy G. Singer, Jerome L. Singer, and Diana M. Zuckerman explain why young children, particularly boys, are so drawn to superheroes. They say that because children are so small, they have little control over their environment and therefore like to identify with characters who do. They point out that in a study which spanned a period of a year, superheroes and other TV characters were the games played most by a group of young children. Imaginary playmates, common to preschool children, are often based on superheroes as well.

Music videos, which are now easily found on MTV, are intensifying in violent and overtly sexual display; and the new reality shows such as *Hard Copy* and *Current Affair* bring real murder, mayhem, matricide, patricide, and fratricide right into our own homes. Even the six o'clock news programs are increasingly showing more violence, and most parents don't remember to shut them off when young children are in the room.

It would certainly be prudent to limit your son's TV viewing for a variety of reasons—not the least of which is that there are many other worthwhile activities to which he could devote his time and energy. However, we are not suggesting that TV in and of itself is bad; in fact, it can play a valuable role in your son's education if it is used judiciously.

There a number of ways you can use TV advantageously for your son. First and foremost, you should monitor the programs your child is watching to be certain of their content. View at least one episode before you allow a child to watch a show. Even this method isn't foolproof, as "trailers" for violent movies can appear on-screen during the most innocuous shows.

You should be aware of the hours in which children's programming ends, and one mother's experience will illustrate the reason. "I was watching a perfectly nice children's show with my son one night," Nancy began, "and then I got a phone call. After the phone call I got distracted in the kitchen talking to my husband. After a while my four-year-old son drifted into the kitchen and said, 'Daddy, can you come watch TV with me? There's one part in this show that I'm a little scared about.' When my husband accompanied my son to the den, he discovered that he was watching the movie *Nightmare on Elm Street!*"

As we previously discussed, don't assume that all cartoons are okay for your son to watch. Although there are some perfectly charming cartoons which are nonviolent, we would guess that at least 50 percent have violence depicted in them. Saturday- and Sunday-morning lineups on network TV are the biggest culprits, so consider going out for brunch or to the park, or sign your son up for some sort of lessons to fill up these time blocks.

Also, be careful about exposing your young son to the six o'clock news, particularly when he is still a preschooler. Kids of this age are too young to understand how what they hear or see on TV affects them personally. Try watching the ten o'clock news instead, when he's safely tucked in bed, or even taping the early news to view later at your convenience. When your son gets a little older, watch the news with him, making certain you discuss what he is seeing and hearing rather than just letting him absorb on his own information that might confuse or frighten him.

Talk to your young son about the difference between what is fantasy and what is real life on TV. Dr. Robert L. Shraig, professor of communications at North Carolina State University, says that "once a child can tell fantasy from reality, almost nothing can scare him or unduly influence him." He suggests you teach your child:

- There is a difference between a TV character and a real character.
- There is a difference between real and make-believe.
- There is a difference between commercials and programs.

This last point may seem obvious to you as an adult, but we know of at least one little boy who, when told to come to dinner one night, blurted out, "But, Mom, I'm going to miss the commercials!"

Encourage your son to watch shows in which the characters care for each other and help each other. If he does view some aggressive behavior on TV, discuss nonviolent ways to solve arguments rather than allowing him to assimilate the behavior he has seen on TV.

We think it advisable to watch TV with your son as much as possible to explain issues and behavior depicted that he may not fully understand, and in this way television can be a wonderful teaching tool. For very young boys, choose some of the excellent children's programming on the Public Broadcasting stations, such as *Sesame Street* and *Reading Rainbow,* and some of the cable programming for kids, particularly on the Nickelodeon Network. For older boys, look for adventure shows that aren't violent, particularly on The Disney Channel, and science and geography programs. There are even some pretty good kids "news" shows that are extremely informative.

In the book *What Parents Should Know About Kids and TV,* the following positive aspects of TV are delineated:

- It can be used to communicate information and education.

- It is useful for dramatizing difficult subject matter, such as divorce (although many excellent books can serve the same purpose).

- It can teach problem solving—seeing boys in shows making decisions can be very instructive.

- Viewing characters that are inspiring will teach your son good ideals.

Needless to say, the same rules apply for movies and videos. Don't let your son watch either unsupervised unless you've seen them first. Even PG-rated movies can have more violence, sex, and bad language than you might expect. Remember that cable TV in particular can provide inappropriate programming at any time of the day.

A few last points to consider. Don't assume that because you know what is good for your son to watch on TV, movies, or videos, others who care for him will have the same good sense. One mother told us her five-year-old son started singing a song in the car one day: "Let's talk about sex, baby." When she asked in surprise where he had learned those lyrics, he told her it was on a teenage sitcom the baby-sitter had allowed him to watch.

Even other parents may have different ideas than you do about what is "good" TV. One mother confided to another in one of our discussion groups that she never let her child watch any "realistic" shows, only cartoons. The cartoons probably had more violence and less redeeming value than the shows she wouldn't let her son watch!

Preadolescents are more likely to see shows you'd rather not have them see at someone else's house because their friend's parents make different judgment calls than you and because they are not supervised as closely as younger children. According to James P. Comer, M.D., "preadolescents who are struggling to develop adequate control over their now more powerful sexual and aggressive impulses" can be overstimulated by sex and violence on TV and in movies.

If your son is a latchkey kid, try to make arrangements so that he can't watch too much or the wrong kind of TV. You could try signing him up for after-school programs or arranging for him to go to a friend's house one or two days a week. If both of these activities are not feasible, there are some products on the market which might help you. One is a "lock" you can put on the TV which will prevent your son from watching it when you're not around. The other is called the TV Allowance and is a device that attaches to your television set. By putting in the code you assign him, your son can watch TV for only the amount of time you have preprogrammed. You can also block out specific time periods when television cannot be viewed.

So the good news about boys and TV is that although it is a disseminator of violence, you can have control and use it as something beneficial to your son. By the way, the less TV your son sees you and your husband watching, the less he will watch. So shut off the set and go do something with your son!

12

Don't Wait for Daddy: Discipline

"The other day I was speaking to my brother on the phone. My son, Jeremy, who is three and a half, asked me to make him an English muffin, but I wasn't paying any attention to him. Suddenly he climbed into my lap and bit my breast hard enough to leave a bruise. I couldn't believe it! He hasn't bitten anyone since he was an infant. And he didn't even seem remorseful that he did it." So wrote our questionnaire respondent Jessica.

When it comes to a battle of wills, mothers often face in their sons what is essentially an alien style of conflict resolution. This is not to say that mothers find disciplining their daughters smooth sailing, only that with their boys they might feel more often at sea. The intent of this chapter is to focus on the singular problems, real or perceived, in behavior associated with boys. Although there is a vast body of literature available that applies to the discipline of children of either sex, we will also cover some of this ground because it is hard to separate general discipline techniques from those that apply to specific issues related to boys. Our goal in this chapter is to give mothers a better understanding of how to work with the problems they may encounter with their little boys precisely because they are boys.

Temper, Temper

"I couldn't control him. I felt like he was deliberately abusing me," said Jessica.

"My son would have fits of craziness; he'd cry so hard, he'd perspire," Ellen recounted.

"He'd have such bad temper tantrums that he would hold his breath when he was crying and actually pass out," Linda told us about her little boy. "We thought there might be something physically wrong with him, but there wasn't. He just wanted his own way."

Disciplining sons offers its own distinct challenges. In the classic book on child rearing, *The Magic Years,* Selma H. Fraiberg cautions: "As part of our education we educate away from raw discharge of aggression, the bullying, the tantrum, the destructive and sadistic acts, but . . . we should never wish to eradicate these tendencies or reverse them so that a boy needs to become passive and feminine in order to win approval." Here is the root of the problem between mothers and sons: mothers aren't as familiar or comfortable with male behavior and unconsciously apply a feminine set of rules to determine proper conduct for their sons. No wonder the quest for obedience from a son often turns into a small battle.

We've already mentioned in previous chapters that most young boys tend to be more physically active and more aggressive than little girls. It's difficult for many mothers to accept and understand this constant movement and level of activity and so they may frequently hear themselves uttering such standards as "You're being too loud, boys, quiet down," "Stop running in the house," "Calm down, you're too worked up," "Stop banging your legs on the table," and so on. Try to imagine what it would be like to be told every day that you're doing something wrong when you're just being yourself. Many boys handle this problem by simply deciding to ignore their mothers' admonishments, which, of course, only further angers the mothers and creates an escalating tension.

Dr. Joan Shapiro describes in *Men: A Translation for Women* how this ignoring of mother evolves into a trancelike state that boys learn to perfect early, a sort of form of self-hypnosis. You may have noticed from time to time that your husband (as well as your son) exhibits this trancelike behavior—it's likely that he learned this technique of playing deaf when he was a boy. Dr. Shapiro explains that males big and small use this as a way to "avoid contact" and "screen out" female stimuli. We've noticed that when boys are watching TV or playing with video games, the trance becomes even more focused and it's almost impossible to get a little boy to even hear you talking to him. This sounds dismaying, but mothers need to remember that there are several underlying factors at play here—their sons are not deliberately setting out to drive them crazy.

In Chapter Four we described how the little boy must begin to separate from his mother around the age of six or seven in order to begin to grow into his future role as a man. Boys often negotiate this passage in their lives by rejecting all that is feminine; this is the stage when they start playing only with other boys and want nothing to do with girls and their mothers, who are part of the feminine world they are rejecting. In addition, most boys spend more time with their mothers than with their fathers. This means their mothers not only reprimand them more, but out of sheer weariness may also fail to follow through on their threats. Both of these interactions undermine mothers' credibility as an authority figure to their sons.

We also need to understand that there is a difference between the ways in which girls and boys use language. Russell Miller, writing in *Sesame Street Parents' Guide,* explains that boys tend to interrupt more, and to issue demands and commands rather than requests. Since our verbal style is different, this behavior may only serve to make us more angry. But we should try to remember that our sons' methods of communication are not specifically a reaction to us.

It has been documented that boys more often than girls fail to respond the first time they are given a command—which is certain to get their mothers' blood pressure rising. As a result, research shows that mothers (and fathers) treat their sons differently than their daughters—they tend to discipline them more often, more firmly, and more physically. Parents also seem to have stricter standards for boys. Diane Baumrind, a psychologist at the Institute of Human Development at the University of California, Berkeley, says, "Once a direction has been given, the [parents] are more likely to follow through to make sure that a boy has complied with it."

Sometimes when a boy gets out of control, physical retaliation may seem like the only way to regain control. When it comes to the subject of spanking and hitting children, child behaviorists and psychologists are in firm agreement—they are vehemently opposed to the idea. Although it seems like a direct way to let a child know that the has gone too far, the use of physical punishment simply teaches a boy that violence is a way to handle violence—undoubtedly not the message you want your son to learn.

Corporal punishment doesn't seem to make sense for another reason: a boy may get used to being spanked, and then the punishment won't have the effect for which it was intended. The purpose of disciplining a child is to help him build a conscience so that he can learn self-control. Being hit or spanked makes a boy feel he has fulfilled his obligation for being punished for whatever he has done. As Selma Fraiberg wrote, in *The Magic Years*, "A child may learn how to avoid successfully any guilt feelings for bad behavior by setting up a cycle in which the punishment cancels the 'crime,' and the child having paid for his mischief is free to repeat another act at another time without attendant guilt feelings."

Because boys seem to misbehave more often than girls, the punishment they receive may be exaggerated. This may be in part because a mother is more frightened when her son is aggressive, fearing he will grow up to be a violent man. When her son is out of control she may deal with him more harshly than she might with a daughter because she needs to feel she can get back in control of the situation. One danger in this is that, depending on the severity and frequency of punishment, a boy may begin to fear exhibiting any behavior that might be interpreted as aggressive. In extreme cases, this could grow so out of proportion that a boy might be afraid to play sports or engage in any rough-and-tumble play. Clearly this should not be the intent of any mother. Breaking the will of her child can expose him to any number of psychological problems.

Having Realistic Expectations

One of the reasons parents are uncertain about how to discipline their children is because they don't understand what their children are realistically capable of responding to at each age and developmental stage. For example, two-year-olds have a tendency to say no most of the time no matter what you ask them to do, which starts to wear on a mother. If she understood that her son was trying to take his first steps toward becoming independent from her, she might handle the situation better and would discipline her toddler with this knowledge in mind.

Psychologist Diane Baumrind suggests that authoritative parenting (as opposed to permissive or authoritarian parenting) is the healthiest style for both parent and child. What this means is that a mother is neither so tolerant that she provides minimal discipline and accepts all behaviors from her son, nor

so strict that she has total control over him. The authoritative
parent sets down rules but also encourages her son's individu-
ality. Baurmrind says that such a parent creates discipline
methods that fit with her child's abilities, interests, and weak
points at each of his developmental stages.

How does this style of parenting directly relate to little boys?
Consider that mothers generally tend to worry more than fathers about their sons' participation in activities in which they
can get hurt. If a mother makes a rule that her son can't go on
a jungle gym when he's physically capable of doing so, they are
going to have to discuss this issue every time they go to the
park, and the child won't understand his mother's rule because
it is not reasonable. She's forbidding her son from participating
in an activity appropriate for his developmental stage. The authoritative mother would probably tell her son that jungle gyms
are fine, but with the caveat that she is making an exception
for playgrounds that don't have a suitable ground surface such
as sand, grass, wood chips, or rubber mats. She would also
explain to him the reason this would be the exception—that
he could be seriously injured.

Mothers tend to worry and care more than fathers about
clean clothes and tidy rooms. With a son, a mother may have
to learn to lighten up a bit. As one mother pointed out to us,
"When you see photographs of your children, the boys are always dirty." The fact is that boys are more likely to engage
themselves in physical activities that will get their clothes and
bodies dirty. A better tactic than constantly telling a boy not
to get dirty would be to suggest that your son change his clothes
as soon as he gets home from school and put on his play
clothes.

As mothers, we need to acknowledge that most of what we
know about discipline is a direct result of how our parents disciplined us. Since our parents were interacting with us as girls,
we received gender-specific instruction which may not work in
exactly the same way with our sons. We're not promoting a
double standard for boys and girls, only suggesting that a
mother needs to understand that boys tend to be more physical, more active, and noisier, and that some adjustment should
be made for this difference.

Because young boys also tend to be less likely to verbalize
their feelings than girls, a mother must be particularly conscious of what is going on with her son. "We always knew with
our son, even though he didn't tell us, to check to see if he was
hungry or tired before we addressed his bad behavior," Michelle

explained. "A considerable amount of the time a snack or a nap helped solve the problem." This advice is true for boys and girls, but we might add that boys tend to need a physical outlet for their pent-up energies. Try to give your son an opportunity to expend this energy every day—by running in the yard, participating in an after-school activity, or riding his bicycle. Many parents find that when they bring young boys into social situations like dining at a restaurant, it helps to let them take a break and go outside for a while to move around.

All young children become frustrated rather easily because there are so many things they can't yet do for themselves and so many aspects of their lives are out of their control. Boys, because they are less likely to say what is bothering them, may be telling their mothers something through bad behavior. It's important to encourage your son to communicate with you. Rather than just responding to his behavior with anger, dig a little deeper for the cause. Allow your son to express his anger and try not to cut him off before he is able to do so. Children who are not allowed to express anger bottle it up inside, and with boys there is a greater likelihood that this will exacerbate an already more aggressive predisposition.

In developing your discipline style, choose which battles are worth fighting—you can't spend all your time in combat. Although teaching your son to pick up his toys is a good way to teach him self-discipline, insisting he do it before bedtime, when he's probably tired and cranky, is self-defeating. Remember too, you don't have to do all the disciplining by yourself. Let your husband share this role, and when you're not certain how to handle situations, talk it over with him. When your son gets old enough, holding family meetings in which everyone gets to air his or her views in a democratic fashion can be very useful—this lets your son know you're all in it together.

A Word of Advice for Single Mothers
As we discussed in Chapter Six, a mother cannot try to take on the role of two parents. If she is left alone to discipline her child, there are times when the responsibility may become overwhelming. Don't try to do it alone; look for help from family members, friends, and support groups. If you're a single parent through divorce, try not to feel guilty because your son is not living with his father. This may lead you to underdiscipline your son, which will not be good for either of you. Boys need a firm hand, especially if their father is not around, so consider bringing an authoritative male figure in contact with your son.

Little Boys and School

When young boys begin either preschool or elementary school, behavior problems often seem to appear. Boys are naturally more active and have a hard time sitting still, which frequently gets them labeled as troublemakers. At this age, boys usually play in larger groups than girls do, increasing the noise level and the likelihood of pushing, hitting, wrestling, and other less than desirable activities. All the while the girls will sit quietly and play house in the corner.

Boys at this stage also tend to be less capable of using their fine motor skills and so are less interested than girls in related activities such as art projects and writing. While most girls of preschool and early-school age will be happy to sit and draw pictures, most boys will prefer to run around the room or throw a ball.

Studies show that teachers, who are primarily women, reprimand boys more often and more harshly than girls. Again, their expectations may be unrealistic—they may be asking males to conform to female standards. Because boys are so active and have difficulty sitting for more than a few minutes at a time, they are often considered disruptive.

There has been a lot of publicity recently regarding sex-related bias in the public school system. Feminist organizations report that teachers encourage and support girls less than boys, particularly in math and science; teachers call on girls less frequently than boys for answers, and girls receive less attention than boys. Perhaps there is some truth to these accusations in the older grades, but from our observations, we feel the bias is actually against boys in the first few years of school. It may be true that boys get more attention, but this is not necessarily to be viewed as positive—they may get more attention because they are being disciplined more. In fact, one school reported that teachers diagnosed boys as having learning disabilities twice as often as girls, when in reality the incidence in boys and girls was about the same.

One mother told us about her son's preschool experience. "My son went to preschool for three years. The first two years, we never heard about any problems. The last year, he unfortunately landed in a class with only two boys. One of the boys came to school only in the afternoon, and the other was extremely docile and preferred to play with girls rather than boys. His teacher started complaining that my son was noncompliant, that he didn't wish to stop whatever he was doing when the group began a new activity. Then my son started coming home crying that he couldn't do things as well as the girls, that he couldn't write or color in the lines as well.

"The problem turned out to be that the classroom was just too feminine for him, and as a result, the teacher saw him as causing problems. We switched him to a class that had somewhat younger children but more boys, and the problems went away!"

Another mother told us that when her son started the morning session of kindergarten in public school, he constantly wound up in the "time-out" chair. He was coming home and describing himself as being "bad" all the time. The very person who was supposed to be building his self-esteem—his teacher—was actually doing the opposite. She learned through talking to her son and to the boy's teacher that almost anything could land him in the chair—talking out of turn, not cleaning up fast enough, not following instructions properly. It seemed that the boys in the class frequently warmed up the chair, but very few girls ever got the honor. The teacher mentioned in a conference with the mother that her morning class needed a lot more "work" than her afternoon class because it was "out of control." The mother subsequently learned that the afternoon class had more girls in it, while her son's morning class had more boys.

After doing some research, this mother decided that her son's teacher was overly punitive to boys. She carefully explained to her son that his teacher was trying to teach him some self-discipline, which was an important attribute to have for the rest of his schooling and his life. She also told him that every person has his own opinion of what is considered acceptable behavior and that this teacher was a bit on the strict side. "If I was your teacher, I wouldn't send you or the other boys to the time-out seat for a lot of things that she does," she explained. "I want you to show her respect, but I want you to know that you're a very good boy, not a bad boy. You're just learning by making mistakes, as we all do."

We relate both of these stories to illustrate how easy it is to believe that your son is misbehaving in school. Certainly you should take seriously any complaints or comments a teacher makes about your son. A mother should weight all the evidence, realizing that there may be a built-in prejudice against boys in the younger grades; armed with that knowledge, a mother can take action accordingly, and if necessary, take her concerns to the principal. As Selma Fraiberg notes in *The Magic Years*, " . . . we need to recognize, too, that a boy is not a girl, that he cannot be bound to the code of women and girls, that his biological make-up disposes him toward greater activity and aggressiveness and that his educators must understand this."

Boys, Attention Deficit Disorder, and Hyperactivity

As we mentioned earlier, teachers sometimes attribute the more active behavior of boys to development disorders. While they tend to "overdiagnose" this problem, it is true that boys are more likely than girls to have development disorders. The opposite problem faces boys as well—at times development disorders are misconstrued as simply bad or resistant behavior.

Attention Deficit Disorder (ADD) is the inability of a child to focus or concentrate. About 5 percent of the American population suffers from this condition, which may be discovered as early as preschool age or not until years later. When children have Attention Deficit Disorder with Hyperactivity (ADDH), their behavior may be noticeable right from birth. They are often colicky babies and are not easily comforted. By the time they reach age two, they become extremely active and hard to control; this behavior is likely to continue unless professional treatment is sought.

Hyperactivity means that the nervous system "can't effectively modulate motor activity," says Dr. Robert A. Moss, author of *Why Johnny Can't Concentrate.* The range of hyperactivity can be as mild as a child who has "ants in his pants" and can't sit still, or as dramatic as the child who seems to be in constant movement. Children can have ADD with or without hyperactivity, and hyperactivity may be seen alone or with ADD.

The mother of a boy with ADD may become angry at her son for behavior which she feels is deliberately confrontational, but the truth is the boy may not be able to help himself. He may have trouble remembering more than one thing at a time and may get distracted in the middle of doing what he has been told to do. Inflexibility is one of the indices of a boy with ADD; he can be particularly demanding and hard on his mother because any change in his life or an upset in his routine can set off temper tantrums.

When hyperactivity is not present, ADD may not become apparent until the school years. At that point, a boy with ADD will have trouble concentrating and won't be able to do well in school; sometimes the condition is undetected until junior high school, when the curriculum gets more difficult.

Dr. Moss describes the following as ADD symptoms in the order of their likelihood:

(1) The child has a short attention span and is easily distracted. He finds it extremely difficult to concentrate.

(2) The child is impulsive or does things without thinking about them.

(3) The child may hear one word that sets him off on a train of thought totally unrelated to what is going on around him. He then misses what is being said to him.

(4) The child can't handle all the pieces involved in one activity because he can't organize them.

(5) The child has a strong desire to have something and then loses interest in it very quickly.

(6) Hyperactivity (in about 30 percent of ADD kids) or constant unfocused motion is apparent.

(7) The child is socially immature, which may make it difficult for him to make friends.

(8) The child can handle a situation or assignment perfectly one day and not be able to do it the next time.

(9) The child gets upset when routines are disrupted.

(10) Mood swings are evident in the child.

(11) Short-term memory is a problem for the child.

If you are aware that a number of the characteristics listed above describe your son, particularly if they seem exaggerated, it would be wise to investigate whether or not he might have ADD. You can ask your pediatrician for advice on how to get your son evaluated. Children with ADD can be helped with treatment—a combination of medication, behavior modification work, and sessions with a certified psychotherapist may be recommended. (Please see Appendix for additional information on ADD and hyperactivity.)

Non-ADD Difficulties

Many kids who exhibit one or more of these tendencies don't have ADD—the normal behavior of young children can be quite similar. In fact, there is a certain percentage of kids, sometimes labeled "difficult children," who have no underlying problems but just seem to be excessively difficult to control and require an enormous amount of patience and attention. Dr. Stanley Turecki, a child psychiatrist and founder of the Difficult Child

Program at Beth Israel Hospital in New York, says in his book *The Difficult Child* that "these children appear to be deliberately defiant. They may act wild when they get excited." This behavior might easily be considered symptoms of hyperactivity; you will need to get some professional guidance for yourself or your son to determine with which problem you are dealing and how to remedy it.

There are a number of other problems and conditions that may be affecting a boy and which are often confused or found in conjunction with ADD. These include learning disabilities, for which a child can be tested and evaluated. Learning disabilities are more prevalent in boys and can involve problems with processing information related to reading, math comprehension, listening, speaking, and reasoning. Like ADD and hyperactivity, these are problems that require treatment but can be greatly improved with professional help.

Chronic anxiety over traumatic events in a child's life such as a divorce or abuse can also cause behavioral and school difficulties. A boy who is suppressing his feelings about such problems may begin "acting out," a psychological term that means in essence the boy is expressing his depression through angry and belligerent behavior. A mother who is depressed herself over a divorce may just return her son's anger without realizing it. If a boy's behavior changes significantly from the way he has always been, this should be a red flag to his mother.

There are also serious psychiatric problems which may be confused with ADD or learning disabilities. One example is childhood schizophrenia, characterized by language problems which usually become apparent by the age of three. Also, such a child does not seem to experience either pleasure or pain. A professional evaluation would again be needed to determine the nature of the problem.

There may also be physiological reasons why a boy's behavior seems uncontrollable. Cold medications, phenobarbital (an anti-seizure medicine), and some asthma medications can cause a child to behave hyperactively. Allergies can play a role in behavior as well, as can lead poisoning and hearing and visual problems. If you suspect that any of these substances or conditions could be affecting your son, see your doctor and you may be able to treat the problem.

Father as Disciplinarian?
In past generations it was very clear in most families that Mother took care of the children's everyday needs and Father was the disciplinarian, particularly when it came to the boys.

The image of a father pulling his belt out of his pants and telling a boy, "This is going to hurt me more than it is going to hurt you," is one that many of us can remember.

Parental roles have evolved a great deal in recent years. Today parents share child-care duties, particularly since many mothers are in the work force.

To our surprise, we still hear mothers utter to sons that old lame standby, "Wait till your daddy comes home!" There are several inherent dangers for a family with the dynamics this statement implies. The first is that punishment is more effective if it is applied immediately after the crime is committed. While a child needs to be remorseful for what he has done wrong, to leave him brooding for hours about facing his father seems excessively cruel both to the son and to the father. A boy should not dread the arrival of his father at the front door because he is going to "get what is coming to him."

Second, a mother should not teach her son she is powerless. Even mothers who are away from home all day need to share disciplinary action with their husbands regardless of whether they are both present when a transgression occurs. If a mother doesn't take control when her son is young, she can't expect him to grow up to be a boy who respects her authority when he gets older.

Third, it is extremely unfair to her husband to base the father-and-son interaction primarily on discipline. In fact, this can damage a relationship which should be loving and supportive. Finally, this family structure also encourages a boy to accept an unhealthy stereotypical view of male-female roles, that the man is stronger and is therefore the punisher.

The best way a mother can control her son is not to get out of control herself when he misbehaves. Using the "time-out" or "go to your room to cool off" technique will give her time to pull herself together and decide how to handle a situation calmly, rather than letting her son see her respond too emotionally. Mothers need to learn to be firm with their sons and not afraid of them because they are male—they are still children who depend on their mothers to teach them how to eventually discipline themselves. There are times when this is easier said than done. As boys become older and bigger, a mother may feel her edge as the grown-up slipping away. If you can't stand firm with a son at this point, it might be useful to get some outside professional help to improve your coping skills.

Lorraine, who is going through some serious marital problems, watched her son, Alan, begin to exhibit almost frightening aggressive behavior because he was aware of the troubles between his parents. A small woman, not even five feet tall, she suddenly became scared that her eleven-year-old, husky son, who had been lashing out at her emotionally, might really hurt her. She was wise enough to get her entire family into counseling, and the situation improved.

Being the mother of a little boy is not always easy. In fact, it can be downright stressful. Some of our discussion group attendees told us:

"He seemed to go out of his way to torture me. He always acted up for me, not his father."

"I couldn't even handle taking him to a grocery store until he was older."

"He was so much harder to handle than my daughter. Sometimes I wanted to send him off to military school."

Yet they also agreed that boys do begin to calm down as they get a little older. Armed with some knowledge of why boys behave the way they do (and maybe some earplugs and aspirin), mothers can discipline their sons empathetically and lovingly . . . and survive.

13

Sons But Not Daughters

"I just had my second son, and strangers are actually offering me condolences. They say things like, 'Well, maybe you'll have a girl the next time,' or, 'Too bad, there's nothing like a daughter!' I'm really flabbergasted and furious." So reports Annie, mother of two boys.

"I wanted a girl so badly the second time that I asked the doctor not to tell me what he saw on my sonogram. I didn't want to know, because I knew that once I saw the baby I would love it no matter what, but if it was a boy and I had time to dwell on the fact, I would be disappointed. You can imagine how I felt when the sonogram technician blurted out, 'Look, you can see the baby's penis!' I was upset until my son was actually born." Georgine related this story almost ten years after her youngest was born—it hasn't left her memory.

While the women we talked to were thrilled to have sons, if they didn't already have a daughter, most desired one. They felt that without a daughter their families were not yet complete. At the same time, some admitted that if they had given birth to a daughter first, they would have not felt the longing for a son.

We overheard a conversation between two women recently. One was pregnant with her second child and knew that she was having a girl. She said to her friend, "I couldn't take another boy. I'm so sick of Ninja turtles and soccer." Her friend nodded in agreement and added, "I know. That's all my son, Eric, does. Sports, sports, sports. And he's only four and a half!"

We also heard similar comments from many of our discussion group attendees. But it wasn't just that these women weren't interested in "boy things"—it went deeper than that. They felt they were missing something by not having a daughter.

Francine felt she was "cheated." "I was very disappointed not to have a girl; I have three boys. I love and adore them, but I have always wished I could have had the chance to share some female growing-up experiences. The boys like G.I. Joe, not Barbie, and their books are boy-oriented, not the books I loved when I was a young girl."

The longing that Francine expresses in her desire for a daughter is in many ways a longing to have her childhood all over again; a desire that is appealing to most of us. Our nostalgic memories are often accompanied by some sadness because we feel too old to participate in these experiences again. Parenting a child of the same gender provides some legitimacy to partaking in these activities and gives a chance to re-create your own childhood.

It's an excuse to pull those Barbie dolls and her wardrobe of little outfits out of the attic and use them again. It's an opportunity to buy pretty clothes instead of all those red-and-blue clothes with sports insignias or dozens of striped T-shirts. Having a daughter gives a mother an opportunity to share advice in areas in which she feels secure in her knowledge—how to braid hair, what it means to be a Girl Scout, why a girl has to have pom-poms on her ice skates, what your first kiss means, and what happens when your body begins to mature.

With a son, a mother doesn't always feel certain she understands his needs or motivations, and she sometimes has to second-guess whether she is giving him the right advice. To many women, raising a daughter seems easier—at least in concept.

The fact is that whether a child is easy or difficult to raise depends on the child and his own personality, not on which sex the child is born. (After all, girls can be colicky too!) We can tell you that the women in our discussion groups were almost equally divided on the subject of whether daughters or sons were easier to raise.

Another reason we may be disappointed in not having daughters is that most of us grow up expecting to have one. When we daydream about getting married and having a family, we envision a family of four, with one boy and one girl. All during most of our childhoods, when we were playing at being mothers with our dolls, we pretended to have girl babies—not boys—and our dolls were female.

Of course, if it turns out we produce only male offspring, we will love our children fiercely anyway. But this doesn't preclude many women from harboring a lingering disappointment. We offer some suggestions that may help in coming to terms with these feelings.

- Today we are fortunate to have technology that offers an opportunity to know the sex of a child in many pregnancies. If you are going to have a procedure such as amniocentesis or a sonogram later in your pregnancy when sexual organs might be visible, you may want to consider being told whether you have a future Einstein or a future Madame Curie doing somersaults and practicing kicks inside you. Psychologically speaking, being prepared for what to expect is comforting for some women.

   "I had hoped for a girl," Anne told us. "When I had amniocentesis, I found out I was having a boy. Knowing the sex of my child almost five months in advance gave me time to get used to the idea of a son and to become enthusiastic about it!" On the practical side, if you do know, you can buy clothes that are "boy" clothes rather than neuter, and decorate his room accordingly. And you only need to argue with your husband over one name decision, not two!

- You might also want to spend time talking to women you know about how they felt having only sons. This might help you to focus on what a wonderful experience it is; when your friends start to complain about the horror of adolescent girls, you can even gloat.

- Take solace, too, in the fact that little boys are usually much more affectionate and loving with their mothers than little girls are—an experience you wouldn't trade for the world. Surprisingly, this positive aspect of mothering little boys doesn't really end after the Oedipal stage, according to many of our mothers. We heard over and over again from mothers of sons that as they got older their sons became extremely protective of them and wanted to take care of them, whereas their daughters were more wrapped up in themselves. We don't believe this should be a motivating factor in having a child, but it's nice to know it might be a residual benefit. As one mother with two sons told us: "I love being the only woman in our house . . . in my family I'm treated like a queen!"

- We'd also like to point out that a mother shouldn't assume with a son that she can't share her childhood experiences. Children are children regardless of their gender, and many childhood pursuits cross sex-typed barriers. On the other hand, learning about the world of boys through her son gives a mother a chance to visit a place she was never privy to as a child.

When Longing Becomes a Problem

For some women, the issue is more complicated and may involve an obsession rather than a nostalgic longing to re-create your childhood through a daughter. It would be wise to reexamine your motives if you are planning to have another child in hopes that you will produce a daughter who can fulfill your need to relive your childhood. A child should be loved for itself and allowed to unfold into its own unique being. A woman with misguided motives for motherhood will be attempting to pre-program her child from birth because of her own agenda. While fantasizing about having a little girl to play Barbie dolls with or imagining buying her first pink ballet slippers might be harmless, there also might be a lot more going on in such a fantasy than meets the eye. Some woman may unconsciously hope with a daughter to rework unsatisfactory relationships they have had with their mothers . . . something that's more difficult to accomplish with a son.

"When I was pregnant I desperately wanted a daughter, because at age thirty-seven, I assumed I'd only have one child," Maureen reported. "I thought this was simply because it would be so nice to have a little girl. My mother more or less abandoned me when I was five and left me to live with my grandparents. I only saw her about once a year. I never allowed myself to get in touch with how much I missed having my mother. Now I'm in my forties, and my husband and I are planning to have another child, and I had to look within myself to make certain that I'm not just making a second try for a daughter, that I really want a *baby*. I think I've finally come to peace with the fact that I can't get my mother back, it's in the past. So I'll be happy even if my second child is another boy. Anyway, I'm in hot water with my son if I don't give him a brother!"

Trying to undo a traumatic situation like a difficult childhood is an unconscious defense. If a mother seeks to relive her life with her mother through her child, she is in a sense making her child into her parent. (Although women are more likely to do this to their daughters, many try to do it with their sons as well.) Additionally, if the disappointment of having a son is too great, a woman may try to treat him almost as if he were a girl, in much the same way we think of fathers who wanted sons turning their daughters into tomboys and nicknaming them "Mike." The problems this could create for a boy are obvious and likely to be permanent. He could suffer from gender-identity issues or have guilt over not being able to live up to his mother's expectations of him. He also is likely to understand that he is a disappointment to her. A mother who can't resolve her feelings of disappointment in having a son should seek immediate professional help to deal with these feelings before she causes emotional harm to her son and so that she can begin to enjoy motherhood.

Disappointment—a Hidden Agenda?

There are a number of other reasons why a woman might be disappointed in having a son, and the disappointment may actually be masking a deep-hidden fear. A woman who has been sexually abused as a girl might be afraid of touching the body of a little boy, afraid of raising a little boy, or afraid of being in a house full of men. This may sound paradoxical, as she has obviously had a sexual relationship with her partner, but emotions related to sexual abuse are often suppressed in the victims and may bring a rise of anxiety during a stressful situation which is not always understood. There may also be other underlying conflicts women face that have to do with absent fathers. If a woman was raised without a father, she could be fearful of mothering a son. Similarly, a woman facing single motherhood and the raising of a son without his father may see the task as much more daunting than raising a daughter.

"I was afraid of the challenge of raising a son. In fact, I was totally terrified," Marla told us when we interviewed her. She became a young widow when her son was only two. Today that son is grown. "The experience has not been what I expected. Although there have been many challenges, I would not have traded the experience for anything. It's been great," she concluded.

There is another reason many women wish they had a daughter. Rita explained: "For me, the hardest thing to accept is that as I get older, I won't have a daughter to go shopping with, to confide in, and to just do the special things mothers and daughters do." Mothers, on the whole, are far more worried about losing their sons when they grow up than they are their daughters. Their fear is based on two assumptions. The first is that grown sons don't usually have the same interests as their mothers, whereas grown daughters are more likely to have at least some activities they can share with their mothers. The second fear is that mothers know that eventually they will be "turning their sons over" to other women. A wife or a girlfriend becomes the primary female relationship in a man's life, so by rights his relationship with his mother has to change. Compounding this fear is the additional worry that they might not get along with the new women in their sons' lives and will consequently be shut out.

We'd like to point out some obvious, but often overlooked, points. First, it is highly unlikely that your children will turn out the way you expect them to. The little girl you want to dress in frilly clothes may prefer patched jeans so she can play football. She could grow up to hate to shop or go for facials. There's no guarantee that you'll have a closer relationship with your daughter than with your son. It's your child's personality and the relationship that you have together that will foreshadow your relationship when your child reaches maturity, not your child's gender.

Parents who have children as their old-age insurance probably shouldn't have had children in the first place. Children should not be brought into this world to provide their parents with companions or to be caretakers for their parents later in life. To long for a daughter simply because a grown son might not be as available to a mother seems like a waste of emotional energy. There are no lifetime guarantees that come with children of either sex.

Your son may actually be the one who's more of your soul mate than your daughter—we were told by many mothers that this was the case in their families. Many reported feeling closer to their sons and having a harder time understanding their daughters.

Our purpose in this chapter is not to suggest that any woman who hopes to have a daughter has emotional problems. Of course, wanting to have a daughter is entirely normal. It is when a mother can't get past the disappointment of only having sons, and appears to be grieving for the daughter she never had, that we think she needs to delve deeper into her emotions and find out what is really going on. Maybe then she can join the circle of mothers who told us that having a son was an exciting adventure that they felt privileged to have shared.

As one mother said, "I've learned so much from having a son. And my son had been a kind and gentle teacher!"

Appendix
A Handbook: Medical and
Developmental Issues

When one of the authors' sons was about eight months old, it was discovered he had an inguinal hernia, a condition commonly found in boys. The child is actually born with it, although the hernia may not become apparent for years. Usually not life-threatening, such a condition nevertheless requires surgery as soon as possible. Suddenly we were researching a medical situation we had never even heard of before, and one we had not recognized in our own son. The hernia was a visible lump in his groin, but we were not familiar enough with how a little boy's body was supposed to look to see that there was a problem. This experience made us realize that mothers of boys need to educate themselves about the physical conditions and problems seen only or more frequently in boys.

Traditional wisdom would have us believe that females are the "weaker sex," but males are actually more susceptible to an array of medical problems. Although 120 males are conceived for every 100 females, the rate of fetal and neonatal deaths in males is higher, so the actual ratio of the sexes that survive is about equal. Boys also have a higher incidence of anomalies than girls because of sex-linked chromosomal defects, some of which we'll discuss later in this chapter, but even

171

many of the most serious anomalies can be treated with medication and surgery.

Some of the topics covered here will be common conditions and not of a serious nature; others are more critical. Our goal is not to scare you; statistically speaking, it is highly unlikely your son will ever suffer from most of the illnesses or conditions we will explore. Yet we feel that it is your right and responsibility to know about these medical and developmental problems for which your son is at higher risk.

Medical Conditions That Occur Only or More Frequently in Boys
Entries that are preceded by an asterisk occur in *boys only.*

Bone Fractures are more common in young boys than in adults because boys still have "open growth plates," the soft cartilage in bones that promotes growth and which don't close until adulthood. A simple fracture means that the bone breaks but the skin is unbroken; when a compound fracture occurs, both the skin and the bone break. Stress fractures are small cracks in the bone which may result from overuse of a limb during a particular sport or activity. Any fracture requires immediate medical attention, especially if a boy is in shock. Symptoms of shock include clammy skin, weak but rapid pulse, dizziness, fast breathing. If a fracture is suspected, do not try to move the affected bone, and put ice on to reduce the swelling.

Breast Swelling at birth occurs in both female and male babies and is caused by the mother's hormone surge. There may even be a white fluid that comes from the baby's nipple and which is sometimes called "witch's milk." The baby boy's penis and testicles may also be enlarged. If the testicles are enlarged, the penis may appear very small.

Cleft Palate and Lip is a condition a baby is born with, resulting in a split upper lip, a split palate (roof of the mouth), or both, sometimes accompanied by teeth problems. The condition is almost always noticeable and most cases are inherited *(two-thirds of which are boys).* The rate of occurrence is about 1 in 1,000 births. Surgery is usually performed as early as possible, because without it children may have trouble receiving nourishment.

Clubfoot (congenital Talipes Equinovarus) is a deformity, present at birth, in which the foot or ankle is in an odd position. It occurs in 1 in 400 babies, with *boys having this problem twice as frequently.* A mild version can be handled with exercises while the child is an infant, but in most cases surgery is required to correct the condition. Although the cause is unknown, it is believed to be a combination of both genetic and environmental factors.

Color Blindness is an inherited trait which *occurs much more frequently in males* than in females—*8 percent of all white males (particularly those of European and Asian descent)* and *4 percent of all black males have it.* It is the inability to distinguish certain colors, usually red and green, but not all colors. In a rare form called monochromatic vision, a child sees in only one color. There is no prevention or treatment for color blindness.

˚Gynecomastia is breast enlargement in males. While this is a normal temporary condition in boys during puberty (particularly in overweight boys), it may be cause for concern in a prepubertal boy and should be brought to the attention of your son's doctor.

Causes of gynecomastia include side effects of medicine, inadequate androgen (male hormone) production, Klinefelter's syndrome, testicular failure and feminizing tumors (usually adrenal, which cause too much estrogen production), breast cancer, neurofibromatosis, hemangioma (a group of blood vessels that come together and form a mass), lipoma (a fatty tumor), abscess (a pocket of pus), bruises, pituitary tumors, testicular tumors, and thyroid disease.

Hypopituitarism *affects boys more often than girls* and happens in the early years. It can be a problem caused by the malfunction of the hypothalamus, which controls a number of functions such as thirst and body-temperature regulation, or by the pituitary gland, which secretes hormones, or by a tumor.

No change in the growth rate of a child who has reached the age of puberty is an indicator that there may be a problem. The child will appear young-looking for his age. Treatment with hormones that promote growth and sexual development is essential.

Inguinal Hernias are tissue defects that will be present at birth in 1 in 20 children, with *nine times as many boys affected.* It is the most common of abdominal wall defects and appears as a bulge or a swelling, frequently not visible until a child is crying. Symptoms also include one or more of the following: continuous pain or a lump in the groin, abdominal cramps, and vomiting.

Surgical repair is necessary to avoid complications which can become a medical emergency, and may be indicated by bloating of the lower abdomen. Although a hernia usually occurs on only one side, it is important for the surgeon to check both sides to avoid a second surgery at a later date.

While present from birth, an inguinal hernia can go undiscovered until adulthood.

Intestinal Polyps account for 90 percent of all childhood polyps and *occur in boys much more often than in girls.* Usually harmless, they can be found in children between ages one and fifteen (but primarily appear in ages three to six) and tend to disappear by puberty without any treatment.

Symptoms may include rectal bleeding, and in older children, abdominal pain and/or diarrhea.

˙Jock Itch (tinea) is a skin infection which is a form of the ringworm fungus. It is commonly found in the groin area or on the skin of the upper leg in teenage boys. Like ringworm, it appears first as round spots which begin to heal from the inside out, creating the ringlike look. When ringworm is located in the groin area, the rings enlarge much faster than when on other parts of the body. It can be treated with an antifungal medicine, but if it continues to spread, a doctor should be consulted.

Kawasaki Disease (mucocutaneous lymph node syndrome) was first described in Japan in 1967 and is believed to be caused by a virus. It is *two times more likely to be contracted by boys* than girls. While it is not a common disease and occurs primarily in boys of Asian-American backgrounds, for undetermined reasons the disease is on the rise and parents of all boys should be aware of it.

Typically, 5 cases per 100,000 are reported, but in 1991, 150 cases per 100,000 were reported. The disease is characterized by prolonged high fevers, a rash, conjunctivitis (pink eye), swelling of the hands and feet, irritation and inflammation of the mucous membranes of the mouth, lips, and throat, and swollen lymph nodes in the neck. Most patients are under the age of five.

The treatment for Kawasaki disease is the administration of aspirin and intravenous gamma globulin (a component of blood plasma), and the sooner it is diagnosed the better. Untreated cases run the danger of causing permanent heart damage, and in a small number of cases aneurysms can occur.

Legg-Calvé-Perthes (aseptic necrosis of the femoral head) is a noninfectious temporary disease of the hip socket. *Eighty-five percent of children affected are boys (1 in 750).* Male infants who weigh less than five pounds at birth are five times more susceptible to getting this disease than those whose birth weight was more than eight pounds. It usually appears from the ages of four to ten.

In the early stages Legg-Calvé-Perthes can be mistaken for muscle strain or bruising, and X-rays are needed for proper diagnosis. The disease results in a loss of blood flow to the hipbone which causes part of the bone to "die." It runs its course in one to several years, after which time the bone usually regenerates. In the early first few weeks it appears as a swollen hip joint with decreased movement.

Treatment is necessary to prevent hip malformation. If a child complains of ongoing hip pain or limps for several days, a doctor should be consulted.

"Little League Elbow" is a condition in which the elbow becomes chronically stressed and inflamed; it is caused by repeated throwing motions and may be connected with throwing curve balls or playing ball too hard at a young age. The primary treatment for this problem is to rest the arm, although in some cases physical therapy may be deemed appropriate.

Night Terrors are most common among two- to five-year-olds, with *boys having them slightly more than girls.* Distinct from simple nightmares, night terrors are not dreams, but incomplete arousals from deep, nondreaming sleep. A child may thrash, cry, kick, or moan in his sleep and will appear confused and/or frightened and not recognize his parents.

Night terrors can last from a few minutes to almost an hour, and children do not remember the episodes. If they

continue past the age of six, they may indicate a problem
that should be addressed.

Nocturnal Enuresis is the name given to bed-wetting that continues in children older than five. Primary enuresis means
a child has never stopped wetting his bed, and secondary
enuresis means that he has stopped and begun again. The
secondary version is often triggered by an illness or a traumatic event.

In primary enuresis there tends to be a family history—almost 75 percent of boys who have this problem have one or
both parents who had the same problem. It is *twice as common in boys* than in girls under the age of twelve. Between
10 and 15 percent of five-year-olds will wet their beds; this
number decreases each year. In some cases, the problem
may continue until adulthood.

Various medications and the use of behavioral modification are available as treatment options, but medical analysis
should definitely be sought before beginning any program.

Osgood-Schlatter Disease is a bump that occurs on the front
of the shinbone, commonly caused by participation in childhood sports. It is actually a microfracture which becomes
inflamed and causes tenderness and pain in the area. Often
occurring during the adolescent growth spurt, it can be the
result of too much physical activity. Treatment consists
mainly of resting the leg, but a cast and/or physical therapy
may be indicated.

Osteochondritis Dissecans is an aseptic necrosis condition
like Legg-Calvé-Perthes, which means it involves death of
some of the tissue of the femur bone from causes unknown,
but not infection. A section of bone or cartilage can partially
or completely detach and lodge in a nearby joint, causing
lack of blood flow. The knee may also be affected. The symptoms include stiffness, swelling, and clicking. It is diagnosed
with an X-ray and over time can lead to arthritis. The disease
may be treated with a cast, and in some cases, surgery.
Males are affected more often than females.

Pigeon Breast (Pectus Carinatum) is a structural deformity
of the chest that usually develops between ages eleven to
fourteen, with three out of four cases being boys. It is a condition in which the breastbone is pushed outward, but it can

be corrected with surgery. A related condition is pectus excavatum, in which the breastbone is pushed inward; if left uncorrected, it can lead to emphysema in early life, because in severe cases the chest is locked in the full inhalation position. It may appear in combination with scoliosis (curvature of the spine).

Precocious Puberty refers to a condition in which a boy (or girl) becomes physically mature at a very young age. If the physical changes associated with puberty occur early, there may be problems, including stunted growth. The appearance of pubic hair or genital enlargement before age ten should be reported to a physician.

In general, the younger the child the more rapid the onset of the condition and the greater the likelihood that there is a medical problem which should be investigated. Even if there is no medical cause, a boy who goes through puberty early may become isolated from other boys. Interestingly, there appears to be no correlation between early puberty and sexual activity.

Scoliosis is a curvature of the spine toward one side of the body. There are a number of different types of scoliosis, but one, infantileidiopathic scoliosis, is more common in male babies. This form usually disappears by itself in a few years. Infrequently, the condition may worsen and must then be treated with shoe lifts, braces, or, in extreme cases, surgery.

Sever's Disease is indicated by a tenderness in the heel, and pain when weight is put on the ball of the foot. Usually occurring between the ages of eight and eleven, it is caused by too much physical activity which places stress on the heel bone—often both heels will be involved. This condition is treated with rest, foot-stretching exercise, and the wearing of footwear proper for an activity.

Suicide in children is more common than might be expected. Girls attempt suicide more often than boys, but boys are more likely to have guns so they succeed more frequently; in fact, they are four times more successful!

Between the ages of twelve to fifteen, for every one thousand children, two will commit suicide. From ages fifteen to twenty-five, the numbers are even higher and still growing. Since 1960 the number of teen suicides in the United States has doubled.

Studies show that the absence of a strong support system or a major change in an important relationship, as well as ongoing problems such as lack of friends, difficulties with parents, or the existence of other stressful situations, may be factors in suicide attempts.

If a child makes a suicide threat, a parent should take it seriously and discuss the problem *immediately,* reinforcing his or her love for the child, and then seek professional help. Though suicide threats are not uncommon in children, they are usually a call for help and should be responded to as such. A child who threatens suicide may not have shown previous signs of depression. The socioeconomic group a child belongs to is *not* a factor. The possibility of a child committing suicide decreases if the parent can help make the child feel hopeful. It goes without saying that keeping guns and unnecessary medication out of the home is wise.

Tics are involuntary rapid and repeated movements of a muscle or group of muscles. This includes behavior such as blinking, throat clearing, sniffing, head shaking, shoulder shrugging, etc. They may appear in children as young as age two, with *boys developing them three times as often as girls.*

Tics usually go away during sleep periods and may be triggered by stress or excitement. In most cases they appear before age six and disappear with adolescence. If a sequence of tics appears and seems to increase in frequency, it might be indicative of Tourette's syndrome and a medical consultation should be considered.

Tourette's syndrome is a rare condition which usually begins to appear between the ages of four and ten but may manifest itself as early as two or as late as fifteen years of age. *Of the approximately 100,000 people who have it in this country, 75,000 are male.* It produces behavior which consists of multiple tics and strange vocal sounds which include throat clearing, coughs, grunts, squeals, etc. Tourette's syndrome is diagnosed on the basis of a group of vocal and motor tics, with symptoms that decrease and then intensify over time. Also, symptoms that change over time and are present for at least one year are part of the diagnosis.

Children with Tourette's syndrome may also have echolalia, which is the compulsion to repeat words voiced by others in a mimicking fashion. Twenty percent of the children who have Tourette's syndrome also have coprolalia, an irresistible urge to utter profanities and/or a phonic tic. From 20 to 50 percent have Attention Deficit Disorder as well (please see section on developmental problems).

Researchers now believe this syndrome is related to a problem in the central nervous system. The symptoms often decrease in late adolescence and can be helped with medication.

Medical Problems Connected with the Male Genitals and Reproductive System

˙Baby Balanitis (inflammation and cellulitis of the glans penis) is a bacterial infection of the penis which is more common in uncircumcised babies in the first year of life. It may follow a bout of diaper rash and will leave the affected area red, swollen, and tender; there may also be pus discharge. Baby balanitis can be treated with an antibiotic cream and heals faster when the diaper is left off whenever possible.

˙Balanitis is inflammation of the foreskin and underlying tissues which occurs frequently in teenagers who may not adhere to proper hygiene. It appears as an oozing patch and is cleared up with the use of antibiotics.

˙Cryptorchidism is the failure of one or both testicles to come into the scrotal sac. It occurs in 20 percent of male premature births, but in only 2 percent of full-term births.

The testicles may remain in the abdomen or the inguinal canal, but in 90 percent of these cases, the problem will rectify itself by a baby's first birthday or will be able to be manipulated into place.

If a testicle periodically retracts, this is a condition known as a **retractable testicle** and does not need surgical correction. An undescended testicle that does not come into place on its own will eventually require surgery (before age five).

˙Epididymitis is an infection of the epididymis (the area of the testicle in which sperm is stored while it "matures") and can cause severe urethritis, an infection of the urinary tract. It is treated with antibiotics.

˙Hydrocele is a swelling from accumulation of fluid in the scrotum; most often it occurs on one side and is not painful. The surrounding areas including the penis, may also be affected. Typically a hydrocele goes away in a few days, but it can last as long as a few months, and may be caused by a minor injury or an insect bite. In young boys it may go hand in hand with an inguinal hernia, while in older boys it may mean an infection of the scrotum. It can occur at any age from infancy on into adulthood although most frequently it appears in the first year of life.

Hypogonadism is the name for impaired testicle function. This condition, caused by a reduction in the production of testosterone, can result in malformed sperm or prevent the production of any sperm. If this happens before a boy reaches puberty, he must receive testosterone replacement therapy or his body may not physically mature. If it occurs *after* puberty, his body and sexual organs will look normal, but he may lose his sex drive and/or fertility.

This condition can be caused by a birth defect, torsion (see separate description), mumps, gonorrhea, or adrenal or thyroid dysfunctions.

Meatal Ulcers are caused by repeated infections of the glans or the tip of the penis, which in turn infects the meatus, the opening through which a boy urinates. Crusty pus and spots of blood may appear. A baby may cry when he urinates. It is important to treat this condition with an antibiotic cream to prevent scarring.

Micropenis is an extremely rare birth defect in which the penis is less than one inch in length at birth. It can be treated with a hormone cream or an oral medication, but may also be indicative of a malfunction of the sex hormones or testicles. The child's pediatrician would run tests to rule out any underlying causes.

Orchitis is a general name for an infection of the testicles. Symptoms include a red scrotum, swollen testicles, pain, and fever. Orchitis can be caused by a sports injury, mononucleosis, diphtheria, scarlet fever, sexually transmitted diseases, mumps, a virus, or use of steroids. It is treated with antibiotics.

Epididymo-orchitis is the inflammation of one or both of the testicles and the epididymis (the area behind the testicles where sperm is stored), and is often associated with venereal disease. This infection is treated with antibiotics.

°Perineal or Scrotal Hypospadias is when the penis is attached to the scrotum or the scrotum is split in two. The testicles may also be undescended and surgery is required for correction.

°Phimosis is tightness of the foreskin, preventing it from being drawn back over the underlying glans (head) of the penis.

°Prostatitis is an infection of the prostate gland. It can attack older boys and may produce pain, fever, shivering, burning, frequent need to urinate, blood in the urine, and pain in the abdomen. It is treated with antibiotics.

°Rupture of the Tissue under the Penis is a slight tearing that can be very painful. A doctor should be consulted if this takes place, but more than likely it will heal by itself.

°Spermatocele is a painless sac containing dead sperm which is found behind the testicle and moves freely. Treatment is not usually necessary.

°Torsion is caused by a birth defect and means that the testicles hang freely in the scrotum. At some point the spermatic cord which connects the testicles to the internal reproductive organs may become twisted, and this can develop into a medical emergency. If the testicle is cut off from a blood supply, it can become gangrenous in as little as twelve hours.

Sixty-five percent of torsion cases happen between the ages of twelve and eighteen but can also occur in the early twenties. If a boy has swelling or pain in the testicles, see a doctor immediately! The symptoms may appear gradually, often during sleep, and cause a very strong pain in the center of the abdomen or the groin. In fact, torsion may be confused with a stomachache, and is often overlooked as a diagnosis. The scrotum will get red or swollen, a boy may have fever, and vomiting is possible. The pain may go away even if it is not treated and the testicle will start to feel smaller. Also, an abscess may form.

In rare cases an infant can be born with torsion. Undescended testicles can predispose a boy to this problem. In infants the scrotum will not be tender, but rather, enlarged and hard, and will be a bluish color.

Although usually only one testicle is affected, if surgery is performed to correct this problem, the surgeon should check both testicles.

˚**Torsion of the Testicular Epididymis Appendix** occurs not when the spermatic cord twists (as described above), but when a small outgrowth of tissue on the testicle twists. This does not cut off the blood supply and does not endanger the testicle. The symptoms may appear the same as those for torsion, but the only thing that can be felt is a pea-sized lump. If this can be found through a scan, surgery will be unnecessary, as the health of the testicle is not compromised.

Reminder to mothers:

Seek medical help immediately if your son has unexplained pain in the groin or if his genitals are swollen or discolored. Be especially watchful for problems if the testicles are undescended. If your son has pain for an obvious reason such as an injury to the groin area, monitor it closely. If the pain gets worse or other symptoms develop, see a doctor.

Undescended Testicles (see cryptorchidism.)

Urethral Stricture is a birth defect in which the urethra is either too small or closed. It may require surgery and, although rare, can be a complication of a "bad" circumcision. Since babies are checked at birth to make certain they can urinate, this problem is usually discovered early on.

˚**Varicocele** is a sac of varicose veins in the scrotum surrounding the testicles, occurring in about 15 to 20 percent of males between the ages of fifteen and forty-five, but most commonly during adolescence. It results from incomplete valves in the veins that carry blood from the testicles to the heart. In rare cases, it can result from a kidney tumor

It produces a heavy or dragging feeling but does not usually require treatment except in extreme cases, in which surgery may be necessary to prevent sterility. It usually is found in the left testicle.

Injuries to the Groin Area

˚**Blows to the Testicle** can be extremely painful but usually don't cause lasting damage. A severe blow such as being hit with a hard ball can cause a boy to fall over in pain, have stomach pains, and vomit. He may also have difficulty walking for a few days, but usually the pain will diminish in a few minutes; the area may continue to be sore for several days. Icc can bc applicd right after the injury to relieve the pain (but don't put it directly on the skin). Several hours later a warm bath may help. Your son can go on with his regular activities as soon as he feels comfortable.

Testicle Rupture or Dislocation as the result of a blow can happen but is highly unusual, and it may require surgery to repair.

Sexually Transmitted Diseases

As mothers of young boys, we find it hard to think about our sons having sex lives, but they will. We feel it is important for you as a mother to know about the various types of sexually transmitted diseases a boy can contract so that you will be well informed and can teach your son early about the dangers of unprotected sexual contact. We have not included all the sexually transmitted diseases, but rather have focused on those that are most common. If you suspect your son has any symptoms of sexually transmitted diseases, have him see a doctor immediately.

NOTE to mothers:

Protective equipment when playing *contact* sports such as football is important for boys. A protective cup for the genital area is an excellent idea. Athletic supporters (jockstraps) do not protect the genital areas, but are worn to allow more freedom of movement than underwear.

AIDS or Acquired Immune Deficiency Syndrome is a disease that results in the breakdown of the body's immune system, which normally fights infections.

AIDS is caused by a virus known as HIV, and is commonly transmitted by sexual contact (either homosexual or heterosexual). It can also bc passcd on by using a contaminated hypodermic needle or by being transfused with blood containing the HIV virus. Hemophiliacs can be exposed by a contaminated injection of a blood-clotting factor concentrate. A fetus can also receive the virus from its mother.

There is no evidence to believe the HIV virus is transmitted through sneezing, coughing, or touching, sharing food, sleeping next to, or living with an HIV-infected person.

Children with AIDS exhibit basically the same symptoms as adults. They begin with swollen lymph nodes, fever, and weight loss, and eventually get weak and fatigued. Other problems that may occur include breathing difficulties, diarrhea, coughing, bleeding, muscle pain, pneumonia, and rare cancers such as Kaposi's sarcoma.

AIDS can be detected with a blood test, the same test that blood banks use to screen the blood supply. A positive test does not mean a person will develop AIDS, only that the HIV virus is present. A person who tests positive should remain under a doctor's care. Patients are treated with several medications, but there is no cure for AIDS.

Chlamydia is a bacterial infection which can affect newborns, adolescents, and adults. Although seen more frequently in females, it is responsible for 40 percent of nongonococcal cases of urethritis (inflammation and/or infection of the urethra) in children. It is transmitted either through sexual contact or from a mother to her fetus.

It begins as an odorless white or gray pus coming from the penis and also produces a burning feeling during urination. In a baby, it appears as conjunctivitis (an eye infection) or pneumonia.

If left untreated in an adolescent, the infection may cause swelling of the epididymis, the area of the testes where sperm are stored. If treated with antibiotics, either orally or with eye drops for babies, it usually causes no further complications.

Genital Herpes is the most common sexually transmitted disease in the United States. When first infected, an individual may have no symptoms or may have blisters for about two weeks. The blisters disappear but can be reactivated from time to time, *more frequently in males than in females.* Headaches, fever, painful urination, and swollen lymph nodes can also be experienced.

Symptoms, meaning blisters, can be passed on to a sexual partner through oral or vaginal sex or by touching one's fingers to the lips and then to the genitals. The virus is very contagious and can be spread for about ten days—from a few days before an eruption until after it disappears.

Genital herpes cannot be cured, but antiviral medicines can decrease the time period for the blisters, lessen pain, and reduce fever after the first breakout.

Genital Warts are an abnormal growth of skin cells in the genital area caused by a virus. They are often found on abused children. The warts can appear on the skin or mucous membranes of the genital and rectal areas and are very contagious. A few masses may be observed, or hundreds of warts may be present. Although not dangerous, they may be uncomfortable and are unattractive.

Gonorrhea is a highly infectious bacterial disease that is sexually transmitted through oral or anal sex, and less commonly by the hands. In males, gonorrhea usually involves the urethra, and early symptoms are more likely to be visible. If left untreated, symptoms often disappear on their own without incident, although the disease can still be passed on to a sexual partner. Young children can contract gonorrhea from adults through sexual abuse and incest. Infrequently, a child may contract it through prepubertal sex play with other children.

Up to 40 percent of afflicted males have no symptoms of gonococcal urethritis, while others may notice pain when they urinate or a discharge of pus. When in the throat, the infection appears similar to strep throat. If it occurs in the rectum or the anus, it may cause pain when relieving the bowels, or a discharge of blood and/or pus. If the eye is infected, there will be a discharge of pus. Gonorrhea can be diagnosed by taking a culture. It is important to be treated as early as possible to prevent the infection from spreading through the body. Treatment for gonorrhea is the use of penicillin or other antibiotics.

Hepatitis B is a very contagious form of viral hepatitis (inflammation of the liver), which in some cases can be transmitted sexually or orally through saliva. It is also transmitted through blood transfusions, contaminated needles, and surgical and dental equipment that is not properly sterilized. Symptoms can include fever, headache, muscle aches, rashes, and loss of appetite, followed by nausea, vomiting, abdominal pain, and joint pain. Jaundice, a yellow color in the whites of the eyes and sometimes in the skin, may appear. Hepatitis is diagnosed by a blood test as well as other tests, such as one that checks if the liver function is abnormal. Bed rest is the only treatment for hepatitis, and the patient should be monitored carefully because there is always a danger of liver failure.

Nongonococcal or Nonspecific Urethritis is an infection of the urethra which is spread through sexual intercourse. Most people have no symptoms, but if they do, the symptoms appear within three weeks after having sex. In a male they consist of burning or pain during urination, or a yellow or white drip from the penis. Without treatment this infection can damage reproductive organs and cause sterility.

Pubic Lice are shorter in length than the type of lice found on the head or body. They look like miniature crabs; hence the colloquial name "crabs" for them. In adolescents or adults they are usually attached to the pubic hair but are sometimes found on the chest, thighs, or beard as well. They can be transmitted through physical contact as well as from clothing, bedding, and towels. Over-the-counter products are available to kill them, but repeated treatment may be necessary to kill eggs that hatch.

Scabies are highly contagious mites that are found anywhere on the body, including the groin area, and can be transmitted by sexual contact. Young children can get them in school through nonsexual contact. The most likely sites to find them are near the penis, wrist, and finger webs. To treat scabies, wash the body with gamma benzene hexachloride, which is sold in the drugstore under the name Kwell.

Syphilis *infects males three times more often than females.* There are two types of syphilis, one which is acquired through sexual contact and another which is transmitted from an infected mother to her fetus.

Syphilis progresses through a number of stages. In the first or incubation stage, which lasts several weeks, there are no symptoms. Then a chancre, or small, hard but painless sore, will appear on the penis or scrotum or, less often, on the lips, fingers, or anus. If a boy is infected before puberty, he will rarely have a detectable chancre. This sore heals in three to six weeks, and there may also be swollen but painless lymph nodes.

The disease becomes "latent" in the next stage, meaning that there are no symptoms, and this stage can last from a few weeks to a few months.

As syphilis progresses, small pink or red spots will appear on the skin; these may turn into inflamed lupus or pimples all over the body or stay confined to one area. Other symptoms may include malaise (a general lack of energy), loss of appetite, weight loss, a low-grade fever, scaly skin, severe pain in the joints, sore throat and/or laryngitis, enlargement of the spleen and lymph nodes, hair loss, and inflammation of the irises.

After this very symptomatic active stage, the disease becomes latent again for as little as a few years to as long as fifty years, and if left untreated, can become fatal.

In the early stages, syphilis can be treated with penicillin.

Developmental Problems in Boys

Boys are far more prone than girls to learning disabilities or difficulties in processing information. A number of different problems come under this heading, such as dyslexia, which is the inability to read properly; dyscalculia, or the inability to do math; dysgraphia, which is a writing problem; and others that involve listening, speaking, and reasoning.

Dr. Gail Ross, a child psychologist and assistant professor of psychology at the New York Hospital/Cornell Medical Center, says: "Boys are more at risk for disturbances of early development. Clearly they are more vulnerable, particularly when you include problems such as ADD and hyperactivity into this category."

In addition, developmental problems are more common in babies who are born prematurely. These problems can often start to be diagnosed as early as age two, with signs including hyperactivity, delayed language problems, inability to follow directions, poor sleeping habits, and excessive dawdling. Some of the other factors a physician looks at when considering the diagnosis of learning disabilities are temper tantrums, moodiness, irritability, stomachaches or headaches related to school attendance, restlessness, dislike of school, inability to concentrate, poor motor coordination, poor memory, and a family history of learning disabilities, particularly in the father.

Bear in mind that all of these behaviors may occur in children without learning disabilities, but when many appear together, this may point to a problem.

When considering the possible diagnosis of learning disabilities, other conditions need to be ruled out, such as deafness, retardation, autism, childhood schizophrenia, seizure disorders, and allergies, particularly to food.

We'd also like to point out that parents should consider the evidence carefully and seek professional advice when a teacher labels a boy as learning disabled. An article written in 1991 by Dr. Sally Shaywitz of the Yale University of Medicine concluded that boys considered "reading disabled" by teachers may be "just acting like boys." She cited a study in which testing showed that there was an equal number of boys and girls in a school with reading disabilities, but the teachers labeled more boys as having problems.

Hyperactive is also a label some teachers place too easily on boys. Young boys have a tendency to be restless, move around a lot, and have trouble sitting still. As Betty Osman says in the book *Learning Disabilities: A Family Affair*, "Some children are perceived as hyperactive in school, particularly by teachers who have a need for order and tranquillity in their classrooms." Again, seek the opinion of an additional professional.

Attention Deficit Disorder (ADD) was once called hyperactivity syndrome or minimal brain dysfunction, but studies have shown there is no brain damage in children with ADD. In fact, it is a neurological problem, and an ADD child may or may not be hyperactive. *Boys are at least three times more likely to have this disorder,* depending on which study you look to for statistics.

The main characteristics of this developmental problem are an inability to pay attention and a propensity for not being able to control impulses, which obviously can cause problems for a boy in school. The child may also have trouble "processing" a lot of information at one time. If hyperactivity is not present, this disorder can be harder to diagnose, and a child could be having trouble in school without the reason being apparent. ADD children may have other learning disabilities as well.

Children with ADD may also have language problems, which include not being able to learn the names of objects or having difficulty understanding what is being said to them. They can be moody and harder to discipline.

The behavioral problems are usually noticeable before age seven and should have lasted six months or more before a diagnosis of ADD can be considered. It is also possible that if a child isn't paying attention or is moody in school, he may just be not getting enough sleep—a problem that can easily be corrected. A change in diet may also be effective.

Treatment for ADD can be a combination of efforts including special-education classes, behavior modification work at home, speech therapy, and psychotherapy.

Autism is a serious developmental disorder which affects 2 in 10,000 children in the United States; *boys are affected at least twice as often as girls.* Autism is primarily diagnosed by observing a child's behavior and is characterized by his lack of responsiveness to other people (having trouble forming emotional attachments to parents and others) as well as problems with development and language. An autistic child may have difficulty making eye contact with people and may even have shown evidence of autism from infancy: unlike most babies, he may not like to be held.

Autism is usually apparent by age three, when it becomes obvious that normal social responses are not developing and speech is either abnormal or not developing at all. The child resists changes in his life and receives comfort from repetition. He may participate in rote activities, as did the character played by Dustin Hoffman in the movie *Rain Man*, memorizing charts such as bus schedules. A child may constantly repeat TV commercials, sing songs at inappropriate times, or mimic other people's speech. Movement disorders such as rocking, head-banging, and hair pulling may also occur.

There are varying degrees of autism, and the severity of the condition may lessen in adulthood, although it does not go away entirely. Some autistic children are also mentally retarded, while others who have higher intelligence and better language development can become somewhat independent as they get older. An autistic child may exhibit very early letter or number recognition or may read early without really understanding what he is reading.

Autism often occurs in combination with medical problems such as encephalitis, meningitis, mental retardation, PKU (a metabolic problem), congenital rubella (the mother had German measles while pregnant), congenital syphilis (the mother had syphilis while pregnant), and retrolental fibrosis (an eye problem that can cause blindness in premature babies).

It was once believed that improper parenting was the cause of autism—the child was rejecting the world around him because his parents had not met his needs as a baby—but this theory has been rejected because it is now known that a child is born with autism. Many experts believe that the "factors" that cause the medical problems mentioned above may also cause autism. Since the incidence of other neurological disorders are higher in autistic children, researchers hypothesize that autism may be caused by a problem with the processing center in the brain or by a malfunction of the central nervous system. There may also be genetic factors at play, as siblings have a much greater chance of being autistic than the general population.

If a child is suspected of being autistic, the best place to seek an evaluation is at a university-affiliated developmental clinic. This type of clinic is usually well equipped to rule out other problems that may resemble autism, such as hearing loss, mental retardation (without autism), and in unusual cases, "social deprivation," caused by parents who are not allowing their child to become socialized. A second opinion is always a good idea.

Autism is a difficult problem to deal with, but treatment has come a long way. There are now special day programs for autistic children and medication may be helpful, although it will not cure the problem. There is also a new and somewhat controversial method of teaching autistic children to communicate by typing on a computer (known as facilitated communication). As this book was going to press, the Children's National Medical Center in Washington, D.C. reported "dramatic results" treating autistic children with the drug naltrexone.

Dyslexia is the term used when a child has difficulty with language and words; it includes reversal, addition, deletion, and substitution of letters. It affects 15 percent of the population of the Western world, but occurs worldwide, *with between four to ten males for every female dyslexic,* according to most studies. Some researchers have recently been suggesting that boys don't have a higher incidence of dyslexia, but are referred for help more often than girls. There is also recent evidence from research conducted at the Yale School of Medicine that in some children dyslexia may disappear over time and in other children it may appear much later than it is usually expected to have been diagnosed.

Postmortem analysis of the brains of males who had dyslexia show an abnormal arrangement of nerve cells in the areas of the left side of the brain associated with language and reading skills. Apparently a certain number of "excess" brain cells are supposed to die off during fetal development, and if they fail to do so, dyslexia results.

Another study indicates that this abnormality may slow down one of two major visual pathways in the brain, so that visual information is not received in the right sequence, hence the mixing up of words and letters. This study suggested that the use of various colors of light filters might help correct the problem.

Dyslexia may be either visual—the reversal of letters or words—or auditory—a child has trouble "integrating" and processing what he hears. Or it may be a combination of both. Misconceptions about dyslexia include the belief that a child's economic background or birth order may cause it, neither of which is true. Although school is harder for dyslexics, with proper help this problem can be overcome. Well-known dyslexics include Albert Einstein, Winston Churchill, and Thomas Edison.

Children with dyslexia require special reading lessons, either with someone provided by the school system or with a teacher hired privately by parents. Parents can also help children with their homework and to learn in other ways at home.

Hyperactivity (Attention Deficit Disorder with Hyperactivity, or ADDH) in children also *occurs about three times more frequently in males.* A hyperactive child has trouble concentrating and staying still and often erupts at inappropriate times.

T. Berry Brazelton, the noted pediatrician, points out that it is a term commonly used for any child who "appears to be out of control," and a true diagnosis of this condition should be made by a health-care professional.

Hyperactivity may run in families, but can also appear following a physical trauma such as birth trauma, head injury, or fetal exposure to alcohol or drugs.

A number of doctors believe that allergies may be a source of hyperactivity. The late Dr. Ben F. Feingold became quite well known for developing the Kaiser-Permanente diet, which he claimed had a 50 percent success rate. His diet advocates avoiding food coloring, artificial flavorings, food additives, and foods containing refined sugar—although there is no scientific proof that sugar causes hyperactivity. A number of studies attempted but failed to connect a direct link to sugar and hyperactivity.

Dr. William G. Crook, author of *Help for the Hyperactive Child,* agrees with Dr. Feingold and adds milk, corn, chocolate, eggs, wheat, peanuts, apples, and yeast to the possible list of food problems. He also believes that other allergies may trigger hyperactivity, including tobacco smoke, chemical contaminants, candida infections (which include the common ear infections of young children), and nutritional deficiencies.

A study done by the National Institutes of Health in 1991 found that hyperactive people don't metabolize enough glucose in the area of the brain that controls attention and movement. This means that part of the brain is less active in hyperactive individuals. About 80 percent of children treated with medication for hyperactivity improve, although many still consider use of medication controversial. Behavior modification programs and possibly psychotherapy are also very useful in controlling a child's behavior. A recent discovery by scientists suggests that a small fraction of cases of hyperactivity is caused by a defective gene that controls the body's use of thyroid hormone.

Half of the children with hyperactivity begin to lose the symptoms as they reach puberty, with the remaining half retaining them into adulthood. In about one-third of children who are hyperactive, there are accompanying learning disabilities as well and these problems must be addressed.

Left-handedness occurs more often in children with learning disabilities. *Males are 2 to 1 more likely to be left-handed.*

The late Dr. Norman Geschwind, a neurologist at Harvard Medical School, linked left-handedness to a number of physical and developmental problems including asthma, dyslexia, stuttering, and autism. All of these aforementioned conditions happen more frequently in boys. He also felt it was linked to genius, particularly in math.

Dr. Geschwind believed that an excess of testosterone during fetal development affects the brain in left-handed children, but further research has not been done to prove his theories. According to Dr. Paul Satz, Ph.D., a professor at the Los Angeles School of Medicine, this theory may have been based on misinformation. He says children who are naturally left-handed but had prenatal or early postnatal damage to the left side of the brain might have switched to their left hand, which worked better. If these children are removed from left-handed studies, the link with developmental difficulties weakens.

It is interesting to note that a recent study by Dr. Charles Graham of the University of Arkansas, Little Rock, indicates that left-handed children are 1.7 times more likely to come to emergency rooms, with male left-handed children twice as likely as "righties" to have accidents. Lefties are also more likely to have accidents that require hospitalization. Although he drew no conclusions as to why this occurs, some researchers believe it is because the world is designed for right-handed people—which makes many things dangerous for those who are left-handed. Lefthander's International, an organization that publishes a newsletter and catalog for lefties, feels the statistics reported by this study may not present an accurate picture and require further research.

In another study done several years ago, the conclusion was drawn that lefties on average die several years earlier than right-handed people. More recent research completed by Harvard and the National Institute for the Aging found no substantiation to this claim.

Schizophrenia affects only 1 in 100,000 children, but is *five times more likely in boys than in girls*. As in the adult form of the disease, it is a "disorganization" of the mind's processes. The cause of this disease is still controversial. Some believe that in young children it is probably biochemical; in older children, stress may be a contributing factor. A recent study by a team of researchers at Harvard Medical School lends credence to the theory that schizophrenia results from damage to the left side of the brain. The study showed a shrinkage of the brain's left temporal lobe, which is partially responsible for hearing and speech.

A schizophrenic child has problems with language, often using words out of context or in a way that they have no relation to one another, and may have serious learning problems. The child's voice may sound flat and without emotion.

He does not exhibit great feelings of pain or pleasure, and tends to have poor muscle tone and coordination. For reasons too complicated to describe here, a child with this condition may begin to suffer from auditory or visual hallucinations and delusions such as paranoia.

Treatment is available. Parents are usually advised to work with a child at home and to combine special education and psychotherapy. Medication may or may not be used. Schizophrenia is a difficult diagnosis to make and is sometimes confused with autism, mental retardation, or learning disorders. The language problems will usually point to a condition that needs to be investigated by age three.

Stuttering occurs when the regular flow of speech is disrupted. While this is common in small children, particularly after they first learn to speak, in about 1 percent of children the problem continues after school age is reached. *Boys are four times as likely to stutter as girls*, and the disorder often runs in families.

Few people become chronic stutterers, but if a problem is suspected after age two and a half to three, a speech pathologist should be consulted.

Selected Bibliography

Books

Aries, Philippe, *Centuries of Childhood: A Social History of Family Life.* New York: Random House, 1962.

Baldwin, Dorothy, *Understanding Male Sexual Health.* New York: Hippocrene Books, 1991.

Balter, Lawrence, with Anita Shreve, *Dr. Balter's Child Sense.* New York: Poseidon Press, 1985.

Berger, Stuart, *Divorce Without Victims.* New York: Signet Books, 1983.

Bly, Robert, *Iron John: A Book About Men.* Reading, Mass.: Addison-Wesley, 1990.

Boston Children's Hospital, *The New Child Health Encyclopedia.* New York: Delta, 1987.

Brazelton, T. Berry, *Touchpoints: Your Child's Emotional and Behavioral Development.* Reading, Mass.: Addison-Wesley, 1992.

Bustanoby, André, *Being a Single Parent.* New York: Ballantine Books, 1985.

Cappolillo, Henry P., *Psychodynamic Psychotherapy of Children.* Madison, Conn.: International Universities Press, 1990.

Chodorow, Nancy, *The Reproduction of Mothering.* Berkeley: University of California Press, 1978.

Cicchetti, Dante, and Vicki Carlson, eds., *Child Maltreatment.* New York: Cambridge University Press, 1990.

Cooper, Kenneth H., *Kid Fitness.* New York: Bantam Books, 1991.

Corneau, Guy, *Absent Fathers, Lost Sons.* Boston: Shambhala, 1991.

Crook, William G., *Help for the Hyperactive Child.* Jackson, Tenn.: Professional Books, 1991.

CTW—Family Living Series, *Understanding Discipline*. New York: Prentice Hall, 1990.

Delamont, Sara, *Sex Roles and the School*. New York: Routledge, Chapman & Hall, 1990.

Elkind, David, *The Hurried Child*. Reading, Mass.: Addison-Wesley, 1987.

Fairchild, Betty, and Nancy Hayward, *Now That You Know: What Every Parent Should Know About Sexuality*. New York: Harvest/HBJ, 1989.

Fausto-Sterling, Anne, *Myths of Gender*. New York: Basic Books, 1985.

Feingold, Ben F., *Why Your Child Is Hyperactive*. New York: Random House, 1975.

Fine, Gary Alan, *With the Boys*. Chicago: University of Chicago Press, 1987.

Forbes, Gilbert B., ed., *Pediatric Nutrition Handbook*. Elk Grove Village, Ill.: Committee on Nutrition—American Academy of Pediatrics, 1985.

Fraiberg, Selma H., *The Magic Years*. New York: Charles Scribner's Sons, 1959.

Franck, Irene, and David Brownstone, *The Parent's Desk Reference*. New York: Prentice Hall, 1991.

Francke, Linda Bird, *Growing Up Divorced*. New York: Ballantine Books, 1983.

Friedman, Richard C., *Male Homosexuality: A Contemporary Psychoanalytic Perspective*. New Haven: Yale University Press, 1988.

Frith, Uta, *Autism: Explaining the Enigma*. Cambridge, Mass.: Basil Blackwell, 1990.

Goldman, Ronald and Juliette, *Show Me Yours*. New York: Penguin Books, 1988.

Goodson, Aileen, *Therapy, Nudity and Joy*. Los Angeles: Elysium Growth Press, 1991.

Goy, Robert W., and Bruce S. McEwen, *Sexual Differentiation of the Brain*. Cambridge, Mass.: Massachusetts Institute of Technology, 1980.

Green, Richard, *The Sissy Boy Syndrome*. New Haven: Yale University Press, 1987.

Greenberg, J.R., and Stephen A. Mitchell, *Object Relations in Psychoanalytic Theory*. Cambridge, Mass.: Harvard University Press, 1983.

Greenberg, Selma, *Right from the Start*. Boston: Houghton Mifflin, 1978.

Grollman, Earl A., *Explaining Divorce to Children*. Boston: Beacon Press, 1969.

Grubman-Black, Stephen D., *Broken Boys/Mending Men*. Blue Ridge Summit, Penn.: HSI and TAB, TAB Books, 1990.

Heslin, Jo-Ann, *No-Nonsense Nutrition for Kids*. New York: Pocket Books, 1988.

Hopcke, Robert H., *Men's Dreams, Men's Healing*. Boston: Shambhala, 1990.

Huesmann, L. Rowell, and Leonard D. Eron, *Television and the Aggressive Child*. Hillsdale, N.J.: Lawrence Erlbaum, 1986.

Hunter, Anne E., Betty Rosoff, and Ethel Tobach, *On Peace, War, and Gender: A Challenge to Genetic Explanations*. New York: Feminist Press, 1991.

Hunter, Mic, *Abused Boys: The Neglected Victims of Sexual Abuse*. New York: Ballantine Books, 1991.

Huston, Anne Marshall, *Common Sense About Dyslexia*. Lanham, Md.: Madison Books, 1987.

Jonas, Gerald, *Stuttering*. New York: Farrar, Straus and Giroux, 1977.

Kaplan, Louise J., *Oneness and Separateness: From Infant to Individual*. New York: Simon & Schuster, 1978.

Keller, Evelyn Fox, *Reflections on Gender and Science*. New Haven: Yale University Press, 1985.

Kempe, Ruth S., and C. Henry, *Child Abuse*. Cambridge, Mass.: Harvard University Press, 1978.

Kutner, Lawrence, *Parent and Child: Getting Through To Each Other*. New York: Avon Books, 1991.

Kurcinka, Mary Sheedy, *Raising Your Spirited Child*. New York: HarperCollins, 1991.

Maccoby, Eleanor Emmons, and Carol Nagy Jacklin, *The Psychology of Sex Differences, Vol. I. Text*. Stanford, Calif.: Stanford University Press, 1978.

———, *The Psychology of Sex Differences, Vol. II. Annotated Bibliography*. Stanford, Calif.: Stanford University Press, 1978.

MacCormack, Carol, and Marilyn Strathern, *Nature, Culture, and Gender*. New York: Press Syndicate of University of Cambridge, 1990.

Madaras, Lynda, *The What's Happening to My Body Book for Boys*. New York: New Market Press, 1988.

Mahler, M., F. Pines Mahler, and A. Bergman, *Psychoanalytic Birth of the Human Infant*. New York: Basic Books, 1975.

Marston, Stephanie, *The Magic of Encouragement*. New York: Pocket Books, 1990.

McGill, Michael E., *The McGill Report on Male Intimacy.* New York: Harper Perennial, 1986.

Miedzian, Myriam, *Boys Will Be Boys: Breaking the Link Between Masculinity and Violence.* New York: Doubleday, 1991.

Milunsky, Aubrey, *Heredity and Your Family's Health.* Baltimore: Johns Hopkins University Press, 1992.

Moir, Anne, and David Jessel, *Brain Sex.* New York: Carol Publishing, 1991.

Money, John, *Love Maps.* New York: Irvington Publishers, 1986.

────── and Anke A. Ehrhardt, *Man and Woman, Boy and Girl.* Baltimore: Johns Hopkins University Press, 1982.

Morgen, Sandra, *Gender and Anthropology.* Washington, D.C.: American Anthropological Association, 1989.

Moss, Robert A., and Helen Huff Dunlap, *Why Johnny Can't Concentrate.* New York: Bantam Books, 1990.

Nelsen, Jane, *Positive Discipline.* New York: Ballantine Books, 1987.

Neubauer, Peter B., and Alexander Neubauer, *Nature's Thumbprint.* Reading, Mass.: Addison-Wesley, 1990.

Neumann, Erich, *The Child.* Boston: Shambhala, 1990 (1st Shambhala ed.).

Ortner, Sherry B., and Harriet Whitehead, *Sexual Meanings.* New York: Cambridge University Press, 1989.

Osherson, Samuel, *Finding Our Fathers.* New York: Ballantine Books, 1986.

────── , *Wrestling with Love.* New York: Ballantine Books, 1992.

Osman, Betty B., *Learning Disabilities: A Family Affair.* New York: Warner Books, 1979.

Parsons, Alexandra, *Facts and Phalluses.* New York: St. Martin's Press, 1989.

Pedersen, Loren E., *Dark Hearts: The Unconscious Forces That Shape Men's Lives.* Boston: Shambhala, 1991.

Pitcher, Evelyn Goodenough, and Lynn Schultz Hickey, *Boys and Girls at Play: The Development of Sex Roles.* South Hadley, Mass.: Bergin and Garvey Publishers, 1983.

Polin, Richard A., and Mark F. Ditmar, *Pediatric Secrets.* Philadelphia: Hanley & Belfus, 1989.

Pomeroy, Wardell B., *Boys and Sex.* New York: Dell, 1987.

Pruett, Kyle D., *The Nurturing Father.* New York: Warner Books, 1987.

Reinisch, June M., and Ruth Beasley, *The Kinsey Institute New Report on Sex.* New York: St. Martin's Press, 1990.

Rich, Adrienne, *Of Woman Born.* New York: W. W. Norton, 1986.

Robins, Lee, and Michael Rutter, *Straight and Devious Pathways from Childhood to Adulthood*. New York: Cambridge University Press, 1991.

Schaefer, Charles E., and Theresa Fay DiGeronimo, *Toilet Training Without Tears*. New York: Signet Books, 1989.

Schreiber, Lee R., *The Parents' Guide to Kids' Sports*. Boston: Time Inc. with Little, Brown and Warner Juvenile Books, 1990.

Schwartz, Kit, *The Male Member*. New York: St. Martin's Press, 1985.

Shapiro, Joan, *Men: A Translation for Women*. New York: Dutton, 1992.

Shettles, B. Landrum, and D.M. Rorvik, *How to Choose the Sex of Your Baby*. New York: Doubleday, 1989.

Singer, Dorothy G., Jerome L. Singer, and Diana M. Zuckerman, *Use TV to Your Child's Advantage*. Reston, Va.: Acropolis Books, 1990.

Solnit, A.J., P. B. Neubauer, S. Abrams, and A.S. Dowling, *The Psychoanalytic Study of the Child*. New Haven: Yale University Press, 1990.

Somers, Leon, and Barbara C. Somers, *Talking to Your Children About Love and Sex*. New York: Signet Books, 1990.

Spock, Benjamin, *Dr. Spock's Baby and Child Care*, 6th rev. ed. New York: Dutton, 1992.

Starer, Daniel, *Who to Call: The Parent's Source Book*. New York: William Morrow, 1992.

Stern, Daniel N., *The Interpersonal World of the Infant*. New York: Basic Books, 1985.

Tavris, Carol, *The Mismeasure of A Woman*. New York: Simon & Schuster, 1992.

Thorn, Mark, *Taboo No More*. New York: Shapolsky Publishers, 1990.

Turecki, Stanley, with Leslie Tonner, *The Difficult Child*, rev. ed. New York: Bantam Books, 1989.

U.S. Department of Education, *Growing Up Drug Free—A Parent's Guide to Prevention*. Washington, D.C.: U.S. Government Printing Office, 1990.

———, *(What Works) Schools Without Drugs*. Washington, D.C.: U.S. Government Printing Office, 1989.

Vogt, Gregory Max, and Stephen T. Sirridge, *Like Son, Like Father*. New York: Plenum, 1991.

Wattleton, Faye with Elisabeth Keiffer—Planned Parenthood, *How to Talk with Your Child About Sexuality*. New York: Doubleday, 1986.

Weiss, Daniel Evan, *The Great Divide: How Females and Males Really Differ*. New York: Poseidon Press, 1991.

Wender, Paul H., *The Hyperactive Child, Adolescent and Adult*. New York: Oxford University Press, 1987.

Whelan, Elizabeth, *Boy or Girl?* New York: Pocket Books, 1986.

Wing, Lorna, *Autistic Children.* New York: Brunner/Mazel, 1985.

Winnicott, D.W., *Babies and Their Mothers.* Reading, Mass.: Addison-Wesley, 1987.

Wyckoff, Jerry L., and Barbara C. Unell, *How to Discipline Your Six to Twelve Year Old . . . Without Losing Your Mind.* New York: Double-day, 1991.

Yablonsky, Lewis, *Fathers and Sons.* New York: Gardner Press, 1990.

Ziai, Mohsen, *Pediatrics,* 4th ed. Boston: Little, Brown, 1990.

Periodicals and Journals

Allen, Eugenie, "Fat Chances," *Parenting,* November, 1992: 89–94.

American Academy of Pediatrics, "The 1992 Child Safety Report," *Woman's Day,* April 1, 1992: 109–123.

Angier, Natalie, "Hormone Imbalance Linked to Behavior," *The New York Times,* April 13, 1989: C3.

———, "Zone of Brain Linked to Men's Sexual Orientation," *The New York Times,* August 20, 1991: A1–D18.

Associated Press Wire Service, "Study: Heavy Teens Face Added Health Risks Later," Gannett Suburban Newspapers, November 5, 1992: 30A.

———, "Technique Screens For Genetic Disease," Gannett Suburban Newspapers, September 24, 1992: 28A.

Graham, C.J., R. Glenn, R. Dick, B. Allen, J. Pasley, "Abstract: Left-handedness As A Risk Factor For Accidental Trauma," Department of Pediatrics, University of Arkansas, Little Rock, AK.

Barrett, Mary Ellin, "Do We Want Baby Boys More Than Girls?" *McCall's,* November 1992: 143–157.

Belgum, Deborah, Allison Stamm, "To Spank Or Not to Spank," Gannett Suburban Newspapers, November 23, 1992: 3C.

Blau, Melinda, "Healthy Sexuality Begins at Home," *Child,* June/July 1992: 52.

Comer, James P., "Sex, Violence, And The TV Set," *Parents,* January 1993: 116.

D'Antonio, Michael, "Words That Hurt," *Child,* October 1992: 108–149.

Donahue, Tim, "Toy Guns Carry Potential Of Tragic Consequences," Gannett Suburban Newspapers, October 10, 1992: 5A.

Erens, Pamela, "Working Mothers and Sexist Sons," *Glamour,* April 1992: 54.

Gallo, Nick, "The Elements of Risk: How Far Must You Let Kids Go To Grow," *Child*, June/July 1992: 98–124.

Gannett News Service, "Children Of Divorce Suffer More, Study Says," Gannett Suburban Newspapers, August 19, 1990.

——, "Psychiatrist: Bad Childhoods Don't Have to Create Bad Parents," Gannett Suburban Newspapers, November 4, 1991: 22A.

——, "Study: TV Leads To More Fat," Gannett Suburban Newspapers, March 26, 1992: 26A.

Gelman, David with D. Foote, T. Barrett, M. Talbot, "Born or Bred?" *Newsweek*, February 24, 1992: 45–53.

George, Liz, "Body Language," *Weight Watchers* magazine, March 1993: 10.

Gomez, Jorge E., and Gregory L. Landry, "How To Prevent Injuries in Sports," *Healthy Kids 4–10*, Fall 1991: 56–60.

Gorman, Christine, "Are Gay Men Born That Way?" *Time*, September 9, 1991: 60–61.

Gross, Linden, "The Right Sport At The Right Time," *Parents*, November 1992: 245.

Hallowell, Christopher, "Maggie's Kisses," *Glamour*, April 1991: 322.

Hickey, Neil, "How Much Violence?" *TV Guide*, August 22, 1992: 10–11.

Igo, Sarah, "Dads Dis Daughters," *Parenting*, February 1993: 22.

Kagan, Julia, "Boys and Dolls, Girls and Trucks," *McCall's*, December 1990: 88.

Kolata, Gina, "Baby Isn't Growing Fast Enough?" Just Wait, A Research Team Says," *The New York Times*, October 30, 1992: A12.

L.A. Times Wire Service, "Drug Found to Treat Autism Successfully," Gannett Suburban Newspapers, November 15, 1991: 24A.

——, "On The Other Hand, Lefties Do Live As Long As Righties," Gannett Suburban Newspapers, February 13, 1993: 22A.

LaForge, Ann E., "The 'C' Word," *Redbook*, August 1992: 138–145.

Leonard, David, "Close Encounters," *Child*, March 1991: 58/122.

March Almanac, "Children And Guns: A Fatal Attraction," *Parents*, March 1991: 20.

Marks, Jane, "We Have a Problem," *Parents*, May 1991: 62–67.

McInnes, Sheryl, "POMBA Survey Results," *Twins*, July/August 1985: 35.

Miller, Russell, "He Said, She Said," *Sesame Street Parents' Guide*, January/February 1992.

Norland, Rod, "Deadly Lessons," *Newsweek*, March 9, 1992: 22–29.

Peterson, Bridgette, "Rough & Tumble," *Smart Kids:* 12–14.

Restak, Richard, "Introducing Your New Smarter, Sexier Brain," *Self*, March 1992: 107.

Rogers, Patrick, "How Many Gays Are There?" *Newsweek*, February 15, 1993: 46.

Samalin, Nancy, with Patricia McCormick, "Meltdown!" *Parents*, January 1993: 40–43.

Schoen, E.J., and A.A. Fischell, "Pain In Neonatal Circumcision," *Survey of Anesthesiology*, June 1992: 172.

Schultz, Dodi (ed.), "Family Fitness," *Parents*, January 1992: 20.

Segal, Nancy L., "The 'Hidden' Twins," *Twins*, July/August 1985: 31–35.

Seligmann, Jean with C. Friday, D.J. Wilson, D. Hannah, "The Wounds Of Words," *Newsweek*, October 12, 1992: 90–92.

Swanbrow, Diane, "Frisky Business," *Parenting*, June/July 1992: 22.

Taffel, Ron, "Your Husband, Your Kids: Could They Be Closer?" *McCall's*, November 1992: p. 80.

Task Force on Circumcision, "Report Of The Task Force On Circumcision," *Pediatrics*, August 1989: 388–391.

USA Today Wire Service, "Researcher: Men's, Women's Brains Are Different," Gannett Suburban Newspapers, July 8, 1991.

Verner, Chris, "The Son Also Dances," *Child*, January, 1992: 76.

Washington Post Wire Service, "Study: Guns Top Killer Of Male Teens," Gannett Suburban Newspapers, March 1, 1991.

Webb, Denise, "Eating Well," *The New York Times*, October 28, 1992: C4.

Williams, Scott, "The Ways Television Teaches Children About Sex Roles," Gannett Suburban Newspapers, October 22, 1991: 11B.

Wlody, Ellen, "TV Viewing Linked to High Cholesterol," *Healthy Kids 4–10*, Spring/Summer 1991: 8.

Helpful Organizations

ORGANIZATIONS

Administration for Children and Families
U.S. Department of Health and Human Services
370 L'Enfant Promenade, SW
Washington, DC 20447
(202) 401-9215

This organization is concerned with improving the well-being of low-income families, neglected and abused children and youth, Native Americans, refugees, and individuals with developmental disabilities and mental retardation. It consolidates related programs that serve the public to meet the needs of children and families.

Administration on Developmental Disabilities
U.S. Department of Health and Human Services
200 Independence Avenue, SW
Washington, DC 20201
(202) 690-6590

The Administration on Developmental Disabilities is responsible for planning programs which promote self-sufficiency and protect the rights of developmentally disabled people.

American Academy of Pediatrics
141 North West Point Boulevard
PO Box 927
Elk Grove Village, IL 60009-0927
(708) 228-5005

> The AAP is an organization of pediatricians dedicated to the health, safety, and well-being of infants, children, adolescents, and young adults. AAP publishes a professional journal, educational journals, magazines, and other publications on subjects related to children.

American Foundation for the Prevention of Venereal Diseases, Inc.
799 Broadway, Suite 638
New York, NY 10003
(212) 759-2069

> This association offers guidance for sexually transmitted disease prevention and personal hygiene information.

American Speech-Language-Hearing Association
10801 Rockville Pike
Rockville, MD 20852
(301) 897-5700 (voice or TDD)
HELPLINE: 1-800-638-8255

> The Consumer Affairs Division of the ASHA is committed to providing information and assistance to Americans who have communication disorders as well as to their families and friends.

Athletic Institute
200 Castlewood Drive
North Palm Beach, FL 33408-5696
(407) 842-3600
Toll Free: 1-800-933-3335

> The Athletic Institute is a not-for-profit organization recognized as the world's largest producer and distributor of sports and physical education programs. It creates and provides major development assistance to amateur sports associations.

Autism Research Institute
4182 Adams Avenue
San Diego, CA 92116
(619) 281-7165

> The Autism Research Institute is devoted to conducting research, and to disseminating the results related to preventing, diagnosing,

and treating autism and other severe behavioral disorders of childhood. It donates to researchers and brings findings to families' attention.

Big Brothers/Big Sisters of America
230 North Thirteenth Street
Philadelphia, PA 19107-1510
(215) 567-7000

Big Brothers/Big Sisters is a one-to-one relationship program
which matches one adult volunteer with one child, of any ethical,
racial, and economic background, in order to establish mentorship,
friendship, and make a difference in his or her life. There are established Big Brothers/Big Sisters agencies nationwide.

Boys & Girls Clubs of America
National Headquarters
771 First Avenue
New York, NY 10017-3506
(212) 351-5900

Boys & Girls Clubs of America is a national, nonprofit youth organization providing support services to 1,340 Boys & Girls Club facili-
ties that help over 1.7 million young people connect with
opportunities for personal growth and achievement. Their primary
mission is service to girls and boys from disadvantaged circumstances, located all throughout the United States.

Carolina Wren Press & Lollipop Power Books
120 Morris Street
Durham, NC 27701
(919) 560-2738

Carolina Wren Press is a nonprofit organization dedicated to seeking out, nurturing, and publishing quality writing that confronts
stereotypes and includes the disenfranchised. Lollipop Power publishes nonsexist, multicultural alternative children's books.

Center to Prevent Handgun Violence
National Headquarters
1225 Eye Street, NW, Suite 1150
Washington, DC 20005
(202) 289-7319
Fax: (202) 408-1851

The Center to Prevent Handgun Violence is a national nonprofit
organization which helps America's young people and their parents
understand the realities of handgun violence and the dangers

posed by loaded, easily available handguns. Information on the STAR Program—Straight Talk About Risks: Pre-K–12 Curriculum for Preventing Handgun Violence—is available. The Center offers information, brochures, and suggested readings.

Center for Disease Control
Office on Smoking and Health
Mail Stop K-50
4770 Buford Highway, NE
Atlanta, GA 30341-3724
(404) 488-5705

This office offers to the public a list of free publications ranging from public information; cessation materials; youth, pregnancy, and infant materials; to posters and technical information.

Center for Early Adolescence
School of Medicine
University of North Carolina at Chapel Hill
D-2 Carr Mill Town Center
Carrboro, NC 27510
(919) 966-1148

The Center's mission is to promote healthy growth and development of adolescents through advocation and by providing information services research, training, and leadership development for those who can have a positive impact on our nation's ten- to fifteen-year-olds.

Child Welfare League of America, Inc.
440 First Street, NW
Suite 310
Washington, DC 20001-2085
(202) 638-2952

The Child Welfare League of America is a national membership organization made up of voluntary child welfare agencies.

CHOICE
1233 Locust Street, 3rd Fl.
Philadelphia, PA 19107
(215) 985-3355

CHOICE is a consumer advocacy organization concerned with reproductive health, sexuality, education, maternity care, AIDS, and child care. This is a nonprofit agency that works with consumers to make sure they receive needed services.

Cleft Palate Foundation
1218 Grandview Avenue
Pittsburgh, PA 15211
(412) 418-1376
Cleft-Line: 1-800-24-CLEFT

The Cleft Palate Foundation is a nonprofit organization which helps patients and families understand birth defects such as cleft lip and palate. It provides publications, information brochures, and fact sheets.

The Feingold Associations of the United States
PO Box 6550
Alexandria, VA 22306
(703) 768-FAUS

The Feingold Associations of the United States are nonprofit organizations whose purpose is to support their members in the implementation of the Feingold Program, and to generate public awareness of the potential role of foods and synthetic additives in behavior, learning, and health problems.

Food and Nutrition Information Center
National Agricultural Library
10301 Baltimore Boulevard
Beltsville, MD 20705
(301) 504-5719

The Food and Nutrition Center is an information source to answer questions and provide consumers with information about food and nutrition. It is open to public visits and inquiries as well; its sources are accessible through interlibrary loan requests.

Hazelden
PO Box 11
Center City, MN 55012-0011
1-800-257-7800 for programs and services
1-800-328-9000 for books, pamphlets, tapes, etc.

Hazelden is a nonprofit organization providing low-cost, quality rehabilitation, education, prevention, and professional services in chemical-dependency and related addictive disorders.

Infant-Parent Institute, Inc.
328 North Neil Street
Champaign, IL 61820
(217) 352-4060

The Infant-Parent Institute is a private teaching and clinical service institute specializing in problems of attachment in infants and adults.

Jervis Clinic
Developmental Disabilities Clinic
1050 Forest Hill Road
Staten Island, NY 10314
Phone Social Service Department
(718) 494-5126 or 494-5151

The Jervis Clinic offers services in the areas of seizure control, behavior management, etiology, and genetic counseling. Clinics and services are for Neurodegenerative Disease, Down Syndrome, and Fragile X Syndrome.

Joint Custody Association
15285 South Keeler
Olathe, KS 66062
(913) 764-8181

The Joint Custody Association offers material kits which provide useful information and recommendations, details regarding legislation, and standardized materials for developing self-help organizations.

Learning Disabilities Association of America
4156 Library Road
Pittsburgh, PA 15234
(412) 341-1515

The Learning Disabilities Association is a national volunteer organization of parents, professionals, people with learning disabilities, and other concerned citizens. Its purpose is to advance education and general welfare of children with learning disabilities; advice, information, and publications are available.

Mothers Matter
171 Wood Street
Rutherford, NJ 07070
(201) 933-8191

Mothers Matter is a mother-focused program which provides educational exchange among mothers—the real professionals in parenting—in order to increase their skills, confidence, and enjoyment as parents.

National Center for Stuttering
200 East 33rd Street
New York, NY 10016
NYS: (212) 532-1460
Toll Free: 1-800-221-2483

The National Center for Stuttering addresses the physical and emotional problems related to stuttering. It uses a phased teaching process for children seven years old and up, which includes workshops and reinforcement techniques. The Center also provides training programs for speech professionals and helpful suggestions for parents of young children who have recently begun stuttering.

National Committee for Prevention of Child Abuse
332 South Michigan Avenue, Suite 1600
Chicago, IL 60604-4357
(312) 663-3520
TDD: (312) 663-3450

NCPCA is a volunteer-based organization dedicated to involving all concerned citizens in actions to prevent child abuse. Its programs include public awareness, chapter networks, education and training, research, and advocacy.

National Down Syndrome Congress
1800 Dempster Street
Park Ridge, IL 60068-1146
Toll Free: 1-800-232-NDSC

The National Down Syndrome Congress is committed to promoting opportunities and resources for all individuals and families. It encourages research related to aspects of Down syndrome and promotes full participation of people with Down syndrome in all aspects of community life.

National Down Syndrome Society
666 Broadway
New York, NY 10012
NYS (212) 460-9330
Toll Free: 1-800-221-4602

The National Down Syndrome Society's mission is to develop public awareness about Down syndrome, to assist families in addressing the needs of children with this genetic disorder, and to sponsor and encourage research. The Society offers printed and video materials, including a free information packet and newsletter, information and referral services, and a 24-hour "800" number hotline.

The National Fragile X Foundation
1441 York Street, Suite 215
Denver, CO 80206
Toll Free: 1-800-668-8765

> The National Fragile X Foundation promotes education and research regarding Fragile X syndrome and other forms of X-linked mental retardation. The Foundation provides information, brochures, and newsletters.

The National Hemophilia Foundation
110 Greene Street, Suite 406
New York, NY 10012
(212) 431-8541

> The National Hemophilia Foundation is dedicated to the treatment and the cure of hemophilia and related bleeding disorders.

National Institute of Mental Health
Information Resources and Inquiries Branch
Office of Scientific Information
Room 15C-05
5600 Fishers Lane
Rockville, MD 20857
(301) 496-4000

> The National Institute of Mental Health offers a list of publications centered on mental illness and mental health.

National Organization of Circumcision Information Resource Centers
PO Box 2512
San Anselmo, CA 94979-2512
(415) 488-9883

> NOCIRC provides parents, health-care professionals, lawyers, and other concerned individuals with information on the practice of routine infant circumcision.

National SAFE KIDS Campaign
Children's National Medical Center
111 Michigan Avenue, NW
Washington, DC 20010-2970
(202) 939-4993

> The National SAFE KIDS Campaign is a nationwide, comprehensive childhood-injury-prevention campaign. It offers material to help increase awareness of the seriousness of childhood injury and to help

develop programs to be implemented in communities to create a
safer environment for children.

National Stuttering Project
2151 Irving Street, Suite #208
San Francisco, CA 94122-1609
(415) 566-5324

National Stuttering Project is a membership organization which
provides support and information to the stuttering community. It
offers support groups, informative brochures, and newsletters.
There is also an established organization for parents and children
called Aaron's Associates.

The New York Association for the Learning Disabled
90 South Swan Street
Albany, NY 12210
(518) 436-5902

Affiliates of The New York Association for the Learning Disabled
provide a variety of services and programs for children and adults
with learning disabilities and their families.

The Orton Dyslexia Society
Chester Building, Suite 382
8600 LaSalle Road
Baltimore, MD 21286-2044
(410) 296-0232

Dedicated to the study and treatment of dyslexia. The Society
shares information with members through publications, conferences, and a network of volunteers across the country.

Parents Without Partners, Inc.
8807 Colesville Road
Silver Spring, MD 20910
(301) 588-9354
Toll Free: 1-800-637-7974

Parents Without Partners is an international nonprofit educational
organization of custodial and noncustodial single parents—widowed, divorced, separated, or never married. There are over 800
chapters which offer mutual support and professional advice. They
offer a variety of programs and events which integrates all types of
occupations, educational levels, faiths, and political beliefs in order
to provide a healthy family environment for single-parent children.

PRIDE
The Hurt Building, Suite 210
50 Hurt Plaza
Atlanta, GA 30303
(404) 577-4500

PRIDE is a nonprofit organization which provides information and
programs to prevent drug abuse. PRIDE aids government, schools,
parents, and business.

**SIECUS—Sex Information and Education Council of the
United States**
130 West 42nd Street, Suite 2500
New York, NY 10036
(212) 819-9770
Fax: (212) 819-9776

SIECUS is a membership organization made up of professionals
and individuals concerned with promoting the delivery of compre-
hensive sexuality education and information and with protecting
individual sexual rights.

Single Mothers by Choice
PO Box 1642
Gracie Square Station
New York, NY 10028
(212) 988-0993

SMC is a national nonprofit organization which provides support
and information to single women who have chosen or who are considering single motherhood.

Sporting Goods Manufacturers Association
Administrative Offices:
200 Castlewood Drive
North Palm Beach, FL 33408
(407) 842-4100
Fax: (407) 863-8984
Legislative Offices:
1625 K Street, NW, Suite 900
Washington, DC 20006
(202) 775-1762
Fax: (202) 296-7462

The SGMA is dedicated to increasing amateur sports participation.
It addresses such problems as funding school sports, product lia-
bility, setting standards, creating guidelines, and generating market data.

Stop Teenage Addiction to Tobacco
121 Lyman Street, Suite 210
Springfield, MA 01103
(413) 732-7828
Fax: (413) 732-4219

STAT's mission is to stop teenage addiction to tobacco by discriminating the sale of tobacco to young people; stop tobacco companies from promoting tobacco addiction among youth; and generate direct social and economic pressure on tobacco companies to force them to stop unethical campaigns to promote smoking.

Stuttering Foundation of America
5139 Klingle Street, NW
Washington, DC 20016-2654
(202) 363-3199
Toll Free Hotline: 1-800-992-9392

The Stuttering Foundation of America is a nonprofit organization that offers brochures, posters, videos, and a free resource list upon request.

The Sugar Association, Inc.
c/o Sylvia Rowe
1101 15th Street, NW, Suite 600
Washington, DC 20005
(202) 785-1122

The Sugar Association, Inc. is a nonprofit organization which funds scientific research and disseminates educational and informational materials on sugar's role in diet and health.

TARGET
National Federation Target Program
PO Box 20626, 11724 NW Plaza Circle
Kansas City, MO 64195-0626
Toll Free: 1-800-366-6667

Target, a service component of the National Federation of State High School Associations, is committed to assisting America's youth in coping with tobacco, alcohol, and other drugs. Target is a service offering training, publications, interactive projects, and a resource center.

United Cerebral Palsy Associations, Inc.
1522 K Street, NW, Suite 1112
Washington, DC 20005
(202) 842-1266 V/TT
Toll Free: 1-800-USA-5UCP V/TT

A publications catalog, support services, information, and referrals are available to the public.

United Cerebral Palsy Research and Educational Foundation, Inc.
Seven Penn Plaza, Suite 804
New York, NY 10001
(212) 268-6655
Toll Free: 1-800-USA-1UCP

The national organization and its network of state and local affiliates share a public trust and commitment to persons with cerebral palsy and to others with severe disabilities. They offer literature, facts, and updates regarding the organization and its affiliated members.

Useful Products

TOILET TRAINING AIDS

TINKLE TARGETS Available From:

Right Start Catalog
Right Start Plaza
5334 Sterling Center Drive
Westlake Village, CA 91361
1-800-LITTLE-1

Perfectly Safe Catalog
725 Whipple Avenue, NW
North Canton, OH 44720
1-800-831-5437

LIL MARC (CHILD'S URINAL) Available From:

Parker Stephens, Inc.
17452 Irvine Boulevard
Tustin, CA 92680
714-730-4145

***ONCE UPON A POTTY VIDEO FOR HIM* Available From:**

Playfair Toys Catalog
Box 18210
Boulder, CO 80308
1-800-824-7255

Hand-in-Hand Catalog
Route 26
R.R. 1, Box 1425
Oxford, ME 04270
1-800-872-9745

TV ALLOWANCE (TV CONTROL AID) Available From:

Randal Levenson
5605 S.W. 7th Street, #21
South Miami, FL 33143
1-800-231-4410

GENDER-FREE TOYS Available From:

Playfair Toys Catalog
Box 18210
Boulder, CO 80308
1-800-824-7255

Index

Elyse Zorn Karlin is a journalist whose specialties include parenting. She is the author of *The Complete Baby Checklist . . . An Organizing System for Parents, Collectible Children Figurines of Bisque and Chinawares 1850–1950,* and *Jewelry and Metalwork in the Arts and Crafts Tradition.*

She also wrote the *Massachusetts No-Fault Divorce Kit* and the *Massachusetts Will Kit.* Karlin was a contributing editor to *Collectors, Clocks and Jewelry Magazine* and has contributed articles to *Heritage Magazine* (a publication on antique jewelry) and *Bride's Magazine.*

She has a degree in journalism from the University of Missouri, Columbia, and she spent fourteen years in the advertising business as a specialist in direct marketing. Her last position in the advertising world was as a senior vice-president at Saatchi & Saatchi Advertising.

Muriel Prince Warren, MSW, ACSW, BCD, is a psychotherapist in private practice in New York City and Rockland County, New York. She is the Executive Director of the Psychoanalytic Center for Communicative Education in New York City and President of the International Society for Psychoanalytic Psychotherapy.

Over the past 15 years Warren has worked extensively with adults, adolescents, children, and families suffering from emotional dysfunctions. She is a doctoral candidate at Adelphi University.

"THE WORLD NEEDS MORE LIKE TOREY HAYDEN"

Boston Globe

GHOST GIRL   **71681-X/$4.99 US/$5.99 Can**
The true story of a child in peril and the teacher who saved her.

JUST ANOTHER KID   **70564-8/$5.50 US/$6.50 Can**
More than a moving story of one woman's personal battle, this is a
loving tribute to all Hayden's "special" children and their remarkable
strength of spirit.

MURPHY'S BOY   **65227-7/$5.50 US/$6.50 Can**
Bestselling author Torey L. Hayden tells the dramatic and moving true
story of her confrontation with a fifteen-year-old boy who refused to
speak—until the miracle of love penetrated the terrible silence.

SOMEBODY ELSE'S KIDS   **59949-X/$4.95 US/$5.95 Can**
This is the true story of Torey Hayden's experience teaching four
disturbed children who were put in her class because no one else
knew what to do with them.

ONE CHILD   **54262-5/$5.50 US/$6.50 Can**
Abandoned by her mother, abused by her alcoholic father, six-year-
old Sheila was placed in a class for the hopelessly retarded and
disturbed. Everyone said Sheila was lost forever...everyone except
teacher Torey Hayden, whose perseverence finally revealed Sheila to
be a child with a genius I.Q.—and a great capacity for love.